Table of Contents

New Close Readings of *The Crying of Lot 49*

This book is dedicated to the many journal editors and anonymous referees, who have read my literary submissions over the past dozen years, were sympathetic enough to commend something they liked, and took the trouble to identify weaknesses and suggest changes that could render the papers publishable. A few of them went so far as to fill the margins of my manuscripts with corrections and instructions, or if they had received the submission as an attachment, to intersperse their comments electronically on the original file. In their generosity, all of the readers, even those that had nothing reassuring to say, enabled me to make up a little for my lack of the more pertinent doctoral degree and to partake in the enduring satisfaction of literary criticism.

New Close Readings of *The Crying of Lot 49*

Robert E. Kohn

Southern Illinois University, Edwardsville

Copyright © 2013

ISBN-13: 978-1492166399
ISBN-10: 1492166391

Front cover design executed by Jason Kleypas.

Cover image: *Tom's Bar and Grill, II* by Jerry O. Wilkerson, 1985.
Acrylic on canvas, 50" by 60"
Tucson Museum of Art, Gift of Ivan and Marilynn Karp, New York, NY
Provenance: The artist, OK Harris Gallery, Ivan and Marilynn Karp, 1999.

Back cover image taken from photograph by Claudia Burris, published in *Webster World*, Winter 2011, page 14.

Back cover design by Jason Kleypas

Book Formatting: Mira Digital Publishing; Anne Schonhardt, Production Technician.

Introduction

> The politics of the page may be part of the inhibiting politics of criticism as an academic institution. The critical article and the scholarly book now reign; they mediate our imagination and knowledge. But why not also the essay, the ideal essay rooted etymologically in risk, trial, examination, balance, rooted in *both* risk and balance? "The essay–"someone always asks, "but is it criticism?" Perhaps it is not. But perhaps also what criticism now requires is a text that puts itself in jeopardy with other texts. (Ihab Hassan *The Postmodern Turn*, 141)

Thomas Pynchon's *The Crying of Lot 49* is one of the most epistemologically complex novels, page for page, ever written. One of the continuing surprises of the 1960s was that such a novel was destined to become a blockbuster. In addition to the two hardcover first editions, by Lippincott, with two American printings in 1966, and by Cape with one British printing in 1967, there has been a flurry of paperback editions–in the United States; by Harper Perennial Modern Classics (Harper Collins, Harper and Row, Perennial Fiction Library, Perennial Classics), with at least eight printings and four different cover designs, and by Bantam (Vintage Classics), with at least ten printings and six different cover designs. This survey was made from online offerings of independent sellers of used-books (through Abebooks.com and Amazon.com), that surely understate the actual totality; some of these offerings mentioned at least twenty printings of a single edition. With the large flow of paperbacks to market and the high prices asked for the hardback editions (now in the thousands of dollars for mint quality specimens, and in the case of one, which includes a letter signed by Pynchon, currently offered by a bookseller in Slingerlands NY for $ 32,500.00), one U.S. manufacturer came out with a new hardback edition in 1997 under the Buccaneer imprint, new copies of which may still be available. In Great Britain, paperback copies were published in 1979 by Picador, which went into at least three printings. In 2002, Random House UK came out with a paperback with the same dust jacket as Vintage Classics in the US, suggesting their joint affiliation. (The variety of imprints available in the United States especially also speaks to the flurry of mergers and acquisitions of book publishers over the last half century.) Most recently, a Kindle edition has been published under the Perennial Fiction Library imprint.

The continual flow of new editions suggests that *The Crying of Lot 49* has remained a major seller well into the first decade of the 21st century. This has led to new editions of some of the major study-aids for this novel (reflecting its continued pedagogical usefulness in college and even high school literature classes), among them a 2008 expanded version of J. Kerry Grant's 1994 *Companion to* The Crying of Lot 49 and a 2010 re-presentation of Patrick O'Donnell's 1991

New Essays on The Crying of Lot 49. There are also Harold Bloom's 2003 *Thomas Pynchon* and Thomas Schaub's 2008 *Approaches to Teaching Pynchon's* The Crying of Lot 49 *and Other Works*. Pynchon studies continue to benefit from the biennial journal, *Pynchon Notes*, edited by John Krafft, Bernard Duyfhuizen and Khachig Tololyan, which is now in its 33rd year of publishing. There is also the phenomenon of the Pynchon Wikis, websites for anonymous page-by-page and alphabetical annotations of Pynchon's novels, including *The Crying of lot 49*. It is not surprising that Grant reported, some "Forty years after its first publication," that *The Crying of Lot 49* "is still selling at the rate of between fifteen and twenty thousand copies annually" (*Companion 2nd*, xvii).

With so much public and academic interest, the study of *The Crying of Lot 49* has continued to flourish. As recently as 2008, Daniel Grausam made the brilliant discovery that the "horror of a fully thermonuclear war" was intimated in Pynchon's "Potsmaster" episode, signifying the "Potsdam Conference in the last days of World War II," where the allies "offered Japan the choice between surrender and total destruction"–that being the first time that the atomic bomb was "mentioned without being named" (Grausam 230; *Crying* 46). This one idiosyncratic signifier, "Potsmaster," which resonates again at the bottom of page 97 of the novel, plus Metzger's brief dismissal of the postal typo–"So they make misprints [...], let them. As long as they're careful about not pressing the wrong button, you know"–are a metaphor for the enormous explosion from a relatively small amount of mass that Earth witnessed in 1945 (*Crying* 47). Alan Wilde has uncovered profound new meanings in this novel, but he was too quick to conclude in 1987 that "*The Crying of Lot 49* has been combed over thoroughly and well for all its possible meanings" (95). Blockbuster interpretations are still being made.

The reader will note that for the present book, I am using the pagination of the Lippincott edition of *The Crying of Lot 49*, which has been maintained in Harper's Perennial Fiction Library. This pagination corresponds to the edition-designation (H) in Grants *Companions*.

The Literary Essay

The literary essay differs from academic criticism because it is a mix of literary criticism and other academic disciplines. The discipline in which I was trained and practiced for 30 years, economics, is necessarily focused on highly complex entities, such as regional, national and world economies. Economists study these complex systems through abstract simulations called models. In my final essay in that field, I modeled the efficient control of global warming in a free-trading, two-country world with only four equations, representing consumption, production, emission, and abatement processes, and two equalities that summed the two countries total endowments of resources (Kohn *A Theoretical Inefficiency*). It is this modeling approach that I brought to literary studies. Where traditional Pynchon scholars–with notable exceptions–are hesitant to make claims that cannot be substantiated, I simply take such claims, if I think they are promising, and *assume* for the nonce that they are true. At the very least, I pose them as hypotheses. The selection of a particular combination of assumptions and hypotheses constitutes a model. If a model is successful, in the words of Milton Friedman, the Nobel laureate from the University of Chicago, it will imply or yield "new facts capable of being observed" (13). If the model works well, it can be used to formulate and corroborate "predictions that are good enough for the purpose in hand" (Friedman 41). Its creation, he avers, is an "act of inspiration, intuition, invention; its essence is the vision of something new in familiar material" (Friedman 43). Friedman's economic model provides another approach to literary criticism that can "mediate our imagination and knowledge" (Hassan 141). Indeed, it is often the case that a different kind of text, which mine is, "puts itself in jeopardy with other texts," but Hassan finds this worthwhile (141). Arnold Harberger, a famous economist at UCLA, where I visited for the winter quarter in 1987, once asked me, with regard to a paper I was writing; "Where are the bubbles?" Harberger explained that a successful paper had to sparkle like a glass of champagne. This was his way of knowing that a model is working. It may be relevant that Harberger got his advanced degrees and taught at the University of Chicago during Friedman's tenure there.

    In the case of *The Crying of Lot 49*, not only is the text exceedingly complex, but its author is famously recluse. The only time that he has publicly commented on his writing was in the uncharacteristic introduction to his 1987 *Slow Learner*, in which all he said about *The Crying of Lot 49* was that it was a story "which was marketed as a "novel," in which

> I seem to have forgotten most of what I thought I'd learned up till then. Most likely, much of my feelings for this last story can be traced to ordinary nostalgia for this time in my life, for the writer who seemed then to be emerging, with his bad habits, dumb theories and occasional moments of productive silence in which he may have begun to get a glimpse of how it was done. (*Slow* 22)

By then, *The Crying of Lot 49* was already famous for its inordinate complexity, and it is apparent from this quotation that Pynchon did not intend to provide much in the way of resolution. However, I will argue in the second essay in this volume that he regretted a particular sentence on thermodynamic entropy *vis a vis* information entropy in *The Crying of Lot 49*. In the first essay, I build on Pynchon's acknowledgement of "ordinary nostalgia," in this case, for what could have been his college introductory text to literary theory, namely E.M. Forster's *Aspects of the Novel*. I know from reading John Maynard Keynes' *General Theory of Employment, Interest and Money* over and over again when I was a college freshman, how nostalgia for a text can nourish one's professional life for decades.

Two years after *The Crying of Lot 49* appeared, Roland Barthes published his most famous essay, in which he exposed the myth of the "Author-God" (146). We know now, wrote Barthes, "that to give writing its future, it is necessary to overthrow [that] myth: the birth of the reader must be at the cost of the death of the Author" (148). For some novels, such as Angela Carter's *Infernal Desire Machines of Dr. Hoffman*, which I write about, I think that Barthes' poststructuralist distancing of the author is extremely relevant, but in the case of *The Crying of Lot 49*, I believe that, as Joseph Carroll put it, "Within his or her own total structure of meaning, each author is necessarily dominant; he or she constitutes a supreme authority" (*Literary Darwinism* 131). Accordingly, I like to believe that Pynchon reads everything that critics write on *The Crying of Lot 49*, hoping to see which of the hundreds or thousands of referents he had in mind have been uncovered. In the third essay in this volume, on the influence of Rachel Carson's *Silent Spring*, I suggest that his 2006 *Against the Day* was intentionally published for the 40th anniversary of *The Crying of Lot 49*, and that he took that occasion to repeat a number of signifiers that had gone undetected in the earlier novel. There are so many signifiers in the 1966 novel, and often so many referents per signifier, that it will take a century for them all to be discovered. Rather than being liberated by the freedom to privilege our own critical interpretations over those of the author, as Barthes advocated, we have the best of both worlds with Pynchon. We feel less hesitant to make assumptions on his intentions, because he will never intervene. Still, we are looking for *his* meanings of the text, *not* our own. I carried this to an embarrassing extreme in a 2009 article when I went so far as to suggest that the mysterious Tibetan seal emblazoned on the dust jacket and one of the fly pages of *Against the Day* was a personal communication meant for me (Kohn *Pynchon Takes the Fork* 162). It is most exciting to critique books whose authors are both dead and alive.

For those who have not read *The Crying of Lot 49*, it might be helpful at the outset for me to provide a synopsis of it. However complex Pynchon's novel may be, it is divided into six chapters with different emphases in each and might therefore lend itself to a generalized synopsis. However, the emphases vary according to which of many models, the text is interpreted. Presumably, the synopses vary from one over-arching model to the next. By declining to provide a synopsis I am acknowledging that this is a book for people who have already read *The Crying of Lot 49*. I have discovered that when I read critical articles on books that I have not read, I tend to skip over the indented (quoted) material because it is unfamiliar. To the contrary, when I read critiques of novels that I have read, these quoted blocks of indented text are felicitous. My selection of a relatively short, 183-page, novel to study and write about was not a random choice. As I skipped from one interpretive model to the next, I have tended to reread the novel with that particular approach in full focus. I am by no means suggesting *The Crying of Lot 49* needs to be reread along with each of the essays presented here; in fact, I am hopeful that the segues from one interpretation to the next and the interesting cross-effects will provide the enriching syncretistic experience that Pynchon might have had in mind.

All but two of the essays in this volume, in their earlier formats, have been submitted to literary journals, anonymously refereed and rejected. Ordinarily, I would have continued to revise them and send them out to different journals, until they finally found homes. But time is closing in on me, and since so many of these essays were on Pynchon and bounced back at about the same time, it occurred to me to accumulate them for a book in which the individual essays might achieve a synergy that had been lacking. I went to special pains to revise the included essays, knowing that this time, there would be no intervening safety net of anonymous readers. There was another motivation for writing this book, and that was the epiphany that struck me in the form of Hassan's quotation which became the epigraph to this introduction. It made me realize that my economics-based approach to literary criticism had been in jeopardy from the beginning, and that something good might come from knowing why. I wasn't sure that I fully understood the epigraph I took from Hassan's book, and endeavored, but failed, to find his email contact on the University of Wisconsin–Milwaukee website. I took the liberty of calling his home on Saturday, November 6, 2010 at 9:43 AM (AT&T keeps a record of long-distance calls, so I know that this one lasted 13 minutes). His wife answered the phone and he was kind enough to turn from his writing, which he told me is now fiction rather than criticism, an incredible turn for a person in his mid-eighties. He explained that an essay differs from literary criticism because it is more general and often multi-disciplinary. He also recognized that one of the problems I was having in my new career was the subject of his 1955 essay, which I hadn't known about, on the problem of influence in literary history. I mentioned his 1971 article on postmodernism, which appears to have been the first paper in the field with that cognomen in its title. Both of these articles by Hassan will be discussed later in this introduction.

On Essay One

My first essay, entitled "The Influence of E.M. Forster," builds on the nostalgia which, from Pynchon's rare confession in *Slow Learner*, I assume to be one of his passions. After his stint in the navy, he returned to Cornell to major in English

5

literature, and most likely studied Forster's seminal *Aspects of the Novel,* dedicated to "literary creation and criticism" (Forster 14). Although it was published in 1927, R.B. Kershner still considers it "Perhaps the most important treatise on the novel by a major English novelist" (18). My English Professor friend, Peter Wolfe, best known for his books on Patrick White, Graham Greene, Yukio Mishima, Iris Murdoch, Raymond Chandler and William Gaddis, remembers from his own college days, he told me, that Forster's book was "very hot in the 1950s," that "any serious student of English lit, graduate or undergraduate, would have read it." In my first essay I assume that Pynchon's first exposure to literary theory was through Forster's book, and that there are pieces of plot in *The Crying of Lot 49* that were consciously or even subconsciously inspired by corresponding plots exemplified in *Aspects of the Novel.*

The three anonymous readers of the preceding version of Essay One, that I had submitted to an interdisciplinary journal, were unanimous in their judgment that the paper should not be published. In general, they all made the point, as expressed by one of them, that he or she "was not persuaded by the paper's basic premise that Pynchon's novel was written as a point-by-point response to Forster's *Aspects of the Novel.* Indeed, it felt like much of the substance of the novel has to be ignored to even make this argument." Hassan explained this kind of adverse reaction when he wrote: "Few problems can prove more vexing to the critic or historian of literature than the problem of influence. [...] For influence presupposes some measure of causality and causality has repeatedly shown itself to be the scholar's Gordian knot" (*Problem of Influence* 66, 68). In the present case, the knot is loosened by simply *assuming* that *The Crying of Lot 49 is* influenced by Forster's *Aspects of the Novel.* If this assumption ultimately yields useful insights, then it is justified.

The anonymous readers' concern that "much of the substance of the novel has to be ignored" in my essay is ameliorated when the essay is put in the context of other essays in this book, which all together deal with a large fraction of the novel's substance. On balance, I have taken all three readers' criticism into account, and the essay is now a very different one than they rejected. With all due respect for their help, each began his or her response with some slight sarcasm, to which I cannot help but respond in Essay One by highlighting their cleverly offending phrases with quotation marks, though necessarily without the usual attribution. I'm happy that they let me have it and then got down to business.

Hassan leaves us with a problem that remains to be resolved. "Authors have been sometimes unaware of works that were supposed to have directly influenced them, a situation painfully embarrassing to all involved" (*Problems of Influence* 73). If my model yields useful results, I shall not be embarrassed if Pynchon reveals someday that he never read Forster's *Aspects of the Novel,* even though my assumption that he had would have been dead wrong. Of such assumptions, Friedman wrote: "Truly important and significant hypotheses will be found to have 'assumptions' that are wildly inaccurate descriptive representations of reality, and, in general, the more significant the theory, the more unrealistic the assumptions" (14). The reason for this is simple. "A hypothesis is important if it 'explains' much by little, that is, if it abstracts the common and crucial elements from the mass of complex and detailed circumstances surrounding the phenomena to be explained and permits valid predictions on the basis of them alone" (Friedman 14). Given Friedman's view of what makes an assumption useful, I am all the more fascinated by Hassan's discussion of the problem of influence in literary criticism, and, to keep it in play for awhile, am including "Influence" in the title of the first four essays in this volume. Hopefully, my readers will make it a practice to read the introductory material on each essay before they read the essay itself.

One of the anonymous readers generously felt that my initial attempt to fulfill Forster's expectation of an underlying visual pattern in *The Crying of Lot 49* "could provide the basis for an interesting reworking of the novel's formal features." What I had proposed in that previous version was a biblical image based on Ezekiel's wheels, because it combined the Forsterian idea of flatness and roundness of *characters*, the Forsterian transcendence of *prophecy*, and the Forsterian supernatural of *fantasy*. It was the "wheel within a wheel," of which there were four, and "they four had one likeness," that the prophet Ezekiel saw when the heavens opened and he saw visions of God (*Ezekiel* 1:16). Each wheel of His chariot consisted of two vertical rings, perpendicular to each other and joined along their flat-sided rims at the top and bottom, so that they symbolized both flatness and spherical roundness. "As for their rings, they were high and they were dreadful; and they four had their rings full of eyes round about" (1:18). The flat characters in *The Crying of Lot 49*, I had suggested, could be represented by the two-dimensions of the circular rings, and the round character of Oedipa, by the three-dimensions of the cross-joined pairs of rings. The eyes around the rings conjure up the "huge eyes" (*Crying* 21), "enormous eyes" (28), "radiant eyes" (42), "little eyes" (43), "suffering eyes" (43), "velveted eyes" (45), "past eyes" (55), "furrowed eyes" (78), "empty eyes" (111), "smudged eyes" (126), "her own eyes" (132), "Hilarius's eyes" and the numerous "his eyes" and "her eyes" (138) that circle through Pynchon's novel. There are only five "wheels" mentioned in *The Crying of Lot 49*, but with a stretch they could be relevant to my hypothesis: "Serge, the driver, not being able to see through his hair [...] was persuaded to hand over the wheel to one of the girls" (55); "two pistons attached to a crankshaft and flywheel [...] violating the Second Law of Thermodynamics" (86); "Wheeler Hall, through Sather Gate into a plaza teeming with [...] bicycle spokes in the sun" (103); "doused himself good with the gasoline [, ...] about to make the farewell flick of the wheel on his faithful Zippo" (114); and Oedipa 'with her forehead resting on the steering wheel" (145). But I don't think I can pull off what this anonymous reader kindly hoped for. In the end, I can't get myself to believe that Pynchon had Ezekiel's biblical Wheels in mind, consciously or unconsciously, when he wrote this novel. There was a time when I bought into Terry Eagleton's view that the most intriguing texts were not those that can be simply read and interpreted but those which are, what he called "writable," which "encourage the critic to carve them up, transpose them into different discourses, produce his or her semi-arbitrary play of meaning athwart the work itself" (quotation from Eagleton in Kohn, *The Fivesquare Amsterdam* 89). I finally realized that the texts that Eagleton had in find were poststructuralist texts like Samuel Beckett's *The Unnamable* and Angela Carter's *The Infernal Desire Machines of Doctor Hoffman*, not Ian McEwan's *Amsterdam* and certainly not *The Crying of Lot 49*. Unless a novel is poststructuralist, it is more productive to assume that the writer has premeditated almost all possible themes in his or her novel. In the case of *The Crying of Lot 49*, I am particularly happy with the Botticelli/Venus pattern which I finally identified in Essay One and, confident that, if Pynchon ever thought about an underlying visual pattern in *The Crying of Lot 49*, that would have been it.

On Essay Two

The original draft, of what in its revised form is now "The Influence of Henry Adams and J.R. Pierce," was rejected by another journal's anonymous reader for four reasons. First, its "enthusiastically ecocritical standpoint […] has a rather curious structure in which the subdivisions help to produce a somewhat disjointed effect." It does appear that I went overboard in my enthusiasm to move, via *The Crying of Lot 49*, from my 1999 economics article on ecological collapse, entitled "Thresholds and Complementarities in an Economic Model of Preserving and Conserving Biodiversity," to Henry Adams' 1910 writings on the extinction of species, which he attributed in part to the second law of thermodynamics. It excited me that my "highly stylized model" of ecological collapse that I had developed earlier served "as a strong metaphor for both the vulnerability of economic productivity to the loss of biodiversity and the vital role that conservation biology and restoration ecology can play in economies where population and production are increasing and wilderness habitat is shrinking" (*Thresholds and Complementarities* 167). I had no idea that I thought in terms of metaphor in my previous career; the transition to literary criticism having been more seamless than I thought. I was also surprised to realize that my economics article, which I wrote before I ever read Pynchon or Adams, contained the term "irreversibility" (160).

Secondly, the anonymous reader of the original version of Essay Two criticized it for my "failure to take proper account of the intervening science which spans the gap between the two writers [Adams and Pynchon] and the differences between the cultural worlds to which they belonged." This was especially useful advice, for it led to my discovery of J.R. Pierce's 1961 book which was exactly the kind of intervening science that the anonymous reader appeared to have had in mind. Pierce's role in connecting Maxwell's box to information theory is not only one of the major contributions of the present book but it also enabled me to recognize that Maxwell's box is a metaphor for the entire novel, and thereby respond to this reader's third contention–that the "literature dimension" of the essay had not been "very well developed."

In Essay Two, I trace Pynchon's famous claim that the "two distinct kinds" of "entropy. One having to do with heat-engines, the other to do with communication," was "a coincidence. The two fields were entirely unconnected, except at one point: Maxwell's Demon" (*Crying* 105). Taking the first name of Oedipa Maas's last lover before her marriage–Pierce Inverarity–as an important signifier, I found in J.R. Pierce's seminal text on information and communication theory, the source for the coincidental connection. I have continued to wonder, given the extravagant new discoveries in contemporary physics, whether or not a physical connection between thermodynamic entropy and information entropy had been established in the almost fifty years since *The Crying of Lot 49* was published. Indeed, in a March 2000 article in *The Astrophysical Journal*, Lawrence Krauss and Glenn Starkman claim that a "decreasing information base in the observable universe is associated with a finite and decreasing supply of accessible energy," which sounds like the two are physically connected over time (22). I was able to email Professor Krauss and learn that he and Professor Starkman focused on the total number of bits of information that could be processed by a computation, which fully accords with Pierce's thesis that the "best way of encoding the messages from a message source [...] calls for the least number of binary digits" (77). I am neither a physicist or a mathematician, but when I look through the 26 equations in the Krauss and Starkman article I find symbols measuring energy but *not* bits of information. I am inclined to presume that in their projections on an ever expanding universe, thermodynamic entropy and information entropy just happen to increase with some independent variable, but are not directly connected, in which case Pierce's (and Pynchon's) finding still holds: "the effort to marry communications theory and physics have been more interesting than fruitful" (24). (I emailed a copy of this paragraph to Professor Krauss, who gave it his approval.)

The journal to which I had submitted the preceding version of Essay Two had a special interest in history and literature, which prompted the reader's fourth observation, namely that the submission "does not strike me as something that really falls within the [journal's] remit." This intensified my interest in the historical integrity of Adams' *Letter*, as republished posthumously in the 1919 Macmillan edition by Henry's brother Brooks. This was the book I purchased for my research, because the original 1910 edition, only a small number of which were privately published by Henry, was rare and costly. Readers will note in Essay Two that I cite page numbers from both the 1910 edition of Henry Adams' *Letter* and the corresponding page numbers from the 1919 McMillan edition, which includes other works by the two brothers. It is fortuitous that I went to the trouble of browsing through the first edition for the original pagination. Washington University Special Collections Department, which archives my literary papers, happens to owns a copy of the 1910 *Letter*, and like Pynchon "brows[ing] through the thesaurus" for "words that sounded cool, hip, or likely to produce an effect," I likewise thought the duplicate pagination would make "me look good" (*Slow Learner* 15). It did much more than that. In every case but one, the wording is identical in both editions; in that one exception, Brooks inserted 46 new lines, beginning with the last five lines on page 252 of the 1919 edition and ending on the sixteenth line of page 254, between two sentences about a Gustave Le Bon that Henry obviously intended to be contiguous. These lines, missing from the 1910 edition, are about an English medical expert, Dr. Forbes Winslow,

> who has scandalized the community by his bluntness: – "On comparing the human race during the past forty years," he says (pp. 376-377), "I have no hesitation in stating that it has degenerated, and is still progressing in a downward direction. We are gradually approaching, with the decadence of youth, a near proximity to a nation of madmen. By comparing the lunacy statistics of 1809 with those of 1909, … an insane world is looked forward to by me with a certainty in the not far distant future." In fact, the statistics show that in 1809 there was one lunatic in every 418 of the total population of England and Wales; in 1909, there was one in every 278 ; so that in three hundred years one half the population should be insane or idiotic. "These are facts!' continues Dr. Forbes Winslow; "they cannot in any way be challenged." (*Degradation* 254)

Three claims in this quoted material from the 1919 edition are suspicious. First: Winslow refers to a comparison over "forty years" whereas the text goes on to specify his beginning and ending years as "1809" and "1909," a full century apart. Second: the author, ostensibly Henry, based his linear regression on normalcy rates, 418/1 in the base year and 278/1 in the latest year measured, rather than on lunacy rates, 1/418 in the base year and 1/278 in the latest year. Third: the result that in three hundred years one half the population should be insane or idiotic, which uses both the incorrect time periods and normalcy rather than lunacy rates, is not in quotation marks and therefore not the calculations of Winslow. This shocking calculation of impending lunacy–the correctly computed date is closer to 40,000 years in the future than 300 years–is not the result that Winslow is quoted by Adams as exclaiming.

History and literature cannot come any closer together than they do here. I assume that Pynchon used the 1919 text when he wrote *The Crying of Lot 49*, discovered the outlandish claims, consulted the 1910 edition, discovered the discrepancy and incorporated the idea of corruptly inserted lines in the narrative of the novel he was working on. This could have been one of the ways that Pynchon responded to the question posed by Forster and repeated in my Essay One: "why has a novel to be planned? Cannot it grow? […] Cannot it open out? […C]annot the novelist throw himself into it and be carried along to some goal that he does not foresee?" (Forster 96, 97). This assumption on Pynchon's response to the discrepancy in the posthumous edition was the basis of the model underlying my article, "The Corrupt Edition of *The Courier's Tragedy* in Thomas Pynchon's *The Crying of Lot 49*," which appeared in the March 2008 issue of Oxford's *Notes & Queries*, my hypothesis being that the 46-line insertion in the 1919 republication of Henry's *Letter* morphed into the corruption of the Whitechapel version of *The Courier's Tragedy*, which "abounds in [...] corrupt and probably spurious lines [...] and is hardly to be trusted" (*Crying* 102).

One of my editor-friends mentioned that he heard that Pynchon was now answering letters from his critics, so when I got an advance copy of my *Notes & Queries* piece I sent it to the reclusive author, via his publisher, in hopes of a reply. Regardless of whether I learned that Pynchon had Brooks's insertion in mind, it was a win-win situation for me. If Pynchon had discovered the 46 additional lines, I was the first to reveal it. If he hadn't, I had uncovered a 90-year-old hoax in American history, though in my case, in contrast to what Pynchon would have had to go through, the discovery was accidental, a simple matter of checking the 1910 edition for lines corresponding to those in the 1919 edition that I was citing. Whatever the reason, I had achieved either a coup in literary criticism or else a coup in American history. Pynchon didn't really have to reply to my letter, because he left enough idiosyncratic allusions in *The Crying of Lot 49* to "go[ing] mad"(22), "like a madman"(68), "freeway madness"(108), "gone mad"(153), "perhaps a madman"(159), "They were all on something, mad"(171), and "temporary madness"(172)–all seven connoting mental derangement–as compared to another four to being or getting "mad" (39, 79, 123, 168), which simply connote anger. Similarly, there are seven allegations of being a "nut" or "nuts," four of being "crazy" and two of "insane." Lest readers miss the message of these repetitions, Pynchon features a used book store named "Zapf's," which he amply reiterates (*Crying* 89, 102, 148, 149, 169, 170) to signify Zipf's law. Zipf's law is defined in the seminal book on communication theory by J.R. Pierce, which Pynchon probably signified in the given part of Pierce Inverarity's name. According to the real Pierce, there is an "empirical inverse relationship between word probability and word rank [, ...] known as Zipf's law" (86). According to this law, the number of times a particular word occurs in *The Crying of Lot 49* can be a measure of its importance as a signifier. Fortunately, Project Gutenberg maintains a complete copy of *The Crying of Lot 49* on its website, freely available for word searches. Lest readers miss the connection of Zapf and Zipf, Pynchon features the "anonymous inamorato," which can be reached "through your WASTE system" at "IA" (*Crying* 116), a patent switching of the two initial vowels.

Pynchon never did reply to my letter to him. I later discovered why my editor friend presumed that he had begun communicating with critics. In the appendix to his 1988 book, *The Fictional Labyrinths of Thomas Pynchon*, David Seed made public a letter that the famous author had sent in 1969 to a graduate student, Thomas F. Hirsch, in reply to the his query as to whether Pynchon had drawn on a particular source in his first novel, *V*, which indeed he had. It was a very long letter, well over a thousand words, in which Pynchon thanked the student for engaging him on the matter, since he planned to refer to it again in another novel he was working on (It turned out to be *Gravity's Rainbow*). When Pynchon generously concluded his letter with "Writing to you has begun to clarify [the matter] a little, so I'm glad you wrote to me. If you want to talk to me about it more, feel free to do so. Good luck on your thesis, though I suspect it's not such a 'little undertaking'" (*Fictional Labyrinth* 242-43), it struck a familiar cord with me. It is well known that Pynchon has great regard for the writings of Rainer Rilke, especially his *Duino Elegies,* which the poet composed while visiting Princess Marie von Thurn und Taxis in her family's Duino Castle. (This may be the "single plausible source for Pynchon's knowledge about the Thurn and Taxis postal monopoly" that Grant found "extremely difficult to track down" in the *Companion* (1st Ed., 59,60; 2nd Ed., 72).) Just as Pynchon alluded to "Rilke" and the coming of "the Tenth-Elegy angel" in *Gravity's Rainbow* (102, 341), so in the final paragraph of *The Crying of Lot 49* (183), the "descending angel" may signify the "assenting Angels" in the tenth and final elegy" of Rilke's great poem.

It is reasonable to assume that, through his reading of Rilke's work, Pynchon learned of "the Thurn and Taxis family, who at one time held a postal monopoly throughout most of the Holy Roman Empire" (*Crying* 66), which he incorporated in *The Crying of Lot 49* along with their feisty competitor, the fictional Tristero. This mixing of real history with fiction is the kind of "interpenetration of worlds," "between fiction and non-fiction and—by extension—between art and life" that Brian McHale (29) and Linda Hutcheon (10) associate with postmodern stylistics (For examples, see my *Pynchon's Transition* 205 and my *Foer's Everything* 247). David Seed is especially perceptive of the ways that Pynchon "straddles fact and fiction" in *The Crying of Lot 49* and gives further examples in the accounts of Admiral Popov and the Confederate gunboats and of Dr. Diocletian Blobb (*Fictional Labyrinths* 124, 126).

Given the importance of Rilke for Pynchon, it is also reasonable to assume that he took Rilke's famous *Letter to A Young Poet* as a model for himself. The young poet was gratified when the first, of what in six years would total ten letters from the renowned Rilke, arrived; it was close to 1500 words and concluded in a spirit similar to the letter that Pynchon sent the young student 66-years later:

> I am returning the verses with which you entrusted me. I thank you again for your unconditional and sincere trust. I am overwhelmed with it, and therefore have tried, to the best of my ability, to make myself a little more worthy than I, as a stranger to you, really am.

> With my sincerest interest and devotion,
> Rainer Maria Rilke
> (Rilke, *Letters to a Young Poet* 13)

Seed has made it possible for us to experience the reclusive author in a one-on-one letter that demonstrates what a kind and caring person Pynchon must be. In order for Seed to get permission from Pynchon to quote this wonderful letter, he too was able to correspond with Pynchon (*Fictional Labyrinths* 244, note 10).

Several pages earlier I offered that Pierce Inverarity was given his first name in recognition of J.R. Pierce, the author of the seminal book on communication theory that Pynchon appears to have used. Richard Poirier has another connection, that is just as good, "to a quite famous, real-life stamp collector named Pierce," who, if you should go to him "for the kind of flawed and peculiar stamps so important in *The Crying of Lot 49* you would ask him for an 'inverse rarity'" (49). This finding of multiple referents (Pierce the communications theorist, Pierce the famous philatelist, etc., see Grant 2nd Ed., 8) for a single signifier, which I find exciting, Poirier of all people, who is so good at it, deems it "an especially inappropriate way to treat Pynchon because each of these elements is in itself highly mobile and dramatic. Each is a clue not to meaning as much as to chaos of meaning, an evidence of the impossibility of stabilization" (Poirier 47). The reader is warned that if I repeat quotations from *The Crying of Lot 49* in different contexts, it is intentional; for me, it contributes to the very "weirdness and pleasure of the reading experience", that for Poirier, it "omits" (46). Both of us are right!

On Essay Three

In the 1998 issue of *Pynchon Notes*, Thomas Schaub, one of the leading Pynchon scholars and by then the editor of a prominent journal of contemporary literature, published: "The Environmental Pynchon: *Gravity's Rainbow* and the Ecological Context." "This essay," he wrote, "explores the influence of ecological discourse in the 1960s on Thomas Pynchon's fiction, especially on *Gravity's Rainbow*"(59), most notably the discourse of the "persuasive [...] Rachel Carson in *Silent Spring*" (61). Schaub acknowledges that waste, as a product of entropy, "is an image in early Pynchon stories like 'Low-Lands' and 'Entropy,' and the central metaphor of *The Crying of Lot 49*; but in *Gravity's Rainbow*, images of waste acquire environmental connotation" (67). I discovered Schaub's article a decade after it was published and formulated a model based on the assumption that *The Crying of Lot 49* was significantly influenced by the environmental movement of the 1960s and especially by Carson's book. When I eventually discovered the words "springing" and "silence" a few lines apart on page 162 of the 1966 novel, I could taste the bubbles that delighted Harberger. Essay Three is entitled "The Influence of Rachel Carson." Originally printed in May 1962, Carson's book achieved such immediate acclaim that by the end of December 1962, there had been five more printings plus the Book-of-the-Month Club Selection in October of that year. If the rising tide of environmentalism that Carson's book helped stimulate was part of Pynchon's motivation in writing *The Crying of Lot 49*, it was also what motivated me at the outset, when I took my first daytime graduate class under the soon to be famous Murray Wiedenbaum, and decided to specialize in environmental economics.

I did not become aware of Thomas Pynchon until the fall of 1998, when I team-taught a course, based on my recently published *Pollution and the Firm,* with Paul Chambers at Central Missouri State University. I mentioned to Paul that I was working on a paper in literary criticism about William Kotzwinkle's *The Fan Man,* and he replied that I should read Thomas Pynchon. I had never heard of Pynchon and Paul didn't know the name of any of his novels, which made me think that his must have been one of the big names in modern literature when he went to college in the 1980s, just like James Joyce, Thomas Mann and Marcel Proust, none of whom I'd yet read, were the big names when I went to college in the 1940s. I started with *Vineland,* which I didn't like as much as *The Fan Man,* and finally found *The Crying of Lot 49,* which I liked more. I kept reading it to figure out its central theme, which was before I read Grant's pronouncement that

> Even after a number of readings, the novel resists interpretation to an extraordinary degree, especially if 'interpretation' is taken to mean the effort to tease out a unitary and more or less comprehensive account of the novel's message from the tangled network of metaphor and allusion that is Pynchon's trademark. (xii)

There are three or four parallels between my career in economics and *The Crying of Lot 49* that made me feel that I was not in completely new territory.

It was in January of 1966, the same year that *The Crying of Lot 49* was published, that the shoe manufacturing company that I helped build and held minority ownership in was sold out, and I decided to enroll in an MS/PhD program at Washington University in economics and prepare for a second career, this time in academia. I immediately became interested in air pollution control, which was one of the hot topics at that time thanks to Carson's *Silent Spring.* Thanks also to Carson's influence on national priorities, the U.S. Public Health Service, predecessor of the Environmental Protection Agency, was completing a pilot study of total emissions of the six major air pollutants in the St. Louis Airshed. The mimeographed results of that emission inventory provided the foundation for my doctoral dissertation, which was completed by June of 1969. Just as Maxwell's box was the major metaphor for Pynchon's novel, so my dissertation had been based on a "Box Formula" in which an "airshed may be viewed as a box in which emissions of each pollutant diffuse completely and there is a uniform concentration of that pollutant throughout the entire box" (Kohn, *A Linear Programming Model for Air Pollution Control* 99). It continues to amaze me that the uniform concentration of a molecule in Maxwell's box coincidently parallels the uniform concentration of each pollutant in the box models of the newly prominent meteorologists M.E. Smith and R.C. Wanta.

In October of the year in which I completed my dissertation, I participated in a symposium in Santa Barbara on the development of air quality standards. I think of my experience there when I read about Oedipa driving on the freeway, heading irreversibly for the Bay Bridge. It was the middle of rush hour [and she] was appalled at the spectacle, having thought such traffic only possible in Los Angeles, places like that. Looking down at San Francisco a few minutes later from the high point of the bridge's arc, she saw smog. Haze, she corrected herself, is what it is, haze. How can they have smog in San Francisco? Smog, according to the folklore, did not begin till further south. It had to be the angle of the sun. (*Crying* 108)

This passage evokes the controversy that raged in California, more than a decade after A.J. Haagen-Smit connected smog to hydrocarbons and nitrogen oxides in automobile emissions. Although car manufacturers finally acknowledged in 1956 that motor vehicles cause *some* of the smog, they maintained until 1960 that its occurrence was a special case confined to Los Angeles. I may have been conflated with some of that controversy when Haagen-Smit, who was present throughout the symposium, turned on me and ridiculed my pie-in-the-sky calculations of optimal air quality standards in the paper I presented (Kohn, *Abatement Strategies and Air Quality Standards* 112-13). He was a no-nonsense, big-picture pragmatist and may have been disaffected by my failure to consider that mass transit and other systemic approaches for reducing gasoline consumption would have made for a more meaningful paper than the fine-tuning of an abstract simulation model that took the magnitudes of polluting activities as given. I have not given up on modeling complex systems, be they polluting economies or tangled literary networks. I am also happy that Haagen-Smit stuck to his guns. The inaugural chairman of the California Air Resources Board, he had been appointed to that position in 1968 by Governor Ronald Reagan, but was fired by him in 1974 for refusing to obey his directive to ease up on pollution control efforts.

The literary journal to which I sent the penultimate version of what is now Essay Three regretted that they "were unable to accept it for publication. Our advisors reported that they found the central comparison interesting but thought the piece wandered too far away from it, into more familiar territory." They didn't say what was already familiar, so in the present revision of this essay, I strive to maintain the tenor of the central comparison.

On Essay Four

The first anonymous reader of the original, much longer version of the fourth essay, then entitled "Thomas Pynchon and Literary Darwinism" and based on *Against the Day* as well as *The Crying of Lot 49*, adamantly recommended

> that the essay be rejected and not reconsidered. The author has no real argument for the structure of meaning in either of the Pynchon novels, and the author doesn't establish much of a context for his work within Pynchon criticism. The author aims chiefly to demonstrate that Pynchon's work can be read in a Darwinist and ecological context. The method is to cite general terms and themes from [a number of writers] and to find verbal echoes in the Pynchon novels. Most of the verbal

echoes are extraordinarily tenuous and doubtful. The essay consists chiefly in a tissue of loose verbal associations. One hardly knows what to make of it. To produce an essay useful as interpretive criticism, the author would need to identify a structure of meaning in Pynchon's novels and connect that structure in explicit, well-articulated ways with substantive formulations from ecology and Darwinism. The tenuous verbal echoes would mostly be irrelevant or marginal to this project. [...] I imagine that this is student work. The author uses quotation marks at the beginning and end of block quotations–a trivial technical mistake, but the sort of mistake that a professional scholar would be unlikely to make."

As to my being a student, the anonymous referee was right on; but "education too, as Henry Adams always sez, keeps going on forever" (Pynchon *Slow Learner* 23);

In response to the criticism that "most of the verbal echoes are extraordinarily tenuous and doubtful," I endeavored to identify the particular verbal echoes that the anonymous reader may have had in mind when he or she used the word "most"–implying that *some* of the verbal echoes were actually convincing–and to tighten the paper around that minority. As a result, Essay Four is a third the length of its rejected predecessor. If this reader were well-versed in Pynchon criticism, he would not have faulted my reluctance to identify a structure of meaning in Pynchon's novels; as I noted earlier in this introduction, the foremost expert on *The Crying of Lot 49* has noted the near impossibility of teasing "out a unitary and more or less comprehensive account of the novel's message" (Grant 1st Ed., xii). As for *Against the Day*, a leading authority on that novel came up with the best reply to the above reader:

It isn't clear whether Pynchon plots by the seat of his pants or has his own secret and impenetrable designs–the hither-thither meanderings of character, the appalling songs, the Rube Goldberg contraptions [...] might all be constituents of some larger, rational order. Such wishful thinking it is criticism's usual duty to propose. "Yeah, yeah," the author might reply. (Logan 233)

My tendency to build on verbal associations from complex novels may be a carryover from my economics career, where I chose to work with numbers, as in the numerical simulation model heuristically based on Costa Rican ecology in my 1999 article on ecological collapse. For me, pieces of text in a novel fulfill a role in literary criticism that numbers and equations did in economics. I am not advocating such an approach to literary criticism in general, but endorsing Hassan's case for an occasional "text that puts itself in jeopardy with other texts" (*Postmodern Turn* 141).

The second anonymous reader of the earlier submission was much more encouraging. He or she began:

From the outset, let me say that I was excited to read this essay, and believe that the topic of Literary Darwinism applied to Pynchon is an

16

important one, that indeed this is one of the directions that Literary Darwinists ought and need to be going, *i.e.*, examining work that does not lend itself easily to a Darwinian analysis, even resists such analysis at some level. Unfortunately I have to recommend that the essay under consideration undergo extensive content revisions before it is ready for publication. Firstly, let me commend the author for driving to the heart of the matter, I think, by identifying 'the need to create cognitive" order early in the essay as one of Carroll's most important contributions to literary discussion. Although this could use a bit more discussion up front as far as conveying what Carroll means by this, this is a good start to the essay. Pynchon's work is notoriously complicated and concerned with issues of order and disorder. [... Secondly,] the essay jumps into connecting *The Crying of Lot 49* with bones and the evolution of human communication. The argument is too loose here, although a full argument might be developed. [...] Finally, we get to cognitive order and natural religion, which connects to order insofar as Carroll views religion as being one way in which order is instantiated in human minds. While I think the above two topics—ecocriticism in a Darwinian context applied to Pynchon and the evolution of communication as applied to Pynchon, are viable (each a potential essay of its own), I think the third argument is the most extensive and has the most potential for this particular essay. [...] In short, my recommendation would be for the writer to home in on the sense of disorder on many levels that Pynchon creates in his work and to explore in much more depth how this relates to Carroll's notion that literary works provide us with a sense of cognitive order. I hope that these suggestions are useful to the writer, and I welcome further dialogue on the topic if it would be helpful.

I am grateful to this reader for the constructive criticism and hope that the revised essay comes closer to meeting his or her standards. The major change in this final version came quite naturally because in the time that has elapsed since this previous version of Essay Four was rejected, I have come to better appreciate the importance of Carroll's interpretation of literary Darwinism. This made it easier for me to answer this second reader's call for more explanation of why I had claimed that Pynchon intentionally exacerbated confusion: "For what purposes? How does this exacerbation of confusion play out is a Darwinian explanatory framework?" I was able to do what the reader requested by drawing on Carroll's own words.

Then this second reader asked a question that I had never considered, even though on some level I had been aware every time I read the last page of *The Crying of Lot 49* that it gave me a sense of relief:

"Are there ways, too, in which Pynchon reins in the disorder? I am thinking in particular of the end of *Crying*, where the last sentence seems to resolve, in a rather game-like way, the reader's confusion as far as what the title can possibly mean … Pynchon seems to almost string the reader along by taking an arbitrary set of words and then eventually allowing them to settle into sense in the final moments, sort of like taking a jet plane and landing it on a dime. Indeed, he lands it at the end, and yet is this an ironic gesture, where one level of order is re-established while others remain in disarray? Are there evolutionary advantages to cognitive disorder, toward the sort of scrambling that Pynchon galvanizes in the reader?"

I have tried to build this interpretation into the penultimate section of Essay Four, but not nearly as well as this reader expressed it. What a wondrous field this literary criticism, where a scholar is willing to anonymously spill out original, eminently publishable ideas for someone else to take credit? I agree with Hassan that the "politics of the page may be part of the inhibiting politics of criticism as an academic institution" (*Postmodern Turn* 141), but it certainly does *not* hold for this anonymous reader and others like him or her.

So that the contribution of this reader will not be lost or appropriated by me, I include here the remainder of his/her thoughts on Pynchon's use of cognitive disorder, skipping back a sentence to where it started:

Are there evolutionary advantages to cognitive disorder, toward the sort of scrambling that Pynchon galvanizes in the reader? Or is this a reflection of society, which has become disorderly and thus maladaptive in the light of the evolved brain, and is Pynchon representing this maladaptivity?"

In his 1970 blockbuster, Alvin Toffler revealed that "In 1965, in an article in *Horizon*, [he] coined the term 'future shock' to describe the shattering stress and disorientation that we induce in individuals by subjecting them to too much change in too short a time" (4). By the time he wrote *Future Shock*, it had become clear to him "that future shock is no longer a distantly potential danger, but a real sickness from which increasingly large numbers already suffer," and he "gradually came to be appalled by how little is actually known about adaptivity" (4). Pynchon may have read Toffler's article in *Horizon* while he was writing *The Crying of Lot 49*, and thought about the maladaptivity. However, he seems to have gotten into that issue much more deeply in his 2006 novel *Against the Day*, which I take to have been his commemoration of the 40th anniversary of *The Crying of Lot 49*. In that novel, I find the influence of Paul Virilio's and Franco Berardi's writing on "the complexity of human life in our disorienting hypermodern world" (Kohn *Pynchon Takes* 176). I also perceive that novel as Pynchon's transition from postmodernism to its sequel "hypermodernism" (*Pynchon Takes* 156, 176-179). More recently, I examine maladaptivity and hypermodernism in the visual context of Van McElwee's disorienting video, "Liquid Crystal" (Kohn, *Motorization of Video Art*).

(At this point in time, I am rereading my manuscript for the last time before it is delivered for formatting. My views as to where postmodernism is headed became more fluid when I got into Essays Ten, Eleven and Twelve. Rather than bring the earlier essays up to date, I would rather let this book record my conceptual development. I'm not even sure that what I thought in these earlier essays might not turn out to be more valid than what I thought in the later essays. It is hard to record literary and cultural change while it is happening.)

On Essay Five

A longer version of Essay Five, now entitled "The Plate Tectonic Revolution," was rejected by an interdisciplinary journal, which was especially disappointing because that is the kind of journal that is generally more receptive to my submissions. The first anonymous reader reassuringly began by acknowledging that *The Crying of Lot 49* contains "a number of oblique allusions to plate tectonics," that this was "the first time, so far as I know, that this argument has been mounted," and that "it is expressed on the whole through a clear discussion," but concluded that "the allusions are so indirect that the argument stretches textual ingenuity to identify them. […] I'm quite willing to believe that there are one or two passing references to plate tectonics, but it isn't clear how this will affect our perception of the novel." The second reader observed that the writer

> "notes the influence of plate tectonics convincingly enough (although at a stretch sometimes) but does not deliver any new reading of the novel in that context.[…] For me, then, the article falls down on two key principles: it does not offer fresh insights into Pynchon's novel (at least not at length) and neither does it interpret the science of plate tectonics in any meaningful way. I would say, in conclusion, that the article would be far better as a short piece that discusses the discovery of a fresh metaphor in Pynchon.

Although both readers recommended rejection, they provided some encouragement as well as constructive criticism. Because my doctorate is not in literary studies, I thrive on this kind of feedback and cannot grow without it. The first reader also suggested that there was an imbalance "between the sections of the essay summarizing plate tectonics and the narrative analysis." The first thing I did in response was to tighten the amount of material on plate tectonics and put it in a separate section. Then I found more allusions in the novel to plate tectonics. Some of these allusions were surely "stretches" of the imagination (Coincidently, both readers used that same word.), but they pervade the novel and average at least one for every ten pages (*Crying* 10, 11, 21, 22, 25, 26, 30, 32, 40, 42, 55, 56, 79, 80, 101, 108, 177, 178, 180, 181).

In response to the second reader's kind suggestion, I reduced the number of pages in the essay, though it is still not short enough to qualify as a note. Both readers were right when they faulted the original submission for its inadequate effort to understand how plate tectonics added to the importance of *The Crying of Lot 49*. The editor had no choice but to reject the article, but softened the blow by adding that "I am very sorry to bring you this news, especially after you have done as much work on it as you have. Indeed I have to admit I am also rather disappointed, as I was enthusiastic about the idea of an article on Pynchon and science and had become involved in it too." It turns out that this editor did us both a favor by not "taking the article any further." Even when all of the constructive criticism is followed, the essay belongs in a volume of essays like the present one. Following Essay Two on the dismal science of thermodynamic entropy and Essay Three on Carson's sad revelations of the effects of dichlorodiphenyl trichloroethane (DDT) on birds, the "gut fear" of the "formless magic" of plate tectonics in Essay Five makes it apparent that, in the context of *The Crying of Lot 49*, Pynchon's "enthusiasm for scientific metaphors" was less general than Grant implied (1st Ed., xi), for all three are specifically dystopian, symbolic of postmodernism's signature repudiation of modernism's utopian views of science and technology. My three earlier essays in concert gave me a "fresh insight into Pynchon's novel" and a meaningful new way "to interpret the science of plate tectonics" that had not occurred to me in the context of an isolated journal article.

Both readers were somewhat tentative in allowing that plate tectonics could be a referent in *The Crying of Lot 49*. The first went along because of the general consensus regarding "Pynchon's polymath reading." Based on my assumption that Pynchon's 2006 novel, *Against the Day*, intentionally but idiosyncratically signifies themes that critics overlooked in *The Crying of Lot 49*, there is a further reason to believe that plate tectonics was one of those overlooked themes. In the vicinity of the south pole, the five-lad crew of the hydrogen airship receive orders "to get up buoyancy immediately and proceed by way of the Telluric Interior to the north pole regions" (*Against* 114). The airship enters "the great portal" near the south pole, into the hollow interior of the earth, whose existence Pynchon correctly tells us had been broached by some "of the greatest minds in the history of science, including Kepler, Halley, and Euler" (*Against* 115). After sweeping "through the interior of the Earth," they exit "at last out her Northern portal" (117-18). We now know that the idea of a hollow earth is contradicted by the presence of densely packed molten magma in the earth's core, as mandated by plate tectonics. This foray through the center of the earth ends Part One of *Against the Day*, which is followed by Part Two, entitled "Iceland Spar," which is the name of a famous calcite crystal. In an article published in 2002 in the *Journal of Geoscience Education*, Leo Kristjansson, a prominent Icelandic geologist, traced the history of this calcite crystal back to 1669 when E. Bartholinus observed its

> strange double refraction. A ray of light entering such a crystal split into two rays: one obeyed Snell's law of refraction, whereas the other acted in an extraordinary manner. Even at a perpendicular incidence upon a cleavage face it was refracted away from the normal inside the crystal, and

when Bartholinus rotated the crystal this [second] ray rotated with it. (Kristjansson 419)

Certain aspects of this refraction may have been vaguely anticipated in *The Crying of Lot 49* when Oedipa stood in front of the painting "Bordando el Manto Terrestre" and, crying, saw "the world refracted through those tears, those specific tears, as if indices as yet unfound varied in important ways from cry to cry" (*Crying* 21). Experiments with Iceland spar, writes Kristjansson, "probably contributed to an improved understanding of tectonic deformations" (423), affirming the link between plate tectonics and Iceland spar, and by extension to *The Crying of Lot 49*. I leave it to the reader of Essay Five to decide whether I now make a believable case for the influence of plate tectonics on *The Crying of Lot 49*.

On Essay Six

Most of my early articles in literary criticism explored Tibetan Buddhist themes in particular postmodern novels. These novels, in the order they were published, were Pynchon, *The Crying of Lot 49* (1966), Don DeLillo, *Great Jones Street* (1973), Ronald Sukenick *Out* (1973), William Kotzwinkle, *The Fan Man* (1974), John Hawkes, *The Passion Artist* (1979) and William Gaddis, *Carpenter's Gothic* (1985). Other postmodern novels that I read and enjoyed–Barth's *Chimera* (1972), Barthelme's *Snow White* (1967), Beckett's *Unnamable* (1958), Carter's *Infernal Desire Machines of Doctor Hoffman* (1972), Coover's *Public Burning* (1977), Elkin's *Living End* (1979), Fowles's *French Lieutenant's Woman* (1969), Gass's *Willie Masters' Lonesome Wife* (1971), Sontag's *Death Kit* (1967), Spark's *Hothouse by the East River* (1973) and Vonnegut's *Breakfast of Champions* (1973),–had no recognizable allusions to either Tibetan or Zen Buddhism. I begin *Essay Six*, "Evans-Wentz and the Tibetan Bardo," with the fortuitous congruence of Pynchon's sojourn in Seattle with the beginning of the period in which the Tibetan lama, Dezhung Rinpoche, was a famous visitor at The University of Washington. Rick Fields alluded to that visit when he wrote that: "Despite the presence of lamas in Seattle, New Jersey and Wisconsin, American Buddhists saw the sixties primarily as the decade of Zen" (294). The fact that Pynchon experienced Tibetan Buddhism before other postmodern writers may explain why his was the earliest, arguably the only, postmodern novel in the 1960s, that incorporated Tibetan Buddhist themes.

Of the six articles identifying Buddhism in postmodern novels, only one that I know of has been challenged on that count. This came close to the embarrassing situation envisaged by Hassan and described earlier in this introduction, in which authors have turned out to be "unaware of works that were supposed to have directly influenced them" (*Problems of Influence* 73). Having come upon Sukenick's email address, I contacted him to ask if I might question him on his 1973 novel, either by email or telephone. At his kind suggestion, I placed a call the following Sunday, September 21, 2003, at noon, confidently expecting that he would be delighted with my Buddhist interpretation of *Out*. It did not go as I expected. When I told him that I interpreted his novel as symbolizing Buddhist

Enlightenment (see *Sukenick's Out* 176), he said that that was never on his mind. The most reassuring information he provided was that he had read "some" of Evans-Wentz's *Tibetan Book of the Dead*, though when I asked him why he spelled "*prahna*" with an h, though Evans-Wentz did not (*Tibetan Book* 214-215), he was nonplussed. He submitted that I had the right to interpret his novel in any way I chose, and several times during our 20-minute conversation, graciously insisted that I knew more about *Out* than he, having written it so many years earlier, did. He spoke very carefully, not without effort, and finally explained that he was disabled by inclusion body myositis, a degenerative muscle disease that he had had for ten years. The reason he preferred talking by telephone, he said, was that he had to struggle with a sound recognition system to communicate by email.

Ten months later, Sukenick died. A year and a half later my article was published in *The Explicator*, and I sent it to his widow Julia Frey, an accomplished author in her own right, for her comments. On May 5, 2007, she emailed the following observations, which she subsequently gave me permission to quote "in any way you want":

> Ron was entirely secular [. …] He had no particular interest in any deity-oriented belief system, including Tibetan Buddhism. [… W]e visited a Tibetan monastery near Darjeeling in 1998, and he showed virtually no interest in or ability to identify the gods in the wall paintings. As he told you on the phone, he had no intentional desire to make Buddhist arguments in OUT or in any of his writing. […] The basic themes of OUT are not "the false illusions of selfhood" or the search for Nirvana [as I had claimed]. Ron was writing about WRITING. He thought that concepts of plot and character are outmoded 19th-Century realist ideas. To him "suspension of disbelief" is a lie, and he's trying to dismantle those expectations in the novel.

Not all of Frey's reply was that discouraging. She also acknowledged that "Ron was widely read and drew his sources from everywhere," that his "writing is a commentary-on / parody-of the historical-social context in which he's writing, so he tunes into all sorts of themes, trends and vocabulary around him. If Tibetan Buddhism is a pop topic in the early 1970's it will be part of his input in a general sense, but there's nothing didactic about it." Most encouraging was her final comment: "I still thought your observations about Vajrayogin were interesting. But the image seems composite to me. Isn't there an Aztec or Mayan scene with amputation of the tongue?" (In my published article, I should note, Vajayogin was spelled without the final "i." I presumed that the copy-editor knew something about eastern linguistics that I didn't and purposely deleted it, which is why I did not dispute the spelling in the proofs. Though both spellings appear on the World-Wide-Web, I would have preferred to follow Evans-Wentz's spelling.)

Because I may have been presumptuous in forcing the compositeness of Sukenick's "girl nude to the waist" and Evans Wentz's Vajrayogini in the *Explicator* article, I shall duplicate the texts of the two writers and let the reader

22

decide whether or not Sukenick's teenager could have been based on Evans-Wentz's sixteen-year-old. In *Out*, Harold and President Nixon (actually a girl called Nixie) are nervously edging their way across a window ledge seven floors above the street:

> They reach a window. Harold winks and motions her to look inside. Inside a blonde girl nude to the waist and wearing bobbysox hovers over a scrawny adolescent boy tied to a wooden chair his head hanging like a wilted flower. As they watch she grabs him by the jaws with one hand forcing his mouth open inserts a gleaming knife and severs his tongue. Blood covers his chin the severed tongue bounces off his chest and lands in his lap where it wags horribly several times in a growing pool of blood. Then she takes hold of her breast and shoves it into the boy's mouth which makes sucking motions. President Nixon looks from the window to Harrold. Is this true she says. (Sukenick 3)

In *Tibetan Yoga and Secret Doctrines*, which the Oxford Press introduced in paperback in 1967, Evans-Wentz presents the following ancient tantric text for "visualizing the physical body as being vacuous," that is, "illusory":

> Then imagine thyself to be the Divine Devotee Vajra-Yogini, red of color; as effulgent as the radiance of a ruby; having one face, two hands, and three eyes; the right hand holding aloft a brilliantly gleaming curved knife and flourishing it high overhead, cutting off completely all mentally disturbing thought-processes; the left hand holding against her breast a human skull filled with blood; giving satisfaction with her inexhaustible bliss; with a tiara of five dried human skulls on her head; wearing a necklace of fifty blood-dripping human heads; [...] nude, and in the full bloom of virginity, at the sixteenth year of her age; dancing, with the right leg bent and foot uplifted, and the left foot treading upon the breast of a prostrate human form; and Flames of Wisdom forming a halo about her. (*Tibetan Yoga* 173-75)

There are four congruities across the two texts: "the blond girl nude to the waist and wearing bobbysox" could be the 20th century equivalent of the 8th century "nude [...] in the full bloom of virginity, at the sixteenth year of her age"; the "gleaming knife [... inducing the] growing pool of blood" corresponds to the "gleaming curved knife [... responsible for the] blood-dripping human heads"; the blond taking "hold of her breast and shov[ing] it into the boy's mouth" is a lurid version of the goddess's "hand holding against her breast a human skull filled with blood"; and finally, "the boy's mouth [... making] sucking motions" is a lascivious parallel to the Vajrayogini "giving satisfaction with her inexhaustible bliss." That the Buddhist text was intended as an exercise in visualizing the illusory seems to explain why Sukenick has Nixie look "from the window to Harrold" and ask "Is this true"? And yet, Sukenick denies that he had Buddhism in mind when he wrote *Out*, and Frey tells us that if Tibetan Buddhism resonates in the text, it is only because her husband tuned "into all sorts of themes, trends and vocabulary around him."

Granted the falsity of my assumption that Sukenick had specific Tibetan Buddhist doctrines in mind when he wrote *Out*, I still believe that it was a productive assumption, capable of fostering a richer reading experience. In my case, it motivated me to reread the novel multiple times for such connections. The Buddhist approach also enabled me to understand Frey's interpretation of *Out*, when she added to the above observations: "If there's any emotional content to Ron's writing, it is paradoxical love/hate relations with women, the dominance of physical desire, and fear and panic in the face of nothingness. He was not much of a Buddhist in this sense." If Frey is right, and she probably is, some of the reassuring Tibetan interpretations offered by Evans-Wentz of the symbolic Vajrayogini icon, *i.e.,* that by her "keen knife, unruliness of mind is dominated, or cut off" and that "the human skull filled with blood symbolizes renunciation of the world, in virtue of which the Goddess bestows success in *yogic* practices" (*Tibetan Yoga* 174n), were not in the least what Sukenick had tuned into. Admittedly, my Buddhist interpretation misled me in this case. However, there is no way that I would have read into Sukenick's novel the particular "emotional content" that Frey ascribes to it. What she identifies as the "paradoxical love/hate relations with women" is a theme that does not resonate with me. Moreover, such relations are so extreme in *Out* that I presumed they had to be symbolic of something philosophical. Because unfounded "fear and panic" is part of my own mental make-up, I may have protectively intellectualized that aspect of *Out*. If indeed Sukenick thought the "'suspension of disbelief' is a lie," as Frey claimed, I wouldn't have recognized it, because I do it all the time with postmodern novels.

My experience with Sukenick's novel tells me that literary criticism can legitimately be a very personal matter. That view is affirmed by views expressed in a multiple-authored cover-page article, entitled "Words About Words About Words," that appeared on pages 9-11 of the January 2, 2011 edition of *The New York Times Book Review*; at least that is how I interpret Adam Kirsch, when he writes that "The serious critic is one who says something true about life and the world, whose will is not to power, but to self-understanding, self-expression, truth"; Sam Anderson, when he asserts that his "favorite criticism always allows itself to imaginatively intermingle with its source text—to somehow match or channel or negate the energy of the text that inspired it"; and Elif Batuman, when she argues that "aesthetic features almost always indicate a hidden level of meaning, a richness of signification, which is itself the very thing that we perceived as beauty to begin with."

Because I can approach Sukenick's *Out* from two different, in some ways conflicting, approaches, the novel acquires a greater richness of signification and contributes in unexpected ways to my self-understanding. Still, I would be disappointed if I learned that my various interpretations of *The Crying of Lot 49* in this book were contradicted by Pynchon, in the way that my interpretation of *Out* were quashed by its late author and his spouse. However, it is much less likely because Pynchon appears to have had multiple referents for many of his signifiers, which Sukenick apparently did not. Surely Frank Kermode, who wrote a critical essay on it himself, would agree that *The Crying of Lot 49* "is loaded with hidden meanings and although there will be a consensus as to certain of these, there is no suggestion that the process of interpretation need ever cease" (36).

Unlike the preceding essays, the present essay is not a revised version of a previously submitted manuscript. It reinforces an endnote of my first published literary article in which I suggested that "the recently deceased lover of Oedipa" is "in the Bardo, while she is the intended conduit for his rebirth" (Kohn *Ambivalence in Kotzwinkle's* 124n). Grant came close to this when he observed that "Critics have noted that Tibetan beliefs include the notion that the soul undergoes a forty-nine day period of 'becoming' after death," and that "it could be argued that Oedipa is in a transitional stage of her life, a kind of rebirth" (*Companion 1st*, 37). It was at this point in writing the present book that I acquired the second edition of Grant and discovered, to my great surprise and delight, that he had cited my "Seven Buddhist Themes in Pynchon's *The Crying of Lot 49*" most generously (*Companion 2nd*, 4, 23, 30, 42, 44, 68, 88, 148, 153, 165, 174). Instead of closing off criticism of *The Crying of Lot 49*, Grant opened it wider than ever. Whereas there were a hundred works, not including Pynchon's, cited under "References" in the first edition of Grant's *Companion*, in the second edition, there are "some seventy new entries in the list of works cited," an amazing increase of 70% (*Companion 2nd*, xviii). In the second edition, Grant deleted the sentence beginning with "While it could be argued that Oedipa is in a transitional stage of her life, a kind of rebirth" and replaced it with "Kohn has made an extended case for reading Buddhist themes into the novel via W.Y. Evans-Wentz's translation of the *Bardo Thodal*" (*Companion 2nd*, 44). Grant was obviously not convinced enough with my argument to convey its essence, that Inverarity may have planned for his soul to be reborn in Oedipa's fetus, and with good reason. For a number of years, I couldn't think of any special reason why Pierce would have engineered such a plot. Finally it dawned on me that Pynchon was making a point of accentuating Inverarity's wealth–"California real estate mogul" (*Crying* 9), "large block of shares" of this (26), "Big block of shares" of that (41), property in "Arizona, Texas, New York and Florida" that he'd "developed" (55)–to support the inference that Pierce had programmed the *bardo*-freighted sexual encounter in the Echo Courts motel so that he could slip in and become heir to the vast fortune that he was leaving in trust to Oedipa (Kohn *Pynchon's Transition* 208). Presumably, as Tracey Sherard suggested, he had arranged for his lawyer, Metzger, to have sex with Oedipa at that time, providing him with secrets of his own seduction of her" (61). To ensure the success of the plan, Pierce had probably hired Metzger because he was "so good looking that Oedipa" would "at first [think that] They, somebody up there, were putting her on" (*Crying* 28). For Essay Six I closely reread *The Crying of Lot 49*, concentrating on evidence that Pierce had plotted his bardo rebirth.

On Essay Seven

The next essay, *"Diagnostic and Statistical Manual of Mental Disorders,"* is a first and final draft, without benefit of anonymous readings and editor's comments. However I recently wrote another essay based on the *DSM-III-R*, one that diagnosed Edna Pontellier in Kate Chopin's nineteenth-century American classic, and received the reader's following three-sentence comment:

> I think it important to publish work on psychobiology and neuroscientific approaches to literature when we have the chance. That said, this very long essay is clunky in the extreme and reads like some sort of clinical manual rather than a piece of literary criticism. The summaries of alterative approaches (queer theory, psychiatric criticism, etc) make criticism seem like a color by number exercise.

The editor softened the reader's curtness by noting that "For better or worse, we have a considerable backlog of accepted manuscripts on hand, so we are at the moment even more selective than usual," but I wonder if this isn't one of those cases, referred to in the above epigraph by Hassan, in which something that isn't pure literary criticism is nevertheless "also what criticism now requires" (141). Surely in my very long, clunky essay, there was at least one useful insight that the anonymous reader could have had the heart to acknowledge.

In Stephen Burn's essay in "Words about Words about Words" in the January 2, 2011 *New York Times Book Review*, he declares that

> it's time to hear less of critics talking about themselves, spinning reviews out of their charming memories or using the book under review as little more than a platform to promote themselves and their agendas. The critic ought to be an obscure, marginal figure. (9)

If the inclusion of one's own experiences in one's literary criticism is a fault, my writing is patently defective, though it seems to me that my memories are more pathetic than charming, hardly self-promoting. If I have any authority to identify particular mental disorders in Oedipa Maas, it is because I have them myself. I would like to think that I am compromising my personal status for the greater interests of literary criticism.

Over the past fifty-five years, I have seen at least five psychotherapists, typically for weekly visits over a period of three to five years. In general, they said very little, just let me talk. I was certain that they saw through my tenebrous neuroses, and though I felt a strong need, like Oedipa, to know what they were, I was apprehensive of what I might learn. But my talk therapists, all except the last one, believed that the cure lay in my talking and their occasional sharp responses, which usually stung but never directly informed. If only I could have been told 45-years sooner that I had obsessive compulsive disorder, recurrent depression, and generalized anxiety, for these are ego-dystonic disorders, easier to confront head-on by the patient than ego-syntonic disorders. Unfortunately it wasn't known back then, that my axis of disorders are to a great extent genetic. More than that, they can be traced back, especially OCD, to pre-human adaptations that contributed mightily to the survival of our species. David Smith explains that

> there was a time when our ancestors believed only what they could see, touch, taste, smell or hear. However, once their brains evolved the cognitive horsepower to move across the landscape of thought from the observed to the unobserved, they became able to make inductive inferences about the world, and this newfound capacity enabled them to anticipate a whole range of dangers and opportunities that would otherwise have remained beyond their ken. (273)

In the context of literary Darwinism, Jeffrey Foy and Richard Gerrig explain how this crucial adaptability to imagining dangers gives rise to behavior that is explicitly maladaptive:

> Thus, as possibilities migrate from the imagination, OCD sufferers begin to engage in behaviors that have a negative impact on their day-to-day functioning. This is a consequence of the human imagination. OCD is just one example of circumstances in which 'believed-in-imaginings' have potential negative consequences. (178)

It speaks to the scholarly conservatism of the professional psychiatric community in America that as late as 1987, under the heading of "Predisposing factors" for OCD, the *DSM-III-R* listed "No information" (246). Not until the fourth edition of the *DSM*, which came out in 1994, was it finally acknowledged that the "rate of Obsessive-Compulsive Disorder in first-degree relatives of individuals with Obsessive-Compulsive Disorder [...] is higher than in the general population," opening the door to the genetic etiology (420).

Only in the last fifteen years, as relatively mild, anxiety-reducing drugs became available, have I reached a point where monthly visits with my talk psychiatrist and semiannual visits with my pharmacological psychiatrist are sufficient. This may in part also reflect recent research suggesting that "depressive and anxiety disorders in the general population decrease with age" (K.M. Scott *et al*). I had thought that my personal experience with pharmacological and talk psychiatry might be unusual, but today's front page article in the *New York Times* treats it as common knowledge that the

> switch from talk therapy to medications has swept psychiatric practices and hospitals, leaving many older psychiatrists feeling unhappy and inadequate. A 2005 government survey found that just 11 percent of psychiatrists provided talk therapy to all patients, a share that had been falling for years and has most likely fallen more since. (Gardiner Harris 21)

Talk therapy, which has come a long way from its Freudian roots and, in my case, revolves more and more about discussions of the *DSM*, continues to be an important adjunct to medications. The combination, according to Paul Caldwell, enables patients to recognize their "panic trigger[s]," desensitize themselves and "give them a sense of control" (60).

Whereas Burn's ideal critic is an "obscure, marginal figure," Katie Roiphe's ideal, in her contribution to "Words about Words about Words," is the opposite: "the critic has one important function: to write well. [...] If critics can fulfill this single function, if they can carry the mundane everyday business of literary criticism to the level of art, then they can be ambitious and brash" (10). I am unable to pose as the obscure, marginal figure that Burn's admires because my work is too personal. If my writing were artful, no scholar would find it "clunky" or compare it to "a color by number exercise." I am nevertheless ambitious, though Roiphe seems to imply that someone like me is not qualified, to "connect books to larger currents in the culture" and to "identify movements and waves in fiction" (10). If I have any success in those endeavors, it is because, in Kirsch's words in the *New York Times* sextet, I have set my "mind [to] working out its own questions–about psychology, society, politics, morals–through reading" (10), and because I try, as Anderson says critics should, to bring together "authors who might never have spoken in touch with other, thereby redefining both," adding my "own idiosyncratic life experiences and opinions and modes of expression– and in doing so, fundamentally chang[ing] the texts themselves" (11). I indentify more closely with the ideals of Kirsch and Anderson than those of Burn and Roiphe. I have mixed feelings about Batuman's contribution to the *New York Times* collection. I like her belief that hidden levels of meaning are aesthetic. I don't agree that the "role of the critic" is "less to exhaustively explain any single work than to identify, in a group of works, a reflection of some conditioned aspect of reality" (11). Both are important; in two of the subsequent essays I do indentify in Pynchon's works, along with those of other postmodern writers, some general aspects of cultural reality. I strongly disagree with what I take to be Batuman's derogation of "books about evolutionary psychobiology and hard-wired behavior" (11), which are at the heart of my Essay Seven. The mental disorders I identify in Oedipa Maas all have a strong evolutionary psychobiological connection and tend to be hard-wired. I disagree with her dismissal of the neuronovel and by extension, the kind of criticism that I present in Essay Seven, which she claims "has nothing to teach us, apart from medical-textbook symptoms" (11), though the three-sentence anonymous rejection cited above seems to affirm her reproach. It is not so much that the psychiatric interpretation of Oedipa is important to me–it does help me understand my own self–but that it was, I believe, important to Pynchon.

My Essay Seven is a close reading of *The Crying of Lot 49* that concentrates on Oedipa's mental disorders. In other cases in this book I have found that close readings from a particular perspective require their own individual, dedicated readings. I have no exceptional reading acuity; my main credential as a literary critic is my willingness to work on a novel by reading it multiple times, each from a different perspective. What Anderson also requires of a critic, which I keep quoting in this book, is that he or she "imaginatively intermingle" with the targeted text and engage with its positive and negative energies (11). That may be a good way of distinguishing the driving forces behind Oedipa's equilibrating and disequilibrating endeavors.

On Essay Eight

This essay began with my accidental discovery that both Roland Barthes, in his acclaimed critical book *S/Z*, and Richard Miller, who provided the English translation of Balzac's *Sarrasine* for *S/Z*, overlooked an arguably strategic repetition of the phrase "*resta pensive*" in Balzac's original French edition. The editor who rejected the previous version of my Essay Eight correctly observed that

> You are suggesting that through the repetition of "*resta pensive*," Balzac directs his audience to reflect on the similarity between the terror-struck La Zambinella and the marquise. [...] Are we supposed to infer that the marquise recognizes this similarity? Does such a recognition extend to thoughts about what she will be like when she is older? Or does the text only invite such questions without answering them? If you answer "yes" to this last question, then is it incompatible to conclude that both you and Barthes are right—you in saying that the "*resta pensive*" conveys an action (and I think you should say something about which of the Barthesian codes the action belongs to) and he in saying that the text holds some larger meanings in reserve? [...] You move from this discussion to your commentary on Barthes' putting "an unexpected but seminal focus on the last line of all fictional works" and you imply that his remaining unaware of the echo made that "happy outcome" more likely. But it seems to me that the outcome would be the same if he had noticed what you noticed, since your argument is that your reading allows us to recognize the final sentence as one of the "most pregnant" ones in the novella. And the examples in your final paragraph reinforce the outcome.

The editor went on to kindly commend my efforts and tell me what needed doing:

> I admire your close reading of both *Sarrasine* and *S/Z*, but in order for the essay to be publishable I think you need to clarify further the nature of your revisionary reading of Balzac and to tie your claims about what Barthes missed more tightly and persuasively to the larger conclusion. By clarifying your reading I mean making more explicit what is now implicit in that reading and commenting more on how it affects the overall understanding of the story. [...]Thus, your attention to the echo actually confirms Barthes' larger theoretical point, and, in that way, limits the theoretical consequences of your close reading. For that reason—and because [literary] theory has moved on from *S/Z*—I'm not inclined to want the essay for [my journal]. But it's possible that you could revise it

for [name of another journal]. I hope that you find some value in these comments. Best regards

I replied several hours later, thanking this painstaking editor for his "close reading of my close reading," and adding that "I'm not sure where I am heading, but your analysis will, I hope, help me find my way." Hardly a day or two passed before I discovered the hear/bear typo in *The Crying of Lot 49*, suspected that it might have an interesting connection to Barthes' oversight of the *resta pensive* repetition, and make for an appropriate essay in the present volume, which had by then become my central project. This kind editor's thoughtful remarks and questions changed the focus of my essay, now entitled "Pynchon's Typo and Roland Barthes' Oversight."

I have one reservation about Essay Eight, which is a concern over my close focus on a faux, if not genuine, typo. No matter how hard I try, I will not be able to eliminate all the typos in this book. I am hard-wired when I proof-read to compensate for failing eyesight by subconsciously relying on my memory of what I wrote and thinking that's what I'm seeing.

On Essay Nine

Essay Nine is a departure from the preceding essays in this book in that it focuses on the turn from Modernism to Postmodernism, which *The Crying of Lot 49* epitomizes. It also builds on the view of Batuman in the *New York Times* sextet, that the "role of the critic" is "less to exhaustively explain any single work than to identify, in a group of works, a reflection of some conditional aspect of realty" (11). Because a group of works is involved in this particular essay, as well as two Buddhist schools, it is less of a close reading than a collection of sweeping generalizations. The latest rejection of this particular essay, read as follows:

> With apologies for the slow reply, I am afraid to report that your manuscript is not right for [the Journal]. There is much that is suggestive in the essay, and I found the sections on late Pynchon and DeLillo quite compelling, but your associations of Zen with modernism, Tibetan Buddhism with postmodernism, [...] feel, in the end, a bit too schematic. Another way of putting this is that the (Buddhist) evidence doesn't bear out such clearly delineated periodization. By the way–and I hope you'll find this gratifying rather than patronizing–your late-career shift in interests is both heartening and promising. I wish you the best in placing this essay.

I thrive on compliments, so of course I did not take this editor's compliment as patronizing. To better concentrate on his disputation of my major thesis, which is postmodernism's complementarity with Tibetan Buddhism and its anticomplementarity with Zen Buddhism, based on writings on the two denominations that were popular during the 1960s and 1970s, I have set aside the "sections on late Pynchon and DeLillo," which the editor found "quite compelling," for inclusion in Essay Eleven, which recognizes the end of postmodernism.

It is ironic that the literary community objected vigorously to my hypotheses on Zen and Tibetan Buddhism, which admittedly are tendentious, but had nothing to say about my narrow interpretation of postmodernism. The latter has been controversial since Paula Geyh, in the lead article of the spring 2003 issue of *College Literature*, declared that "By this point in history, there are so many ways of seeing postmodernism, and the term is used by so many people in so many disparate ways, that it seems almost to mean or describe everything" (2, 3). Whether or not Zen continues to be complementary with modernism and Tibetan Buddhism with postmodernism, the hypotheses provide a good introduction to the dynamics of the modernist turn. The dynamics as I present them in Essay Nine are compatible with Huyssen's view that postmodernism "casts a new light on [modernism] and appropriates many of its aesthetic strategies and techniques, inserting them and making them work in new constellations" (49), with Fredric Jameson's view of postmodernism coming "into being on the basis of a fundamental hostility towards and repudiation of modernization as such" (391), with McHale's thesis that "postmodern fiction differs from modernist fiction just as a poetics dominated by ontological issues differs from one dominated by epistemological issues" (xii), with Hutcheon's conception that postmodernism "can both self-consciously incorporate and equally self-consciously challenge that modernism from which it derives and to which it owes even its verbal existence" (52), with Hassan's tracing of the term back to the 1934 Spanish *postmodernismo*, which was meant "to indicate a minor reaction to modernism already latent within it" (85), with Chris Barker's association of modernism "with the enlightenment philosophy of rationality, science, universal truth, and progress," in contrast with postmodernism's "questioning of these categories" (13), and with Lyotard's definition of the "*postmodern* as incredulity toward metanarratives" (xxiv), in which modernity was steeped.

On Essay Ten

Essay Ten, now entitled "Paul Virilio's Hypermodernism and Jerry Wilkerson's Pointillism," is focused on Pynchon's 2006 novel *Against the Day* rather than *The Crying of Lot 49*. It has turned out, however, that Petruta Lipan has associated Wilkerson with postmodernism (4), and that his painting on the cover of this book evokes scenes in *The Crying of Lot 49*. This painting, executed in the middle of the signature decade for postmodern American art (Kohn, *Pynchon's Transition* 194), features a crisp pack of Camel Cigarettes, the brand that more doctors smoked than any other back in the 1950s. It was the "Golden Age of Smoking," when advertisements led us to believe that cigarettes nourished healthy, energetic adult bodies. Postmodernism's backlash to modernity's euphoria is sarcastically characterized in *The Crying of Lot 49* by "Beaconsfield Cigarettes" featuring "the very best kind of filters," made, of all things, aged human bones (*Crying* 34). The study of Pynchon's turn from postmodernism in *Against the Day* and especially in his latest book, *Inherent Vice*, are part of an extended close reading of *The Crying of Lot 49*. Essay Ten has gone through five revisions. An anonymous reader's comments on the second draft included the following remarks which, that reader all-too-truthfully warned,

> were being put […] ungenerously: this is an essay in art-historical comparison by someone with a meager grasp of art history. Worse, the comparison is between a real contemporary print-maker (Jerry O. Wilkerson) and novelistic ekphrases of imaginary paintings by a fictional painter (Andrea Tancredi in Pynchon's *Against the Day*). Since the paintings of Andrea Tancredi don't actually exist, and we have only Pynchon's rather indeterminate descriptions to go on, there is (to say the least) considerable latitude for someone intent on finding real-world parallels. Considerable latitude, but not unlimited latitude. Pynchon associates Tancredi with Futurism. He says that, having absorbed the lessons of pointillism, Tancredi has moved beyond the latter to a more dynamic and "explosive" use of paint. He describes Tancredi aiming "controlled spatter[s]" of paint at his canvas. None of this sounds remotely like Wilkerson's practice, which seems (on the evidence of the images reproduced in the paper) coolly contained and witty, not remotely Futurist, not at all "explosive," despite the alleged resemblance of his image of a muffin to a mushroom cloud. If anything, Pynchon seems to be positioning Tancredi as an unheralded precursor of Abstract Expressionism - and Wilkerson's prints, engaging and witty though they may be, seem about as far from Abstract Expressionism as one could get.

The remaining half of this reader's report is no longer relevant because it persuaded me to eliminate the text therein disparaged. I consider such disparagement constructive and am grateful for it. This reader, who appears to have a background in art history, is probably correct that Pynchon seems to be positioning Tancredi as a precursor of abstract expressionism, and that Wilkerson's prints seem about as far from abstract expressionism as one could get. This did not surprise me because I already knew from Carlo Lamagna's article on Wilkerson's art that it "was a reaction to the hegemony of abstract art" (12). I also knew from Lamagna that many of Wilkerson's paintings "recall the opulence of 17th century still lifes teeming with abundance and underlying approval of conspicuous consumption" (14), but I believed, because Wilkerson used advanced print-making technologies and inks, that he could be considered a Futurist, like the fictional Tancredi. For such reasons and in accord with Tancredi's technique of "stabbing tiny dots among larger ones" (*Against the Day* 587), I hypothesized that Pynchon might have had Wilkerson in mind when he developed Tancredi's persona, and used that hypothesis as one of my models for interpreting *Against the Day*. In none of my three earlier drafts of this essay did I ever mention "abstract expressionism." My assumption that Wilkerson was the model for Tancredi was a simplification, an abstraction. The reader was correct when he argued that "there is (to say the least) considerable latitude for someone intent on finding real-world parallels. Considerable latitude, but not unlimited latitude." This is true of economic-type modeling in general. There was a lot of useful advice in this reader's report, and it enabled me to revise my draft accordingly and send it to a second journal. Subsequently I received the following reply from that journal's editor:

> Sorry for the delay with the assessment of your paper on Pynchon's *Against the Day* for [Journal's name]. We have to deal with a considerable backlog – without exemption from courses or any other duties. The editorial team read the paper with interest, particularly enjoying the pictures and your comments about them. Ultimately, however, it found the paper's promise that Virilio and Wilkerson might elucidate Pynchon's novel unfulfilled, and the claim that Wilkerson mediates between Virilio's theory and Pynchon's fiction not convincing. The text of the paper also displays methodological problems, especially with its claims about Pynchon's hypothetical interest in or knowledge of Wilkerson. This paper's profile is, unfortunately, not for [this journal]. I would suggest journals where there is a greater emphasis on art. Thank you for getting us acquainted with Wilkerson's works. He is, indeed, a fascinating painter.

This rejection was less specific than the preceding one, but it did make clear that I had not yet achieved, what this editor correctly presumed was the "paper's promise that Virilio and Wilkerson might elucidate Pynchon's novel" and its "claim that Wilkerson mediates between Virilio's theory and Pynchon's fiction." That this editor and his or her editorial team would thank me "for getting us acquainted with Wilkerson's works" and would volunteer that "He is, indeed, a fascinating painter" was reassuring, for this was one of the major goals of my essay. My brother, who was one of Jerry's teachers in art school, thought very highly of him and especially admired his ability to achieve prominence in the highly competitive New York market. By this time, I wanted to publish my essay as much for lovely Gail Wilkerson's sake as for my own. Once again I revised it, this time sending it to a journal with "a greater emphasis on art," as the second editor had advised. The third editor, without sending it out for review, turned it down because: "Basically, interesting and well-written as your essay is, it does not fit with our current editorial priorities, as we do not presently publish essays organized around the kind of close reading that you perform here." Intrigued, I responded to the editor with the following email:

> Thank you for reading my manuscript. I do not have a doctorate in literature so I hunger for the kind of feedback you gave me–in this case, making me aware of "close reading." I googled that term and discovered two kinds of close reading, both of which I use. I also learned that there is a book on the subject by Frank Lentricchia and Andrew DuBois, which

I plan to buy [. ...] According to the definition of close reading on the internet, I used it in my essay when I closely read the 50 or so pages on the artist Andrea Tancredi to find connections to Jerry Wilkerson's work. Then I used it to scan *Against the Day* for possible allusions to close readings of Paul Virilio. I have had a number of my Pynchon papers rejected because readers are not convinced that my readings of *The Crying of Lot 49* are valid. Does that connect to one of these two kinds of close readings, either with respect to specific hot spots in the novel or to connections in the novel to hot spots outside of it? I take it that close readings can be problematic. I know that they violate your own current editorial policies. Is one of the two kinds of close readings my problem, or is it both? Or am I not using the approach convincingly? I would be very grateful for your guidance on this matter, which I think is especially relevant for me.

I'm not sure what I meant by "hot-spots" at the time, but most likely, these are places in the texts that are rich in information that require close reading. The editor–by now, we were on a first-name basis–responded as follows:

Dear Bob. Apologies for the delay in reply. It is not so much that you use one particular type of close-reading, and we do sometimes publish work that relies on close-reading. Over all, we look for rigorous, original work that is engaged with current debates and that addresses other contemporary criticism. When we do publish work that relies on close-reading, the work always engages current debates. I can't be sure of others' editorial policies, and you no doubt do reference a number of contemporary scholars, but it seems to me that your close-readings would work better if they were woven into arguments that more effectively engaged current debates. That is, it's not so much that we avoid publishing any close-readings, but rather that we tend to publish essays in which any close-reading is not the focus. Hope that helps, and thank you for your interest in [Journal's name].

To this, I replied on February 23, 2011:

Dear [...], Thank you for the helpful reply. I am working on a book that was originally entitled "Nine New Essays for the 49th Anniversary of *The Crying of Lot 49*." Most of the essays are previously rejected essays that I have revised. When I got your rejection and realized that you were connecting my work to what appears to be a hot new term, I changed the title of the book to "Close Readings of *The Crying of Lot 49*." I feel even better about the new title after receiving your [last email] because each of my essays is a close reading from a different perspective. Thank you for taking the time to help me.   Sincerely, Bob

At the time, I did not understand what this editor was telling me to do differently, and so I simply tried harder, in this case, by expanding my exposure to Virilio's writings, to Wilkerson's paintings, and to relevant Pynchon criticism. I acquired the recent English translation of one of Virilio's early books, *Negative Horizon*, which turned out to have intriguing complementarities with *The Crying of Lot 49*, further justifying my including this essay on *Against the Day* in the present book, which, thanks to the above third editor, now has a more compelling title. Because Virilio's *Negative Horizon* has parallels to *The Crying of Lot 49* rather than to *Against the Day*, these are best included in the current introductory material for Essay Ten, rather than in the main body of the essay itself, which draws on Virilio's later writing.

An early chapter of *Negative Horizon* has to do with nostalgia for past wars, exemplified by "clothing from the last world wars" and "trophies and banners" in "the *Imperial War Museum in London* and the *muse de l'Armée* at les Invalides" (*Negative* 81). "The army presents itself to us in the French capital like a department store with its summer fashions, its winter collections, and its springtime sales, while in Great Britain we picture instead a travel agency" (81). "Tremaine's Swastika Shoppe" in San Narciso anticipates by several decades, some of the strange nostalgia evoked by Virilio's imagined department store in Paris or travel agency in London (*Crying* 168). Its spirited entrepreneur, Winthrop ("Winner, for short") Tremaine, hustles Oedipa:

> This season now it's your rifles. Fella was in just this forenoon, bought two hundred for his drill team. I could've sold him two hundred of the swastika armbands too, only I was short, dammit. [...] Listen, now we're getting up an arrangement with one of the big ready-to-wear outfits in L.A. to see how SS uniforms go for the fall. [...] Next season we may go all the way and get out a modified version for the ladies. How would that strike you? (*Crying* 149)

Both Virilio and Pynchon connect "the soldier's equipment" with "certain politics of the fighting body" (*Negative* 82), except that the connected politics are much more sinister in Tremaine's Swastika Shoppe.

Virilio's *Negative Horizon* is "An Essay in Dromoscopy," the relationship between speed and seeing that focuses on "the violence of speed" (113). In the case of the automobile, "accelerated traffic [has] triggered and developed a new catastrophe, the collision: that is the disappearance of one vehicle into another" (113). Pynchon, like Virilio in *Negative Horizon*, involves darkness and alcohol in the equation of speed and danger, when he has Oedipa "drink bourbon until the sun went down and it was as dark as it would ever get. Then she went out and drove on the freeway for a while with her lights out, to see what would happen" (*Crying* 176). Both writers see a connection here to the transcendent. For Virilio, "speed finally provides for a crossing over, without any problem, of the distance between the physical and the metaphysical" (119), while Oedipa's hazard was crossed-over because "angels were watching" (176).

Finally, there are five references to the "void" in *The Crying of Lot 49* and at least ten in *Negative Horizon* that demonstrate further shared interests by the two authors. For Pynchon, there is the "seeking hopelessly to fill the void" (*Crying* 21), "galleons sailing west into the void" (45), and Oedipa's sitting "for hours, too numb even to drink, teaching herself to breathe in a vacuum. For this, oh God, was the void (171). For Virilio, there is "the void" that "is no longer an absence" but a "presence" (*Negative Horizon* 136), "the last resource of space" that is "the void" (146), and "the void of the ground" that "causes the fullness of the sky" (146). Both writer's recognize the transcendental aspects of the void.

It did not occur to me until the penultimate page of *Negative Horizon*, when Virilio raised the issue of *"technological excesses"* and finally *"scientific excess"* (199), that his 1984 book anticipated hypermodernism, but was not about it. It is in his later books, *The Vision Machine*, *The Art of the Motor*, *Open Sky*, *The Information Bomb*, *Ground Zero*, and *Art and Fear*, which are the others that I have read so far, and especially in his interview with John Armitage, that the specter of hypermodernism and Virilio's fear of science and technology are expressed. Even dromoscopy is raised to the higher alert level in the latter, where information transmission is "no longer concerned with the bringing about of a relative gain in velocity, as was the case with railway transport compared to horse power, or jet aircraft compared to trains, but about the absolute velocity of electromagnetic waves" (Armitage 36).

Just as it informs Essay Ten that Pynchon and Virilio have interests in common that precede *Against the Day*, so also is it informative that the same is true of Pynchon and Wilkerson. My search for more Wilkerson paintings led me to the Tucson Museum of Art, which owns a major work by him entitled "Tom's Bar and Grill, II" after one of Jerry's favorite haunts located at 20 South Euclid Avenue in St. Louis's Central West End. As soon as I saw the painting, I recognized images reminiscent of *The Crying of Lot 49*. At the center of the painting are what could be the "fluted gold lens of a beer pitcher," through which Oedipa and Mucho "faced each other" in the "pizzeria and bar" in downtown San Narciso (*Crying* 141). In the foreground is a pack of Camel Cigarettes, which brings to mind the competing brand, Chesterfield Cigarettes, which Pynchon must have had in mind when Oedipa and Metzger are watching TV in the Echo Courts motel, and into "the break now roared a deafening ad for Beaconsfield Cigarettes, whose attractiveness lay in their filter's use of bone charcoal, the very best kind" (*Crying* 34). What a great day that was for me when Susan Dolan, the Tucson Art Museum's Collection Manager, wrestled that fifty-by-sixty-inch painting out of storage so that I could see it, fall immediately in love with it, and tell her then and there that I wished to reproduce it on the cover of this book.

It was on this same visit to Tucson that I read Seed's *Fictional Labyrinths of Thomas Pynchon* for the first time and Bloom's *Thomas Pynchon* for the second, roused by the editor's rejection of my third draft to find more substantive connections of Virilio and Wilkerson to Pynchon. It was in the former that I discovered that Pynchon had created in his novel *V.*, long before Virilio in *Open Sky*, "an important motif around the erotic satisfactions of the mechanical," in which robots "and automata symbolize the possible inanimate end-points to such

36

a process" (*Fictional Labyrinths* 4). The corresponding passage in *V.* softened my view in Essay Ten of Pynchon's take on Virilio.

The extended readings of Virilio, Wilkerson and even Pynchon that the final editor fostered when he advised me that my "close-readings would work better if they were woven into arguments that more effectively engaged current debates" finally enabled me to understand what he meant when he concluded that "it's not so much that we avoid publishing any close-readings, but rather that we tend to publish essays in which any close-reading is not the focus." It appears that I had mistakenly presumed that close reading was not only necessary but sufficient. My problem, as Virilio himself put it in the foreword to *Negative Horizon*, is that "One only really sees what one already has in mind," and what one already has in mind depends on what one has read and how he or she has reacted to it (36). Virilio recognized that the problem lay in "the clandestine voluntarism at work in the most ordinary vision" (36). When I revised the third draft of Essay Ten it struck me how much text I was deleting that was based almost entirely on close reading for its own sake, before I happened upon Virilio's *Negative Horizon* and especially its foreword, upon Wilkerson's *Tom's Bar and Grill II,* upon the last three chapters and epilogue of Pynchon's *V.*, and finally upon rereading the brochure for Wilkerson's posthumous retrospective, all of which fostered new perspectives requiring specially dedicated close readings.

When I finally took in the importance of what Lipan had to say in her piece in the brochure about Wilkerson's "employ[ing] intertextuality," still another cycle of discovery began for me (4). All of my essays on *The Crying of Lot 49* depend specifically on close *intertextual* readings. This is where I get the hypotheses that motivate my models. The connection of intertextuality, hypotheses and models explains the "clandestine voluntarism" at work in my writing, as it is "in the most ordinary vision" and therefore not so special after all (*Negative Horizon* 36). "[E]ducation too, as Henry Adams always sez, keeps going on forever" (Pynchon *Slow Learner* 23)

On Essay Eleven

The earlier Essay Nine on the complementarity of Tibetan Buddhism and postmodern fiction built on John McClure's hypothesis that the turn from science-based secularism to new spiritualities was a distinct attribute of postmodernism. The two principal postmodern novelists that McClure discussed in that regard were Pynchon and DeLillo. In *Essay Nine* I argued that these two writers, together with Kotzwinkle, Hawkes and Gaddis, were particularly influenced by Tibetan Buddhism, whose coming to America in the 1960s coincided with the rise of postmodernism. The latest of my drafts, on which *Essay Nine* is based, concluded with a section on Pynchon's 2009 *Inherent Vice* and another on DeLillo's *Point Omega,* both of which evinced a significant cooling toward Tibetan Buddhism as well as corresponding, possibly related retreats from postmodern stylistics. The latter were the kind of change that could have been predicted from the hypothesis underlying *Essay Nine*. The editor who rejected the preceding draft of that essay (see "On *Essay Nine*" above) did find "the sections on late Pynchon and DeLillo [i.e., *Inherent Vice* and *Point Omega*] quite compelling, … ." These two sections, recent additions to the last draft of *Essay Nine*, reflected a change in my thinking prompted by a letter from John Knapp, the editor of *Style*, dated March 26, 2008, in which he noted that, as a critical concept, postmodernism had come and largely gone, and that for the most part, treatises on postmodernism are "really dealing with a moment in critical history rather than something current." Alerted by Knapp, I began to wonder what might follow postmodernism, the ethos of which was explained by Huyssen as a philosophical response to the ideology of modernization, which had to do with a "rational design for a rational society" (14). The problem of modernism, as Huyssen saw it, was that "the new rationality was overlaid with a utopian fervor which ultimately made it veer back into myth" (14). It was the repudiation of that myth that, for Huyssen, "goes by the name of the postmodern" (49). Because modernization was most closely associated with advancements in science and technology, these spectacular advancements more than anything else, it seemed to me, explained modernity's confidence in its innate rationality and its utopian expectations for humanity. On the premise that the present cycle from modernism to postmodernism would lead to a sequel based on the next cultural attitudes toward science and technology, particularly those of Virilio and Berardi regarding the dangers of extreme science and technology, the likely sequel could be what Virilio called hypermodernism and what Berardi saw as the incompatibility of human receptivity and digital electronic connectivity.

I was astonished to learn that Pynchon had completed a new novel, *Inherent Vice*, in 2009, only three years after he had published the gigantic *Against the Day*. Because the 2006 novel showed signs of Virilio's and Berardi's influence, I thought that Pynchon may have developed full-blown thoughts about hypermodernism that he urgently needed to publicize, and I thereupon acquired a copy of *Inherent Vice*. But the verification I wanted to find and expected to find was not there. There is a reference to a "very weird hypercolor" that is "as far beyond our everyday color as Technicolor is beyond black and white" (*Inherent* 286), which could herald the kind of breakthrough I was expecting to find. But if anything, Pynchon's characters went out of their way to mock hypermodernism, dismissing the "wave of the future" as "a whole 'nother strange world–time, space, all that shit" (*Inherent* 195). So much for "One only really sees what one already has in mind," the old "maxim" for which Virilio provided an experiential rationale (*Negative Horizon* 36).

Not unlike the fake history that Pynchon wrote in *Against the Day*, he has taken to dabbling in fake science in *Inherent Vice*, as when some "lab people" explain that "the universe " has been "like, expanding, […] with all the molecules further apart" (106), which incorrectly implies that the space inside of molecules as well as outside of them is expanding. That Pynchon is now writing fake science is a strong charge to make in print, so I immediately emailed my two physicist experts, asking them: "As the universe expands, do all molecules become further and further apart. Does the space within molecules also expand?" Lawrence Krauss replied "No.. all things that are gravitationally self bound do not expand. . our galaxy does nor expand.. the earth does not expand.. only the space between objects that are not bound by gravity to each other expands." John Stachel wrote that "cosmological models deal only with smoothed out, averaged distributions of matter, not even with the stars and galaxies, let alone molecules. One assumes that the expansion applies to the distances between galaxies, since we can observe galactic red shifts (*i.e.*, red shifts in the spectrum of light received from galaxies); but the expansion can't apply to everything. If it did, then our measuring rods would also expand, and there would be no way to notice any expansion!" Pynchon appears to have anticipated the imaginative problem of measuring human dimensions in an expanding universe when he fancied "that they'd just invented intergalactic time travel and that he [Doc] was about to be sent across the universe and maybe 3 billion years into the future [, ... so that] you'll be the same size and density. Meaning you'll be about a foot shorter than everybody else, but much more compact. Like, solid?" (*Inherent* 106). Like his fake history in *Against the Day*, Pynchon's fake science of expanding molecular space is followed by the seemingly absurd question, "Can I walk through walls?" (106), which quantum mechanics actually says that we can if the spaces between our own molecules and those of the wall are lined up just right–it's called tunneling–though the probability of that is infinitesimally small. Besides the above-mentioned discussion of "hypercolor," there are also arcane references to Doc's "new hyperdensity," "to a sort of hyperdimensional pattern" and to Einar's "hypersensitive hands" (*Inherent* 107, 217, 226) that suggest that Pynchon may be acknowledging the buzz about hypermodernism at the same time that he appears to be distancing himself from Virilio's extravagant fears of hyper-science and hyper-technology. Still it's strange that Sparky's apprehension that "someday everybody's gonna wake up to find they're under surveillance they can't escape" seems to have been inspired by Virilio's fear that "with the advent of globalization, it is everywhere that one can be under control and under surveillance" (*Inherent* 365; Armitage 38).

The sea change between *The Crying of Lot 49* and *Inherent Vice* suggests that Pynchon in 2009 is marking the end of postmodernism and possibly the beginning of something new. This cultural sequel, it appears however, has less to do with science than with a shift to a different form of modernism. Whereas the old modernism was enraptured with humanity's potential for moral good, Pynchon's new modernism has not only, like postmodernism repudiated that potential, but has awakened to a newfound ubiquity of vice and evil. When Denis worries that Doc is putting trust in evil people, Doc retorts: "What, I should only trust good people? man, good people get bought and sold every day. Might as well trust somebody evil once in a while, it makes no more or less sense. I mean I wouldn't give odds either way" (*Inherent* 349). That Pynchon places the novel from late 1969 to early 1970, only three or four years after *The Crying of Lot 49*, suggests that he would have taken it almost literally when Knapp called postmodernism but "a moment in critical history" (*supra*). That Pynchon's world fluctuated so quickly from utopian goodness (the old modernism) to teeming evil (the new modernism) may have been the message that Bigfoot told Doc: "What goes around may come around, but it never ends up exactly the same place, you ever notice? Like a record on a turntable, all it takes is one groove's difference and the universe can be on into a whole 'nother song" (334). Presumably Pynchon's new modernism is as dystopian as the old modernism was utopian, and will likewise be eventually repudiated by a different postmodernism, which may conform to Huyssen's view that in "some ways, the story of modernism and postmodernism is like the story of the hedgehog and the hare: the hare could not win because there always was more than just one hedgehog. But the hare was still the better runner …" (49).

I was intrigued when DeLillo came out with a new novel in 2010 entitled *Point Omega* and wondered if it too heralded a significant cultural shift. DeLillo was as interested in Tibetan Buddhism as Pynchon, maybe even more so. One of my forthcoming essays, "Tibetan Buddhism in Don DeLillo's Novels: The Street, The Word and the Soul," which builds on Joseph Dewey's classification of DeLillo's novels, finds allusions to Tibetan Buddhism in every one of his fourteen novels. Thanks to an anonymous reader for *College Literature* whose "key recommendation for revision [was] to explicate how the current author's Buddhist take on the street, the word, and the soul is different from Dewey's, notably by defining the Buddhist meaning/version of each section, street, word, an soul, respectively," I was able to connect Dewey's "the street" to the Tibetan Priesthood, "the word" to the Buddhist Scriptures–and "the soul," to the Buddha. I would be remiss not to credit this wonderful suggestion, which had never occurred to me over the years I kept revising that paper. It would be unusual if not significant if DeLillo stopped alluding to Tibetan Buddhism in *Point Omega*. I was also eager to see how DeLillo treated hypermodernism. At the time that Virilio was expressing his fears of futuristic science and technology in French, DeLillo was independently portraying comparable fears in his 1985 novel *White Noise*: a railroad tank car gets "rammed and something punch[es] a hole in it;" then "a lot of smoke" and "a heavy black mass hanging in the air" (110). "It's called Nyodene Derivative or Nyodene D. […] At first they said skin irritations and sweaty palms. But now they say nausea, vomiting, shortness of breath" (111). The area is ordered evacuated and people crowd the highways in cars and buses. Hours later, there's a rumor that

> Technicians were being lowered in slings from army helicopters in order to plant microorganisms in the core of the toxic cloud. These organisms were genetic recombinations that had a built-in appetite for the particular

toxic agents in Nyodene D. They would literally consume the billowing cloud, eat it up, break it down, decompose it. (*White Noise* 160)
Babette Gladney tells her husband Jack, the narrator, that she doesn't like this latest rumor:

"What scares me is have they thought it through completely?"
"You feel a vague foreboding," I said. [...]
"Every advance is worse than the one before because it makes me more scared.' "Scared of what?"
"The sky, the earth, I don't know."
"The greater the scientific advance, the more primitive the fear."
"Why is that?" she said. (*White Noise* 161)

Jack does not answer. It remained for Virilio to do so in his books.

Today is May 25, 2011. Steven Moore is in town, searching the Gaddis archives in Washington University Libraries' Special Collections for material for a book in progress featuring his favorite writer's correspondence; last night, I was able to meet him in person for the first time and have dinner with him. I showed him a copy of the front and back cover material for the present volume, and was pleased when he said that this is a book he will definitely read. He was a little taken aback at the title, "Close Readings of *The Crying of Lot 49*," remarking that he thought that *all* literary criticism is based on close reading. That prompted me to add "New" to the title. Steve had read *Inherent Vice* and loved it because he was born in southern California and knew the area, even the actual surf bands, that Pynchon talked about. He told me about the amazing 26-page review of the novel by Bill Millard in the *College Hill Review* that I would probably have discovered on my own, but to my great dismay *after* my book had been printed. I learned that last year, Steve authored a 700-page tome entitled *The Novel: An Alternative History, Beginnings to 1600*, to be followed by a second volume, more than half of it already completed, continuing the history to the present. Because he is a proven scholar on the history of the novel I was apprehensive when he told me that in the last ten years, some critics have tired of literary theories such as deconstruction, structuralism and reader response theory, fearful that he might be including modernism and postmodernism in his list, but not mentioning them because he saw them displayed in the table of contents I had shown him. He hastened to assure me that he was OK with terms like modernism and postmodernism, even hypermodernism, because they describe historical periods.

On May 26, two nights after my reassuring discussion with Steve, my wife and I fortuitously attended a panel discussion intended to prepare the community for the performance next month of the potentially divisive 1991 opera, "The Death of Klinghoffer"–music by John Adams, libretto by Alice Goodman. The speakers were Gerald Early, Director of the Center for Humanities at Washington University, Timothy O'Leary, General Director of Opera Theatre of St. Louis, Ghazala Hayat, former chairwoman of the Islamic Foundation of Greater St. Louis, David Greenhaw, President of Eden Theological Seminary, and Batya

New Close Readings of *The Crying of Lot 49*

Abramson-Goldstein, Executive Director of the Jewish Community Relations Council. I did not appreciate how skittish the Panel was about their central mission until I asked them a question during the open-mike session. It had to do with one of the excerpts from the opera that was explained and then played for us: Mamoud, one of the hijackers, tells of the tragic death of his mother and brother in the Palestinian refugee "Camps at Sabra/ and Chatila/ Where Almighty God/ in his mercy showed/ My decapitated/ Brother to me/ And in his mercy/ Allowed me to close/ My brother's eyes/ And wipe his face" (Goodman 10). Although the refugee camps were in Lebanon, the Israeli's, who had invaded the country were said to have been complicit in the massacre. The captain of the Achille Lauro is moved by Mamoud's story and tells him: "I think if you could talk like this/ Sitting among your enemies/ Peace would come" (11). Mamoud's reply was an epiphany for me for it had never occurred to me that Palestinians might feel this way: "The day that I/ And my enemy/ Sit peacefully/ Each putting his case/ And working towards peace/ That day our hope dies/ And I shall die too" (11). When the mike was passed to me, I remarked on the power of criticism to inform art, as exemplified by the panel's discussion of Mamoud together with the excerpt from the opera, which made me understand Yashir Arafat in a way that I had never thought. When Ehud Barak in 2000 offered a peace agreement in which Israel would completely withdraw from the West Bank, return to the pre-1967 borders, and negotiate the problem of the Palestinian refugees, who had been forced to flee their homes in 1948, all in return for Palestinian recognition of Israel, Arafat turned him down without even making a counter-offer. At first I thought that Arafat was being unreasonably stubborn, but then I was told that if he accepted the agreement he would have been assassinated by his own people. Mamoud's speech to the Captain suggested something very different, that Arafat couldn't make peace for the same reason that Mamoud would have preferred to die. While I deeply regret that his refusal to negotiate may have helped the right-wing come to power in Israel and accelerate the unfortunate colonization of the West Bank, at least I understand better why he did what he did. O'Leary immediately replied that by invoking Barak and Arafat, I had crossed the line into politics that the conference had pledged to avoid. In a front page article of the May 28 *St. Louis Post-Dispatch*, Sarah Miller put it more starkly: "'We're going to stay away from the political,' said Hayat firmly, in response to an audience member who stood to denounce the late Palestinian Liberation Organization leader Yasser Arafat" (A10). Perhaps Hayat as well as O'Leary had come down on me for being political–I don't remember–but I couldn't fathom the misunderstanding, for I had intended my comment to be an example of how art, informed by criticism, enhances our understanding of ourselves and others. I tell this story to prepare the reader for the emphasis that I put on "The Death of Klinghoffer" in *Essay Eleven*–it exemplifies dystopian modernism–and on panelist Early's opening comments on the opera–which may presage a new kind of postmodernist response, this time to dystopian rather than utopian modernism.

On Essay Twelve

In rejecting an earlier version of Essay Eight, an editor kindly admired my "close reading of both *Sarrasine* and *S/Z*" (*supra*), but it was not until another editor rejected the penultimate version of Essay Ten because "we do not presently publish essays organized around the kind of close reading that you perform here" (*supra*), that I took careful note that I perform this special kind of reading, and that this could either be or not be advantageous. I consulted Eagleton's *Literary Criticism* and learned that "[F.R.] Leavis's name is closely associated" with "close reading" (45), and that the term itself

> meant detailed analytic interpretation, providing a valuable antidote to aestheticist chit-chat; but it also seemed to imply that every previous school of criticism had read only an average of three words per line. To call for close reading, in fact, is to do more than insist on due attentiveness to the text. It inescapably suggests an attention to *this* rather than to something else: to the "words on the page" rather than to the contexts which produced and surround them. It implies a limiting as well as a focusing of concern–a limiting badly needed by literary talk which would ramble comfortably from the texture of Tennyson's language to the length of his beard. But in dispelling such anecdotal irrelevancies, "close reading" also held at bay a good deal else: it encouraged the illusion that any piece of language, "literary" or not, can be adequately studied or even understood in isolation. It was the beginnings of a "reification" of the literary work, the treatment of it as an object in itself, which was to be triumphantly consummated in the American New Criticism. (Eagleton 44)

I like it that the American New Criticism was based on close readings that focus on specific aspects of a work, not simply, though unrealistically at least for me, on *every single word* and phrase. I do NOT at all like it that such close readings focus *exclusively* on the words in the text being interpreted and necessarily disregard the contexts which produced and surround the text. I reject the presumption that any literary text "can be adequately studied or even understood in isolation" (Eagleton 44). The present book is evidence that my close readings of *The Crying of Lot 49* are narrowly focused, but typically on something else that I had read, and read closely, that had to do with the subject text. I would never have written Essay One the influence of Forster's *Aspects of the Novel* on *The Crying of Lot 49*, if I hadn't read the latter. The same holds true for Adams' *Letter* and Pierce's book on communications in Essay Two. All of the above eleven essays are based on dedicated close rereadings of *The Crying of Lot 49* or selected portions of it and comparably dedicated close readings of other sources including artworks. I am not alone in this; Edward Mendelson's classic essay, "The Sacred, the Profane, and

The Crying of Lot 49," republished at least the second time in Harold Bloom's edited volume, carefully explains Pynchon's novel in terms of Mircea Eliade's *The Sacred and the Profane: The Nature of Religion* (Mendelson 20).

Because my essays draw eclectically on other sources, and are alien to the American New Criticism which Eagleton defines in terms of close reading, does this mean that I jumped too quickly when, in the midst of Essay Eleven I proudly featured close reading in the title of this book? Before jumping to the conclusion that I had, I read Leavis's *The Living Principle*, which Paul Dean, in his introduction to the book, called Leavis's "*summa*, the book in which, for the last time with full vigor, he expounds his view of humanity, language, and art" (8). As I explain in Essay Twelve, I am proud to associate this book with Leavis's. I feel the closer to him because, in some significant ways, he shares my attitudes. Lest I come down to strongly on the American New Criticism, I should acknowledge that it has helped me understand Jacques Derrida's *The Truth in Painting* (see Kohn *A Derridean Look*).

Acknowledgements

In addition to the unnamed editors and anonymous readers to whom I dedicated this book at the outset, I am indebted to a great number of non-anonymous professionals who in one way or another made it a better book and/or nurtured my commitment to literary criticism. They include Craig Abbott, Glenda Abramson, Anne H. Bader, Matthias Bauer, Jeffrey Chimene, James Dougherty, Allen Dunn, Chatham Ewing, Cynthia Florin, David Gorman, Frank Grady, Geoffrey Green, George Griffing, Ihab Hassan, John Hodge, Linda Horne, Robert Karsh, John Knapp, Leo Kristjánsson, Van McElwee, Brian McHale, Kostas Myrsiades, Carolyn Perry, Anne Posega, Deborah Scaperoth, James Schick, Howard Schwartz, Doris Sloan, Bob Smith, Gary Storhoff, Helen Strang, Leona Toker, John Whalen-Bridge, Martin Willis, Peter Wolfe and Kenneth Womack.

Essay One

The Influence of E.M. Forster

> Then through the sunned gathering of her marjoram and
> sweet basil from the herb garden. (*Crying* 10)

Because of the likelihood that Thomas Pynchon had been schooled in E.M.
Forster's *Aspects of the Novel* when he attended Cornell in the 1950s, I shall assume
that *The Crying of Lot 49* was influenced by Forster's text and test whether that
assumption and the following corollary hypotheses are productive. That
Pynchon's novel begins with Oedipa Maas's discovery that she "had been named
executor, or she supposed executrix, of the estate of one Pierce Inverarity" (9)
could reflect the fact that Forster's book was an exact transcription of lectures
made possible by "a bequest in [William Clark's] will" to Trinity College,
Cambridge that "provided for a series of lectures, to be delivered annually 'on
some period or periods of English Literature not earlier than Chaucer'" (Forster
5). I don't think this assumption is disqualified, as one of the anonymous readers
in the above Introduction argued, because it would follow that "any book which
mentions that it has been made possible by a bequest has influenced *Lot 49*." That
Forster wrote of the Grecian beauty's "face, as Botticelli knew her when he
painted her risen from the waves, between the winds and the flowers" (88, 89),
explains the painted sheet metal representation of the famous

> nymph holding a white blossom towered thirty feet into the air; the sign,
> lit up despite the sun, said "Echo Courts." The face of the nymph was
> much like Oedipa's, which didn't startle her so much as a concealed
> blower system that kept the nymph's gauze chiton in constant agitation,
> revealing enormous vermillion-tipped breasts and long pink thighs at each
> flap. (*Crying* 26)

The Grecian beauty is of course Aphrodite, or Venus to the Romans; the fact that
the face of the nymph was much like Oedipa's and that the sight of it caused her
to remember "her ideas about a slow whirlwind, words she couldn't hear"
suggests that Oedipa symbolizes Venus being blown to shore (*Crying* 26, 27). Lest
readers miss the devious connection to Forster, Pynchon conjured up the name
"Strip Botticelli" ten pages later (36). Nor do I think that this assumption is
violated, as the anonymous reader argued, because "Botticelli is far more
important in *V.* than in *Lot 49*, so maybe the importance of Forster would loom
larger in Pynchon's first novel?" Forster began his theoretical discussion of "plot"
with fragments of plots" from André Gide's novel, *Les Faux Monnayeurs* (*The
Counterfeiters*): "The main fragment concerns a young man called Olivier" (97). The
Crying of Lot 49 is likewise built on fragments of plots, and the name of its main
character similarly begins with an O. Nor am I embarrassed by this assumption

because the anonymous referee chided: "As to the -O: now really!!!" One of these fragments of plot had to do with a "forgery," a ten-franc piece made of glass, but "worth more than a couple of sous, as it's coated in gold" (Forster 100). This could explain, if my initial assumption is correct, the references to "forgery" and "forgeries" in The *Crying of Lot 49*, especially the stamp with "the gold once-knotted horn" that was "obviously a counterfeit. Not just an error" (*Crying* 97, 98, 96). Nor do I cringe because "*The Recognitions* (1955) by William Gaddis is all about forgery too, so does that mean *Lot 49* has a strong connection with that novel as well?" Actually, it may.

It's likely that Pynchon would have agreed when Forster questioned whether the framework of a novel has to be the best possible framework:

> After all, why has a novel to be planned? Cannot it grow? Why need it close, as a play closes? Cannot it open out? Instead of standing above his work and controlling it, cannot the novelist throw himself into it and be carried along to some goal that he does not foresee? (Forster 96, 97)

"As for a plot," Forster wrote, "to pot with the plot, break it up, boil it down. Let there be those 'formidable erosions of contour' of which Nietzsche speaks. All that is prearranged is false" (101). But *The Crying of Lot 49* also reveals disagreement with Forster, especially with the latter's strong assertion that: "We shall all agree that the fundamental aspect of the novel is its story-telling aspect" (25), and several pages later, that "the backbone of a novel has to be a story" (27). In contrast to his mentor's disparagement of "the detective element as it is sometimes rather emptily called" (87), Pynchon's masterpiece is often identified as a detective novel.

Forster has two chapters on character, "People" and "People (Continued)" (43, 65). The second of them is best known for

> dividing characters into flat and round. Flat characters were called 'humorous' in the seventeenth century, and are sometimes called types, and sometimes caricatures. In their purest form, they are constructed round a single idea or quality: when there is more than one factor in them, we get the beginning of the curve towards the round. (67, 68)

One of the advantages of flat characters, according to Forster,

> is that they are easily recognized when they come in–recognized by the reader's emotional eye, not by the visual eye, which merely notes the recurrence of a proper name. [... T]hey never need reintroducing, never run away, have not to be watched for development, and provide their own atmosphere–little luminous disks of a pre-arranged size, pushed hither and thither like counters across the void or between the stars; most satisfactory. (69)

Among the flat characters in *The Crying of Lot 49*, readily recognized by their names, are Mike Fallopian, Stanley Koteks, Emory Bortz, Genghis Cohen, and Manny Di Presso, though some of these names mean more than the obvious that Forster had in mind. That the "air suddenly went cold" and "the sun was blotted out" while Di Presso was "tipping his shades" suggests that Manny symbolizes the third-century Persian gnostic Mani, who proclaimed himself the "Paraclete of the Truth," sent by Jesus in the person of the Holy Ghost, whom Pynchon may have alluded to ten pages later:

> *Thy pitiless unmanning is most meet,*
> *Thinks Ercole the zany Paraclete.*
> *Descended this malign, Unholy Ghost,*
> *Let us begin thy frightful Pentecost. (Crying 58, 59, 68)*

Even Oedipa, the main character, seems flat; Pynchon keeps us so busy looking for the signifiers which she evokes that we seldom think of her roundness. Such an interpretation accords with R.B. Kershner's view that: "If modernist writers [which Forster was] see character as a more complex, contradictory, and tentative matter than do their nineteenth-century predecessors, those writers we call postmodern often seem to reject the idea of novelistic characters outright" (107). In that vein, Samuli Hägg's argues that "Pynchon is in reality probably no more a narratologist than the author of these pages [himself, of course] is a novelist" (250), to which Luc Herman agrees in "Pynchon is Not a Narratologist," the title of his review of Hägg's book. In *Slow Learner*, Pynchon had this to say about the narratology in his 1961 short story "Under the Rose": "I think the characters are a little better, no longer just lying there on the slab but beginning at least to twitch some and blink their eyes open, although their dialogue still suffers from my perennial Bad Ear" (19).

Because of the general impression that Pynchon has more on his agenda than character delineation, I was taken aback when Alan Palmer, in his 2004 book, *Fictional Minds*, drew twenty brief excerpts from *The Crying of Lot 49,* most of them centering on Oedipa, to demonstrate how narratologically rounded she actually was. Among Oedipa's subtle qualities of consciousness that Palmer identified were "horizontal unity," having to do with "the remembered present," which he illustrated with the sentence that includes part of the epigraph for the present essay:

> Through the rest of the afternoon, through her trip to the market ... then through the sunned gathering of her marjoram ... into the layering of a lasagna ... eventually, oven on, into the mixing of the twilight's whiskey sours ... she wondered, wondered, shuffling back through a fat deckful of days. (Palmer 100)

Palmer illustrates Oedipa's ability to manage "different levels of attention within conscious states" when Metzger picked her up on the parking lot after her private conversation with Driblette: "She got in and rode with him for two miles before realizing that ... the disc jockey talking was her husband, Mucho" (Palmer 102). In this case, the radio went from the periphery of Oedipa's attention to the center "once the aspect of familiarity [was] represented" (102). "The description of characters' moods," writes Palmer, "is clearly an important element in narrative discourse," and he gives this example from *The Crying of Lot 49*: "There had hung the sense of buffeting, insulation, she had noticed the absence of an intensity, as if watching a movie, just perceptively out of focus, that the projectionist refused to fix" (104). Not surprisingly, Palmer "found it significantly more difficult to illustrate this feature from the Pynchon novel than [he] did the others" (Palmer 104). He explained that "in a subtle and oblique novel such as *The Crying of Lot 49*, it would be inappropriate for the narrator to state in bald and explicit terms that Oedipa's moods progress from restlessness, curiosity, excitement, and unease to anxiety, fear, and terror" (104). Pynchon knew that his narratological skills had burgeoned, for he wrote that "[w]hat is most appealing about young folks [read "Oedipa" ...] is the changes, not the still photograph of finished character but the movie, the soul in flux" (*Slow* 23). Though he turns out to be a master narratologist, Pynchon's greater interest is in ideas; for fifty years, readers of *The Crying of Lot 49* will have wrestled with the relationship between thermodynamic and information entropy–"The equation for one, back in the '30's, had looked very like the equation for the other"–and wondered why it was significant in the context of this novel (*Crying* 105). This is an aspect of the postmodern novel that Forster did not anticipate. The closest he got to what we are calling ideas were "logic" and its "derivatives" (Forster 106).

From characters and the derivatives of logic, the first two aspects of the novel, Forster moves on to plot, which he defines as "a narrative of events" over time, tied together by a "sense of causality" (86). Oedipa perceives herself at the center of four possible, mutually exclusive plots: (I) her accidental discovery of the secret communication network called the Tristero, (II) her hallucination of such a network, (III) a plot set up by Inverarity before his death, "so labyrinthine that it must have meaning beyond some practical joke," or (IV) she was "fantasying some such plot, in which case you are a nut, Oedipa, out of your skull" (*Crying* 170-71). Although Pynchon appears to have agreed with Forster's expectation that a novel's "[e]very "action or word ought to count [, that] it ought to be economical and spare; [and that] even when complicated it should be organic and free from dead-matter" (88), he violated Forster's rule that "the plot requires to be wound up" (95). The reader never learns for sure whether any of Oedipa's four possible plots is (or are) real, although Forster left room for Pynchon's evasiveness when, as noted near the beginning of the present paper, he questioned whether the framework he was advocating was in fact "the best possible for a novel" (Forster 96). "Cannot fiction devise a framework that is not so logical yet more suitable to its genius?" (97) It is not surprising that Leona Toker observes that Forster's *Passage to India* "anticipates the tendencies that will become manifest [...] in American post-modernist fiction" (144).

The next aspect of the novel, after plot, that Forster addressed is fantasy. "The power of fantasy," he wrote, "penetrates into every corner of the universe, but not into the forces that govern it" (110). "It implies the supernatural, but need not express it" (112). The paragraph in which Pynchon first mentions fantasy is set in a little room with "a couple of religious tracts" and a "picture of a saint, changing well-water to oil for Jerusalem's Easter lamps" (*Crying* 127). The kind of "fantasy" in which Oedipa "was so lost" was more mundane, having to do with finding the old sailor's landlord, bringing him to court, and buying "the sailor a new suit at Roos/Atkins, and shirt, and shoes, and giv[ing] him the bus fare to Fresno" (*Crying* 127). Or, when plagued by her memory of seeing all the WASTE symbols "saturating the Bay Area [, …] she wanted it all to be a fantasy" and to have Hilarius tell her "that there was no Trystero" (132). The most common kind of fantasy that Oedipa experiences—Forster (108) refers to it as "something that could not occur" naturally—is what she calls miracles. She encounters the first miracle at the Tank theatre when the roll of parchment, written by Angelo, the evil Duke of Squamuglia, and given to Niccolò to deliver to Gennaro, is read "aloud. It is no longer the lying document Niccolò read us excerpts from at all, but now miraculously a long confession by Angelo of all his crimes, closing with the revelation of what really happened to the Lost Guard of Faggio" (*Crying* 74). The good Niccolò could not have rewritten the lying document because he was murdered as soon as he finished reading it and because the document foretold his own assassination by the Tristero:

> But now the bones of these *Immaculate*
> Have *mingled with the blood of Niccolò,*
> *And innocence with innocence is join'd,*
> *A wedlock whose sole child is miracle; (74)*

The miracles are especially prescient in *The Crying of Lot 49* because they satirize the kind of utopian expectations whose repudiation would subsequently define postmodernism. Jesús Arrabal called it "An anarchist miracle" when "revolutions break out spontaneous and leaderless, and the soul's talent for consensus allows the masses to work together without effort, automatic as the body itself" (*Crying* 120; see also Kohn, *Pynchon Takes* 167-68). Oedipa herself experienced what Arrabal "would have called […] an anarchist miracle" when, swept up in a ballroom dance of deaf-mutes, she "followed her partner's lead, limp in the young mute's clasp, waiting for the collisions to begin. But none came" (131-32). The only explanation she could think of was some utopian though "unthinkable order of music, many rhythms, all keys at once, a choreography in which each couple meshed easy, predestined. […] She was danced for half an hour before, by mysterious consensus, everybody took a break, without having felt any touch but the touch of her partner" (131). Oedipa's disk-jockey husband Mucho had a similar "vision of consensus" that he called "a flipping miracle" when he described himself as "an antenna, sending your pattern out across a million lives a night, and they're your lives too. […] The songs, it's not just that they say something, they are something, in the pure sound. Something new" (143-44). Oedipa, not on LSD like her husband, finally feels something utopian in the "secular miracle of communication, untroubled by the dumb voltages flickering their miles, the night long, in the thousands of unheard messages" (*Crying* 180). She knows that she is on the verge of something spiritual that would reveal itself "out of the roar of relays, monotone litanies of insult, filth, fantasy, love whose brute repetitions must someday call into being the trigger for the unnamable act, the recognition, the Word" (*Crying* 180).

That brings us to Forster's fifth aspect of the novel, which is "Prophecy [, …] a tone of voice [that] may imply any of the faiths that have haunted humanity," but has more to do with

> an accent in the novelist's voice, an accent for which the flutes and saxophones of fantasy may have prepared us. His theme is the universe, or something universal, but he is not necessarily going to 'say' anything about the universe; he proposes to sing, and the strangeness of song arising in the halls of fiction is bound to give us a shock. (Forster 125)

Pynchon appears to have responded to this strange pedagogy as literally as a novelist can—with songs. There are six of them in *The Crying of Lot 49*, all transparently labeled in capital letters: "MILE'S SONG," "BABY IGOR'S SONG," "SERENADE," "HYMN," "GLEE" and "SERGE'S SONG" (27, 30, 39, 83, 147). Except to scan them for arcane signifiers, I originally paid little attention to these songs, considering them beneath Pynchon's level of sophistication. William Logan accordingly said of Pynchon's lyrics that

> The songs rarely function as the comic relief the porter scene in Macbeth is said to provide, because they're funny only in a strained and sniggering way. There's little more embarrassing than to see a writer of genius fail at something trivial (it's difficult to prevent the shiver of *Schadenfreude* that follows). (234)

Forster appeared to have anticipated criticism like Logan's when he wrote: "How will song combine with the furniture of common sense? [W]e shall ask ourselves, and shall have to answer 'not too well'" (125). Still, Foster helped to temper the questionability of such songs when he recommended that we "neglect as far as we can the problem of common sense" and recognize that "the prophetic aspect [of the novel, particularly as it is expressed in song,] demands two qualities: humility and the suspension of the sense of humor" (126). From time to time I re-read "the songs Miles, Dean, Serge and Leonard sang," with Foster's sobering admonishment in mind, trying to be open to "either some fraction of the truth's numinous beauty (as Mucho, on LSD, believed) or only a power spectrum" (*Crying* 181).

Forster identifies two final aspects of the novel for which there appear to be no literary words; "We will borrow from painting" and call the first "pattern. Later we will borrow from music and call [the second] rhythm" (149). If we adopt the recommended attitudes toward the songs, we can better appreciate their rhythm. But there is rhythm in Pynchon's text as well. This description of Mucho Maas verges on blank verse: "He had believed too much in the lot, he believed not at all in the station" (*Crying* 15), as does Driblette's admonition: "You could waste your life that way, and never touch the truth" (80), as do the words of the anonymous inamorato: "A whole underworld of suicides who failed. All keeping in touch through that secret delivery system" (116). Such poesy verges on song.

To exemplify pattern in fiction, Forster perceives the novel *Thaïs* by Anatole France as being in "the shape of an hour-glass" and the novel *Roman Pictures* by Percy Lubbock "in the shape of a grand chain in that old-time dance, the Lancers" (150). But why "borrow from painting first and call [that borrowing] the pattern," as Forster did (149)? Why not let the painting itself, complete with all its content, be the Forsterian pattern for Pynchon's novel? Why would Pynchon not have followed his mentor's lead and chosen for his painting Botticelli's Venus "risen from the waves, between the winds and the flowers," as Forster himself described it (88, 89)? No critic to my knowledge (at least none is recorded by Grant in either edition of his *Companion to The Crying of Lot 49*) has explained the significance of "the sunned gathering of her marjoram and sweet basil from the herb garden" reproduced in the epigraph of this essay. If Oedipa symbolizes Venus, whom she looks like, she is the goddess of vegetation and gardens as well as the goddess of love and lust (*New World Encyclopedia*). Pynchon must have had a reason for emphasizing that the herb garden was Oedipa's when, in the first paragraph of the second chapter, he has Mucho tell her to "look after the oregano, which had contracted a strange mold" (*Crying* 23). This is in keeping with evidence, reported by P.R. Coleman-Norton that "Venus was worshipped in Rome at an early date as a spirit that particularly increased the fertility of vegetation."

That Oedipa symbolizes the goddess of lust explains why almost every male she meets thinks she's coming-on to him: Roseman, "her trusted family lawyer [...] tried to play footsie with her under the table. [...] 'Run away with me,' said Roseman when the coffee came" (*Crying* 18, 19). "Do you want what I think you want? [...] I have a smooth young body,' said Miles, 'I thought you older chicks went for that'" (28). "'Feel,' said Driblette, extending his arm. She felt. [...] He stuck his head out of the shower. The rest of his body was wreathed in steam, giving his head an eerie, balloon-like buoyancy" (77, 78). "You could fall in love with me," Driblette suggested (80). At the Yoyodyne stockholders' meeting, "Oedipa sat on a long bench between old men who might have been twins and whose hands, alternately (as if their owner were asleep and the moled, freckled hands out roaming dream-landscapes) kept falling onto her thighs" (82). John Nefastis abruptly "put an arm around her shoulders. 'Come on in on the couch. [...] We can do it there.' 'It?' said Oedipa. 'Do it? What?' 'Have sexual intercourse,' replied Nefastis. 'Gah,' Oedipa screamed, and fled" (107-8). Oedipa inspired lust throughout the novel; when Genghis Cohen "rung [her] up" and asked her to "come over," it could have been an accident, when she arrived at his apartment/office, that "his fly was half open" (94). But it happened again on the last page of the novel, when the two of them were preparing to enter the auction room: "'Your fly is open,' whispered Oedipa" (183). Emory Bortz invited her to "come in and see some dirty pictures"(154), and Mike Fallopian, though "surrounded by broads, drinking champagne cocktails, and bellowing low songs," as soon as "he spotted Oedipa he gave her the wide grin and waved her over. [...]: "Go on, now, all of you. I want to talk to this one" (166, 167). All of this may have been uncomfortable for Oedipa, but the worst part of being the goddess of lust was that it had the opposite effect on her husband, Mucho, and her "one extra-marital fella [Metzger]" (153). Early in the novel, she knew that her husband was lost to "a Sharon, Linda or Michelle, seventeen," hanging out at a KCUF record hop in high heels,

> whose velveted eyes ultimately, statistically would meet Mucho's and respond, and the thing would develop then groovy as it could when you found you couldn't get statutory rape really out of the back of your law-abiding head. She knew the pattern because it had happened a few times already, though Oedipa had been scrupulously fair about it, mentioning the practice only once, [...] asking if he wasn't worried about the penal code. 'Of course,' said Mucho after awhile, that was all; but in his tone of voice she thought she heard more, something between annoyance and agony. She wondered then if worrying affected his performance. (*Crying* 45, 46)

Likewise, Metzger, soon after getting her drunk and winning her over at Echo Courts, "eloped with a depraved 15-year-old" (153). Oedipa, of course, has no sense of her Venus powers; she believes that it was the "Tristero" that had gotten rid of Driblette, for the same "reason they got rid of Hilarius and Mucho and Metzger—maybe because they thought I no longer needed you [and them]" (162).

Forster asks us to accept beauty "as part of a completed plot" (88). Botticelli's Venus, floating to shore on her large clamshell, does "look a little surprised; it is the emotion that best suits her face, as Botticelli knew when he painted her" (Forster 88). Likewise, Pynchon's narrator said that Oedipa was "startled" (*Crying* 26).

Concluding Remarks

The seven aspects of the novel, which Forster deems the most important, are story, characters, plot, fantasy, prophecy, pattern and rhythm. I have assumed that Pynchon read Forster's text, was influenced by it, and nostalgically took themes from it, especially from its first chapter on story, to embellish *The Crying of Lot 49*. Has my model been productive? The idea of flat versus round characters was new to me and made me much more open, than I would otherwise have been, to Palmer's unexpected discovery of roundness. Because of Forster, I continue to ponder the songs the Paranoids sang, especially their message of loneliness and the longing for love, which signifies Venus, the goddess of love. While Pynchon rejected Forster's advice for "a completed plot" for *The Crying of Lot 49*, his Oedipa is the "beauty at which a novelist should never aim, though he fails if he does not achieve it" (Forster 88). The opposite of the "prima donna" demanding "her due," she is the exact pattern of beauty that Forster called for (89).

Was this first model useful, even if the hypothesis on which it was based—that Pynchon had studied Forster's *Aspects of the Novel* and drew on it for themes in *The Crying of Lot 49*—turns out to be spurious? My answer would be an emphatic "Yes!" The prospect, *inter alios*, that Oedipa was a stand-in for Botticelli's Venus, which Forster made so much of, predicted all kinds of interesting new insights on Pynchon's novel. Given the mixture of the sacred and the profane in this mimesis, Pynchon may have anticipated the novel's foremost interpretation by Edward Mendelson. For me, such mimetics are the bubbles in Harberger's celebratory glass of champagne.

Essay Two

The Influence of Henry Adams and J.R. Pierce

> [T]here were two distinct kinds of this entropy. One having to do with heat-engines, the other to do with communication. The equation for one, back in the '30's, had looked very like the equation for the other. It was a coincidence. The two fields were entirely unconnected, except at one point: Maxwell's Demon. As the Demon sat and sorted his molecules into hot and cold, the system was said to lose entropy. But somehow the loss was offset by the information the Demon gained about what molecules were where. (*Crying* 105)

The above passage from *The Crying of Lot 49* is arguably the novel's most challenging for Pynchon scholars. Grant devotes almost fourteen full pages of the first edition of his *Companion* to the boldfaced entry–H105.14, B77.13 two distinct kinds of this entropy–as compared to an average rate of a little more than a quarter of a page per entry for all 482 of them. In his 1981 article, David Seed described how in Pynchon's writing "the concept of entropy can be applied to human behavior" (135), while in his 1988 book he usefully traced Pynchon's fascination with thermodynamic entropy back to Henry Adam's *A Letter to American Teachers of History*. The importance of information *per se* was recognized by Maurice Couturier when he suggested that *The Crying of Lot 49* can "be read as an elaborate textbook on communication in its various aspects" (6). Given that Adams attributed the decline in global biodiversity, long before it started becoming a popular issue in the 1970s, to thermodynamic entropy, I shall assume that *The Crying of Lot 49* connects the extinction of species to the second law of thermodynamics. In a companion model I shall assume that Maxwell's box is a metaphor for the extreme complexity in *The Crying of Lot 49*.

Thermodynamic Entropy and the Extinction of Species

Pynchon flippantly concluded his famous introduction to *Slow Learners* with the remark that "education too, as Henry Adams always sez, keeps going on forever" (23); but the flippancy itself may signify the importance that Pynchon attached to Adams' writings. Around the middle of the nineteenth century, according to Adams, a new school of physicists announced two laws of thermodynamics:

> The first law said that Energy was never lost; the second said that it was never saved; that, while the sum of energy in the universe might remain constant, – granting that the universe was a closed box from which nothing could escape, – the higher powers of energy tended always to fall lower, and that this process had no known limit. (Adams 2 [140-141])

It follows from the second law that "within a finite period of time to come, the earth must again be, unfit for the habitation of man" (4 [141]). The double-page references here to Adams' *Letter* are respectively the pages of the 1910 self-published edition followed [in brackets] by the page numbers of the posthumously printed 1919 Macmillan edition, that included additional material by Henry's brother Brooks Adams, who edited it. The essence of Adams' theme was that "the entire universe, in every variety of active energy, organic and inorganic, human or divine, is to be treated as clockwork that is running down,[...] terribly narrowed by thermodynamics" (Adams 203 [261]). Because of the repetition of Adam's "clockwork" and "running" in the following passage of *The Crying of Lot 49*, it appears that Pynchon wrote it with the antecedent text in mind: "The rest ran off some opposite Principle, something blind, soulless; a brute automatism that led to eternal death [, ... a] brute Other, that kept the non-Scurvhamite universe running like clockwork" (*Crying* 155, 156). It follows that the brute Other is the "Second Law of Thermodynamics," to which Pynchon had already referred (*Crying* 86). Based on this compelling parallelism, I hypothesize that there are other parallels between Adams' *Letter* and *The Crying of Lot 49*.

To "the frequent and tragic outbursts of physicists, astronomers, geologists, biologists and sociological socialists announcing the end of the world," Adams adds their expectation that "[t]he sun is ready to condense again at any moment, causing another violent disequilibrium, to be followed by another great outburst and waste of its expiring heat" (70, 71 [180]). This could be one of several interpretations–the other being the ancient Manichaean fear of the "tricks of the Darkness, there to distract us from seeking union with the Light" (*Against* 438)–of Manny Di Presso tipping his shades whereupon the "air suddenly went cold [and] the sun was blotted out" (*Crying* 58-9). A natural consequence of the second law of thermodynamics was thought to be "social decrepitude [, ... an] increase of insanity or idiocy, [...] enfeebled vitality, [...] deterioration in the race" (Adams 81, 82 [186-87]) and "a universal tendency to the [...] degradation of thought" (85 [189-90]). "Worse than all, such is [man's] instinct of destruction that he systematically exterminates or degrades all the larger forms of animal life in which nature stored her last creative efforts"(Adams 133 [217]). It may be relevant that, among the fifty or more animals mentioned in *The Crying of Lot 49*, there are the "Tiger" (15), "shark" (37), "seal" (38), "Jaguar" (58), "Whale" (82), "Gorilla" (106), all of which, for one reason or another are endangered species, and finally the "dinosaur" (141), which is their sad standard-bearer. I am taking words out of context, but Pynchon appears to have intended that kind of selectivity over and over again in *The Crying of Lot 49*. Perhaps the vanishing species were among the things that "would truly cease to be, forever," another "irreversible process" that Oedipa lamented: "It astonished her to think that so much could be lost" (*Crying* 128). When Pynchon refers to the "Antarctic loneliness and fright," he may be signifying the expeditionary team of scientists that began measuring the ozone layer over Hadley Bay in Antarctica in 1957 for changes that might threaten the photoplankton and krill, on which the world's food chain is based (*Crying* 129). Because species are interdependent, the death of any one species undermines the vitality of others. The "dead ocean of energy [...] incapable of doing any work," that the second law of thermodynamics predicts for the far-off future, can also be a metaphor for the decrease and collapse of biodiversity (Adams 10 [145]).

Adams lamented man's having "largely deforested the planet, and hastened its desiccation" (131-2 [216]). Pynchon may be signifying this desiccation when he refers to "earth-moving machines" and "a total absence of trees" in the glamorous new Fangoso Lagoons estate (*Crying* 56). The pervasiveness of automobiles in *The Crying of Lot 49* and their part in accelerating entropy–Oedipa's Impala is mentioned four times (24, 56, 94, 104)–is reinforced by the bad dream Mucho used to have about the car lot:

> It was only that sign in the lot, that's what scared me. In the dream I'd be going about a normal day's business and suddenly, with no warning, there'd be the sign. We were a member of the National Automobile Dealers' Association. N.A.D.A. Just this creaking metal sign that said nada, nada, against the blue sky. I used to wake up hollering. (144)

Adams may have been one of the earliest historians, just as Pynchon may have been one of the earliest novelists, to express concern over the human-induced extinction of species.

Information Entropy

In the abstruse context of thermodynamic and information entropy, I found a sentence in *The Crying of Lot 49* that could have made the self-deprecating Pynchon in *Slow Learner* regret having forgotten some rule or other that he "thought [he'd] learned up till then" (22). The sentence, "But somehow the loss was offset by the information the Demon gained about what molecules were where" (*Crying* 105), has caused unnecessary misunderstanding. If there were a rule or commandment forgotten, it might have been something like: Writer, thou shalt not intentionally muddle a concept that is confusing to begin with. Pynchon may actually have apologized when he wrote that "people think I know more about the subject of entropy than I really do" (*Slow* 12). Yet, the offending sentence forces the reader to give special regard to what is arguably the most famous metaphor in postmodern fiction.

James Clerk Maxwell conceived the thermodynamic aspect of the metaphor in 1871 when he imagined a vessel full of a gas, whose molecules are

> moving with velocities by no mean uniform. [...] Now let us imagine that such a vessel is divided into two portions, A and B, by a division in which there is a small hole, and that a being who can see the individual molecules, opens and closes this hole, so as to allow only the swifter molecules to pass from A to B, and only the slower ones to pass from B to A. He will thus, without expenditure of work, raise the temperature of

B and lower that of A, in contradiction to the second law of
thermodynamics. (Maxwell 338-39)

What Maxwell called "a being," William Thompson (Lord Kelvin) chose to call a
"demon" in a journal article in 1874.

The information aspect was first associated with Maxwell's box by J.R.
Pierce in his 1961 text on information theory, entitled *Symbols, Signals and Noise:
The Nature and Process of Communication.* Pierce provided the segue to information
theory in a framework somewhat like Maxwell's box,

> in which all the molecules of a gas are initially on one side of a partition
> in a cylinder. If the molecules are all on one side of the partition, and we
> know this, the entropy is less than if they are distributed on both sides of
> the partition. Certainly we know more about the position of the
> molecules when we know that they are all on one side of the partition
> than if we merely know that they are somewhere within the whole
> container. The more detailed our knowledge is concerning a physical
> system, the less uncertainty we have concerning it (concerning the
> location of the molecules, for instance) and the less the entropy is.
> Conversely, more uncertainty means more entropy. (Pierce 23)

Some critics have already suggested that Pierce Inverarity's given name was
Pynchon's way of signifying J.R. Pierce. It was an important signifier because
Pynchon was now able to assert, with the authority of science, that
thermodynamic entropy and information entropy "were entirely unconnected,
except at one point: Maxwell's Demon" (105). Except for that, the only
connection between the two equations was purely formulaic, each a summation of
individual probabilities times the logarithm of the probabilities (see Grant 1st Ed.,
89). Whereas thermodynamic entropy defines the relative potential for work in a
closed system, such as the solar system or the universe, information entropy
measures the potential information content of an individual communication.
Pierce clarified the latter as follows:

> In communication theory we consider a message source, such as a writer
> or a speaker, which may produce on a given occasion any of many
> possible messages. The amount of information conveyed by the message
> increases as the amount of uncertainty as to what message will actually be
> produced becomes greater. A message which is one of ten possible
> messages conveys a smaller amount of information than a message which
> is one out of a million possible messages. The entropy of communication
> theory is a measure of this uncertainty, and the uncertainty, or entropy, is
> taken as the measure of the amount of information conveyed by a
> message from a source. The more we know about what message the
> source will produce, the less uncertainty, the less the entropy, and the less
> the information. (Pierce 23)

The twofold consequence of the Demon's sorting (assuming as Maxwell did in
1871 that sorting itself entails no energy) is to lose thermodynamic entropy

(building toward a system with greater potential for performing work) and at the same time to convert a system with a high potential for information to one in which that potential for information (as to "what molecules were where") has been drawn down. The novel's claim that a "loss was offset" but "information […] gained" implies that the loss was undesirable, which of course it was not, but that the gain was truly a gain, which it was not, at least not from the perspective of classic information theory. For this twisted sentence to make sense, it must be that the gain in information, the knowledge of which molecules were where, is undesirable, which is counter-intuitive. Pierce acknowledged that information theory can be counter-intuitive to the lay person, because it "is still a confused and confusing matter; […] information is sometimes associated with the idea of *knowledge* through its popular use rather than with *uncertainty* and the resolution of uncertainty, as it is in communication theory" (24). It may have been–contrary to my interpretation of what I take to be his apology in *Slow Learner*– that Pynchon knowingly chose to confuse readers in this subtle way, purposely conflating the popular interpretation and the esoteric theoretical interpretation in his presumably offending sentence. He must have known too that Warren Weaver, in the article in *Scientific American* signified in *The Crying of Lot 49* (10), wrote that "greater freedom of choice, greater uncertainty, and greater information go hand in hand" (Weaver 13). It would have made more sense, but had less literary impact, if he had inelegantly written: "But somehow the loss, which was actually a heightened potential for useful work, was offset by the gain in knowledge, which actually reduced the original reservoir of potential information." Fortunately, Edward Mendelson made it clearer than I am making it when he explained, amazingly early in the game, that "the two meanings of the term 'entropy' are in opposition" (25). He didn't even have to say that it was "[m]etophorically" true (25), for it is true by definition; more thermodynamic entropy in a mature system like our own is undesirable whereas more information entropy in any given message is desirable. (I add these last two sentences in the final reading of the manuscript, having finally, in Essay Eleven, worked out a numerical example that greatly clarifies the matter for me, and hopefully for you too, dear reader. If you want to skip ahead and look at it, I use the symbols ♣, ♦, ♥ and ♠ to represent either molecular-level microstates or informational components.) Maxwell's box, arguably the greatest metaphor in postmodern fiction, is Pynchon's "metaphor of God knew how many parts" (109). But what does it mean or do for *The Crying of Lot 49*?

Maxwell's box had little relevance to thermodynamic entropy in the real world. It depended on the superhuman molecule-sorting capability of a demon, who would have been "able to do what at present is impossible to us," which is to sort molecules of a gas with no more effort than thought (Maxwell 338). As Pynchon's narrator put it, "Since the Demon only sat and sorted, you wouldn't have put any real work into the system. So you would be violating the Second Law of Thermodynamics, causing perpetual motion" (*Crying* 86). But even Oedipa knew that sorting was work: "Tell them down at the post office" that it isn't and "you'll find yourself in a mailbag headed for Fairbanks, Alaska, without even a FRAGILE sticker going for you" (*Crying* 86). Physicists, writes Grant, have been uneasy with Pynchon's "attempts to link thermodynamic and information theory" in more than a metaphorical way" (1st Ed., 91). Of course they would be uneasy! Why should thermodynamic entropy which is the basis for a universal law of nature, have anything to do with the total information potential of an individual message? Then, how can Maxwell's box possibly be the greatest metaphor in postmodern fiction? Anne Mangel starts us in the right direction with her brilliant insight of "Maxwell's notion of the Demon as a metaphor for Oedipa's [...] sorting masses of information" (196). From that, we can go much further.

Maxwell's box, before sorting, is the metaphor for *The Crying of Lot 49* itself! The entire novel is crammed full of signifiers–tiger, shark, seal, jaguar, whale, gorilla, the irreversible process, potsmaster, the finger on the button, post horn, WASTE, *et cetera*–for the reader to sort out. Nor is it as simple as fast and slow molecules, for a single signifier such as the "irreversible process" can represent the extinction of species, the running down of energy, and the destruction of information when the sailor's mattress flares. The most polysemous of all the signifiers is the "Tristero," which Grant found characterized by such terms as "shadowy organization," "anarchic underworld" (1st Ed., 43), "agent of [Oedipa's] liberation" (44), "the idea of the sacred," "analogous to Christianity" (45), "revelation," "vital, regenerative energy," "demiurgic hierarchy" (46), "'Augustinian' entropy" and "the closed system of America,"(47). These ten are from Grant's entry H44.3, B28.3 Tristero, and there are another 101 such entries listed under "Tristero" in the index of his *Companion 1st Ed.* volume. Oedipa's own conceptions of the Tristero vary as often as Pynchon changes the first vowel of its name from an *i* to a *y* and back to an *i*.

Mangel adds hyperbole to the novel's polysemy: "symbols, such as WASTE and its emblem, the muted post horn [...] point in a thousand different directions and never lead to a solid conclusion" (198). It would take a veritable demon of a reader to sort and resort all the possible themes that *The Crying of Lot 49* was meant to signify. That the reader is the "Demon makes the metaphor not only verbally graceful, but also objectively true" (*Crying* 106). The best symbolic evidence that Pynchon had something like this in mind is the dot-filled <u>49</u> in Figure 1, which is taken from the right-hand side of the double-spread title page of the Lippincott first edition.

Figure 1. Page 3 of the Lippincott Edition,
1966, of *The Crying of Lot 49*

Concluding Remarks

Although thermodynamic entropy and information entropy have nothing tangible in common, they come together in Adams' *Letter*, where he writes: "If Thought is capable of being classed with Electricity, [...] it seems necessarily to fall at once under the second law of thermodynamics as one of the energies which most easily degrades itself" (Adams 101-2 [199]). "From the beginnings of philosophy and religion, the thinker was taught by the mere act of thinking, to take for granted that his mind was the highest energy of nature.[. ...] Society must still continue to act upon it, [...] for the obvious reason that it was and is their only motive for existence,–their title to their identity. [... though, as an energy,] it must submit to the final and fundamental necessity of degradation" (Adams 114 [207, 208]). Contemporary physicists now know that the heat death of the solar system is more than three billion years in the future (Krauss and Starkman *Fate of Life* 61), long after the human species is statistically expected to disappear–the average species lasts a million years, and the age of *homo sapiens* is already a fifth of that. We also know that thought does *not* fall under the second law of thermodynamics. Norbert Wiener has made us aware "that in considering such a local process as the growth of a tree or of a human being, which depends directly or indirectly on radiation from the sun, an enormous local decrease in entropy may be associated with a quite moderate energy transfer" (24). He refers to these local processes as "islands of locally decreasing entropy" and chooses "to give a much higher weight of importance to the regions of decreasing entropy and increasing order than to the universe at large" (25). Perhaps this is what Pynchon had in mind when he concluded his introduction to *Slow Learner* with the sentence: "But as we all know, rock 'n' roll will never die, and education too, as Henry Adams always sez, keeps going on forever" (23). Forever clearly implies the duration of *homo sapiens*, and in contributing to his readers' education, Pynchon is enhancing what Adams called "the highest energy of nature" (114 [207]). Perhaps, the idea of his readers sorting the mass of jumbled information from *The Crying of Lot 49* into separate vessels, is Pynchon's metaphor for Wiener's "islands of locally decreasing entropy."

I am not the first to suggest that Maxwell's Box is a metaphor for the entire novel, overflowing with information meant to be sorted out by readers. Seed writes of Pynchon's "reader [taking] the time to sort out the information," because in his view, "sorting, in various senses, is the book's true subject" (*Fictional Labyrinths* 125). In the face of this immense complexity, which almost defies sorting out, George Levine has an "uncomfortable feeling [...] that not knowing is an important qualification for participating imaginatively in [Pynchon's] fictions. Only by surrendering our demands for order can we be released into the terror of the moment" (67). His view is valid, but I prefer to sort out the information in *The Crying of Lot 49*, as I do in this book, into separate vessels, *i.e.*, essays, even though it is frightening to think that the number of vessels to sort into may be too great for generations of readers to fill.

Essay Three

The Influence of Rachel Carson

> She thought of a hotel room in Mazatlán whose door had just been slammed, it seemed forever, waking up two hundred birds down in the lobby; a sunrise over the library slope at Cornell University [...] (*Crying* 10)

Environmentalism can be said to have begun with the publication of Rachel Carson's *Silent Spring* in 1962; *The Crying of Lot 49* was written in the wake of its enormous impact. In his latest novel *Against the Day*, Pynchon revisits themes from *The Crying of Lot 49* that critics appear to have overlooked. Elsewhere I argue that the idiosyncratic allusion in *Against the Day* (766) to "a variant currently for sale, which contains lines that do not appear in other versions," seems to be signifying the reference to "the 'Whitechapel' edition" in *The Crying of Lot 49*, which "abounds in such corrupt and probably spurious lines, as [...] hardly to be trusted" (*Crying* 102; Kohn *Corrupt Edition* 83, 86n). An equally suspicious idiosyncrasy, this one having to do with Carson's *Silent Spring*, pops up in *Against the Day* when Lew Basnight croons "a tune from the third act of *Waltzing in Whitechapel*," that contains the woeful, but strangely-silly lyrics:

> Oh Sing-
> -ing Bird,
> Of Spital-fields—
> How lonely i'-all-feels,
> Wiv-out your mel-
> o-dee! When shall my
> Brick Lane bunt-ing
> Chirp-again,
> To my throbbing-brain,
> Her dear refrain,
> Soft-leee? Al-
> though it's spring
> In Stepney, so-we're-told,
> Here in my
> Heart-it's-cold
> As any-win-
> try sea—until my
> Singing Bird of
> Spit-alfields,
> Perched on her lit-tle heels,

63

Comes trip-ping back,
To meee!
  —(My dar-ling) (*Against* 684-85)

William Logan, who has written the most perceptive review of *Against the Day* to date, is nonplussed by the novel's "appalling songs" (234). "Pynchon obviously delights in writing dreadful lyrics," Logan concludes, "otherwise he would stop. He's hardly unaware of how bad they are" (234). I assume that when Pynchon included the outlandish "Oh Singing Bird of Spitalfields" in the generally sophisticated *Against the Day*, he was signaling the long overlooked influence of Carson's book on *The Crying of Lot 49* that had yet to be discovered by critics. The premise in the "Singing Bird of Spitalfields," of the same birds returning every spring, is all wrong, and Pynchon knew it was. Charles Knight reveals that the weavers in Spitalfields, an area in eastern London, were known for their skills in snaring songbirds such as linnets, woodlarks, goldfinches, greenfinches, and chaffinches for the cages of London homes in the nineteenth century (386).

There is another bird-related red herring in *Against the Day*: "Birds here had not sung for generations, no one alive in fact could remember a time when they had sung, and these skies belonged now to raptors" (*Against* 955). The implication, intuitive but wrong, is that raptors have decimated the songbirds. To the contrary, England's Royal Society for the Protection of Birds insists that there "is no scientific evidence that sparrowhawks or other birds of prey have had population effects on British songbirds." Such intentionally flawed assertions in *Against the Day* have a parallel in the exaggerated forecast of *Silent Spring*, entitled "A Fable for Tomorrow," which reads:

> There was a strange stillness. The birds, for example—where had they gone? Many people spoke of them, puzzled and disturbed. The feeding stations in the backyards were deserted. The few birds seen anywhere were moribund; they trembled violently and could not fly. It was a spring without voices. On the mornings that once throbbed with the dawn chorus of robins, catbirds, doves, jays, wrens, and scores of other bird voices there was now no sound; only silence lay over the fields and woods and marsh. (*Silent* 2)

That "dawn chorus" is evoked in *The Crying of Lot 49* when Oedipa remembers "waking up two hundred birds down in the lobby," while on the final page, the mention that "Loren Passerine, the finest auctioneer in the West will be crying today" signifies the first name of another early icon of the environmental movement, the naturalist Loren Eiseley, while the last name of the auctioneer denotes the ornithological *passerine* order, which includes more than half of all living birds, most of them songbirds (10, 183). A haunting story of woodland song birds is recorded in Eiseley's *The Immense Journey* ; on one of his hikes the author sights "an enormous raven with a red and squirming nestling in his beak," that it had wrested from a nest, amid "the outraged cries of the nestling's parents, who flew helplessly in circles about the clearing. [...] Up to that point the little tragedy had followed the usual pattern. But suddenly, out of all that area of woodland, a soft sound of complaint began to rise. Into the glade fluttered small birds of half a dozen varieties drawn by the anguished outcries of the tiny parents. (Eiseley 174)

No one dared to attack the raven, but then, in the midst of the protest,

the crystal note of a song sparrow lifted hesitantly in the hush. And finally, after painful fluttering, another took the song, and then another, the song passing from one bird to another, doubtfully at first, as though some evil thing were being slowly forgotten. Till suddenly they took heart and sang from many throats joyously together as birds are known to sing. (175)

"In simple truth" Eiseley concludes, "they had forgotten the raven, for they were the singers of life, and not of death" (175).

There are several idiosyncratic paragraphs in *The Crying of Lot 49* that make good sense in the context of corresponding paragraphs in *Silent Spring*. The first of these pictures Mr. Thoth in a nursing home with

a black fly browsing along the pink, dandruffy arroyo of the neat part in the old man's hair. A fat nurse ran in with a can of bug spray and yelled to the fly to take off so she could kill it. The cagy fly stayed where it was. 'You're bothering Mr Thoth,' she yelled at the little fellow. Mr Thoth jerked awake, jarring loose the fly, which made a desperate scramble for the door. The nurse pursued, spraying poison. (*Crying* 91)

Although the list of DDT "resistant species now includes practically all of the insect groups of medical importance," Carson wrote, "the blackflies, sand flies, and tsetse flies have not yet become resistant to chemicals" (267). Presumably, that is why Pynchon's "black fly" made its "desperate scramble for the door." It's a hermeneutic stretch, but the out-of-control caroming of the "can of hair spray" earlier in the novel may have been a metaphor for DDT, like the poisonous "can of bug spray" in the above excerpt (*Crying* 36).

Another enigmatic scene in *The Crying of Lot 49* depicts Oedipa with the old sailor. "She knew, because she had held him, that he suffered DT's. Behind the initials was a metaphor, a delirium tremens, a trembling unfurrowing of the mind's plowshare" (128). Critics have offered many interpretations for the paragraph that contains this line, but none have related it to Carson's observation that the action of DDT

is primarily on the central nervous system of man; the cerebellum and the higher motor cortex are thought to be the areas chiefly affected. Abnormal sensations as of prickling, burning, or itching, as well as tremors or even convulsions may follow exposure to appreciable amounts, according to a standard textbook of toxicology. (192)

Another interpretation of the "DT's" in *The Crying of Lot 49* is Dichlorodiphenyl Trichloroethane, the chemical more familiarly known as DDT, which the sailor could have absorbed during his service. Pynchon, a former sailor himself, may have chosen a sailor for this role in the novel to commemorate the two British scientists of the Royal Navy Laboratory, whom Carson credited with furnishing "[o]ur first knowledge of the symptoms of acute poisoning by DDT," to which they "deliberately exposed themselves in order to learn the consequences" (*Silent* 192-93). As might be expected in *The Crying of Lot 49*, the old sailor has multiple connotations, not only of Pynchon's service in the navy and that of the two British scientists, but also of "the old sailor" in Pynchon's first novel (*V.* 437), as well as of Homer's Odysseus, who could have been the model for Oedipa's old sailor, who "left [his wife in Fresno] So long ago, [he couldn't] remember" (*Crying* 125).

The spraying of insecticidal poisons is a major theme in *Silent Spring*, and Pynchon appears to have signaled it by his frequent use of the words "spray, sprayed, spraying" and "poison, poisons, poisoning"—at least seven times each for the two sets of terms (*Crying* 32, 36, 37, 38, 51, 91, 91, 65, 66, 68, 69, 91, 138, 174). The novel's iconic post horn could even double as a spray can—the oval representing the tank and the trapezoid, the funnel emitting the spray (52, 84). "[T]he legend DEATH," that Oedipa finds "scratched on the back of a seat" in a San Francisco bus (121), along with a post horn, could also be an acronym for D(ieldrin), E(ndrin), A(ldrin), T(oxaphene) and H(eptachlor), the five insecticides that Carson identifies as "the most dangerous of all chlorinated hydrocarbons" in "agricultural use" (87, 139). All that Pynchon says in *The Crying of Lot 49* about "the legend DEATH" on the back of the bus seat–perhaps to throw off readers, in accordance with "the resistance of modern writers to having their archetypes 'spotted'" (Frye 102)—is that "somebody had troubled to write in, in pencil: DON'T EVER ANTAGONIZE THE HORN" (121).

So carefully did Pynchon conceal this archetype that as late as 1994, twenty-four years after the first Earth Day, when Grant's first companion volume to *The Crying of Lot 49* was published, it included no references to Rachel Carson or *Silent Spring*. Nor, for that matter, does his 2nd edition. The closest Pynchon came to mentioning that title was near the end of the novel, when

> "the bright winged thing had actually made it to the sanctuary of her heart—perhaps, springing from the same slick labyrinth [. ...] She waited for the winged brightness to announce its safe arrival. But there was silence" (162).

In this passage, "silence," "springing," "the bright winged thing," and the "safe arrival" may all be Pynchon's covert way of signifying Carson's influential book.

Concluding Remarks

The Crying of Lot 49 was one of the first, if not *the* first, novels to address environmental contamination. Inspired by the writings of Rachel Carson and Loren Eiseley, it was published four years *before* U.S. Senator Gaylord Nelson of Wisconsin spearheaded the nation's first Environmental Teach-in, called Earth Day, on April 22, 1970. Whereas modernism had long heralded the benefits of science and technology through shibboleths like "Better Living through Chemistry," Carson was the first to make the world aware that agricultural chemicals and pesticides posed significant dangers for humans and for biodiversity. By taking up Carson's cause, Pynchon took up the standard that became known as postmodernism, which replaced modernity's confident utopian vision of science and technology with one of skepticism. The third avatar of environmentalism was Aldo Leopold; I assume that Pynchon was likewise influenced by his writing, especially *A Sand County Almanac* published in 1949 and *Round River* in 1953. However, I can find no allusions to his name in *The Crying of Lot 49*, as I could to "Loren," nor to Leopold's books, as I could with Carson's "silence" and "springing." Except that there is a faint possibility, based on Zipf's Law, that "sand" is being subtly signified in four repetitions: "the sky, the sand, the moon, and the lonely sea"(*Crying* 40), "shimmying for the sand roads" and "the trucked-in white sand"(56), and the "rakings in the sand of a Japanese garden" (108). What may be more convincing is the sarcastic designation in *Round River* of "entire biotic communities" such as "marshes, bogs, dunes, and 'deserts,'" as "'waste' areas," and Leopold's disgust of "those devoid of imagination" for whom "a blank place on the map is a useless waste; [whereas] to others, the most valuable part" (Leopold 228, 269). This may be one of the referents for the many allusions to WASTE in *The Crying of Lot 49*. In the Lippincott edition, there is a row of "w.a.s.t.e. w.a.s.t.e. w.a.s.t.e. w.a.s.t.e." along the paste-down endpaper and free endpaper, at both the front and back ends of the novel. I started this essay with the assumption that *The Crying of Lot 49* was influenced by Rachel Carson. In the follow-up research, I am pretty well convinced that he was influenced by Loren Eiseley and Aldo Leopold, as well—the three major avatars of the environmental movement of the 1960s who, by repudiating modernism's unconditional acclaim for science and technology, brought postmodernism in its wake. Eiseley expressed this repudiation twenty-years before postmodernism first entered fiction in *The Crying of Lot 49*, when he wrote:

> There is another magazine article on my desk that reads "Machines Are Getting Smarter Every Day." I don't deny it, but I'll still stick with the birds. It's life I believe in, not machines. (*The Immense Journey* 181)

Essay Four

The Influence of Loren Eiseley and Charles Darwin

"A paperback," Driblette yelled back, "Don't ask me the publisher. I found it at Zapf's Used Books over by the freeway. It's an anthology, Jacobean Revenge Plays. There was a skull on the cover." (*Crying* 78)

When Maurice Couturier describes *The Crying of Lot 49* "as an elaborate textbook on communication in its various aspects," especially those that "weld together the members of a cultural group"(6), he connects Pynchon's novel to Loren Eiseley's thesis that communication was fundamental to the survival of pre-humans and early *homo sapiens*. Signifiers of Eiseley's 1946 monograph, *The Immense Journey*, abound in Pynchon's allusions to "bone," "bones," "forgeries," "hoax," and "skull" in *The Crying of Lot 49*, as well as to the first name "Loren" of the auctioneer who "spread his arms in a gesture that seemed to belong to the priesthood of some remote culture; perhaps to a descending angel" (*Crying* 183). Eiseley called himself the "bone hunter," and the many references – more than thirty – in his book to "bone" and "bones" is almost equaled by the number of similar repetitions (more than twenty) in *The Crying of Lot 49*. Oedipa, who attended a play at the Tank Theatre "to ask about bones" and "to see about the bones," was something of a bone hunter herself (*Crying* 68, 80). Whether consciously or unconsciously, Pynchon's accounts—first, of the cornered "handful of American troops, [...] huddled on the narrow shore of the clear and tranquil" Lago di Pietà, somewhere between Naples and Rome, whose "water was too cold to swim: you died of exposure before you could reach any safe shore. [...] But they died, every one [; ...] the Germans came down from the cliffs, and their enlisted men put all the bodies that were on the beach into the lake" (*Crying* 61, 62); second, of the Lost Guard of Faggio [...] massacred by Angelo and thrown in the lake" (74); and third, of the "bones of the GI's at the bottom of Lake Inverarity" in Fongoso Lagoons, that had been pirated from Italy– all may have been inspired by Eiseley's poetic reference to "the treasure of countless piracies, the dead of innumerable battles [that] had gone down into the green gloom of the mermaids' kingdom"(*Crying* 74, 181: Eiseley 32). It is relevant to both books that bones are a key to the long-hidden. That bones are mentioned so many times in Eiseley's book on paleontology would be expected, but in *The Crying of Lot 49* such an inordinate number of repetitions evoke Zipf's law and constitute Pynchonesque signaling. The references to the "Tristero 'forgeries' [...] to be sold, as lot 49" and to the "hoax, maybe something that Inverarity set up before he died" in *The Crying of Lot 49* (175, 167), correspond to a "forgery, a hoax [...] the famous Piltdown cranium, known in scientific circles all over the world since its discovery in a gravel pit on the Sussex Downs in 1911" in *The Immense Journey* (80). It was a "skull, a supposedly very ancient skull, long used as one of the most powerful pieces of evidence documenting the Darwinian position upon human evolution" (Eiseley 80). In fact, "an unscrupulous but learned amateur" had attached the lower jawbone of an orangutan to the upper skull of a modern man, giving the impression that an unknown early human, having "an antiquity of something over a million years," already had the large brain of modern man (80). By the fall of 1953, the famous Piltdown cranium "was jocularly dismissed by the world's press as the skull that had 'made monkeys out of the anthropologists'" (80). The "skull on the cover" of *The Courier's Tragedy* is especially suggestive of the Piltdown skull because this particular edition of the play is spurious. (*Crying* 78, 89) A subliminal reminder of the skull appears in the novel, when "the founding figure enters the scene: Hernando Joaquín de Tristero y Calavera," where "Calavera" is "Spanish for 'skull'"(*Crying* 159). It might be thought that the Piltdown deception was in the long-run of no significance to the understanding of human evolution, but to the contrary, Eiseley argued that

> The true secret of Piltdown [...] lies in the fact that it has forced science to reexamine carefully the history of the most remarkable creation in the world – the human brain. [...] If we accept the evidence of evolution, we must assume that man became man by degrees, that he emerged out of the animal world by the slow accumulation of human characters over long ages – save for that seemingly rapid spurt in brain growth, which has carried him so far from his other relatives. (Eiseley 94, 105)

This "seemingly rapid spurt in brain growth" is much better understood because of a surprising discovery in 2004 by Stedman *et al.* of a mutation that occurred approximately 2.4 million years ago, which led to the "marked size reductions in [...] masticatory muscles" that distinguish humans from chimpanzees (415). This "decrement in masticatory muscle size removed an evolutionary constraint on encephalization" (418). Because the large muscles that encircled the head and constrained the growth of the skull were weakened by the mutation, early humans could accommodate further genetic changes that increased brain size.

It was Eiseley's insight that Darwin's theorized struggle of man against man for survival did not explain the rapid development of the human brain for, to the contrary, "man is totally dependent on society [...] Man's competition, it would thus appear, may have been much less with his own kind than with the dire necessity of building about him a world of ideas" (92, 93). Despite its physical vulnerabilities, the human species was able to survive because "Enlargement of the cerebral hemispheres by 50 per cent seems to have taken place, speaking geologically, within an instant, and without having been accompanied by any major increase in body size" (Eiseley 94). Because pre-humans lacked powerful jaws and protruding teeth, they were extremely vulnerable, and Eiseley believed that man's survival depended on developing skills for cooperating with other humans. He was being

> as rigorously selected for survival […] as the first fish that waddled up the shore on its fins. […] He was becoming something that the world had never seen before–a dream animal–living at least partially within a secret universe of his own creation and sharing that secret universe in his head with other, similar heads. Symbolic communication had begun. (Eiseley 120)

The descent of the human species from the "fish that waddled up the shore on its fins" was the beginning of the "journey […], difficult, immense, at times impossible," that explains the title of Eiseley's book (12). Perhaps, somewhere in our genetic makeup there is a memory of that beginning that Pynchon may have had in mind when, in the context of "the unimaginable Pacific," he wrote of "something tidal [that] began to reach feelers in past eyes and eardrums, perhaps to arouse fractions of brain current your most gossamer microelectrode is yet too gross for finding" (*Crying* 55). This "dream animal – living at least partially within a secret universe of his own creation"–resonates in Oedipa's query "*Shall I project a world?*" (Eiseley 120; *Crying* 82, 87). "[S]haring that secret universe in his head with other, similar heads" (Eiseley 120) connotes the "secret richness and concealed density of dream; onto a network by which X number of Americans are truly communicating," into which Oedipa had "stumbled" (*Crying* 170).

"'Communication is the key,' cried Nefastis" (*Crying* 105), not only to directing Maxwell's Demon but, more importantly, as it turns out from Eiseley's speculations, to the survival of the human species, for "in this new societal world communication meant life" (Eiseley 121) Communications are signified again and again in *The Crying of Lot 49*, from the lowly "marginal try at communication latrines are known for" to the massive "world of information flow" (*Crying* 70, 106). Had it not been for "the sudden growth of the human brain which fostered the communication of ideas, "the bones of man would lie abortive and forgotten in the sandstones of the past" (Eiseley 94, 122). In terms of the Thurn and Taxis postal service, which lasted six centuries:

> The salvation of Europe […] depends on communication, right? We face this anarchy of jealous German princes, hundreds of them scheming, counter-scheming, infighting, dissipating all of the Empire's strength in their useless bickering. But whoever could control the lines of communication, among all these princes, would control them. (*Crying* 164)

When the influence of Eiseley on *The Crying of Lot 49* is taken into account, Couturier's description of Pynchon's novel "as an elaborate textbook on communication in its various aspects" applies as much to the innate organic ability of humans to initiate, receive and understand messages as to the different technologies for sending them. In the context of the present close readings of *The Crying of Lot 49*, it is appropriate that we appreciate the ability of *homo sapiens* to formulate and comprehend messages as well as understand the mathematical complexity and subtlety of messages themselves. The former took two million years to evolve, the latter, less than a hundred.

Revelation and Religion

The assumption that Pynchon was familiar with Eiseley's *Immense Journey* opens further vistas for interpreting *The Crying of Lot 49*. On the page facing that of his discussion of the Piltdown skull, Eiseley writes about the two great evolutionary theorists Charles Darwin and Alfred Wallace, the first of whom believed that because

> the reproductive powers of plants and animals potentially far outpace the available food supply, there is in nature a constant struggle for existence on the part of every living thing. Since animals vary individually, the most cleverly adapted will survive and leave offspring which will inherit, and in their turn enhance, the genetic endowment they have received from their ancestors. (Eiseley 81)

Whereas Darwin saw in the evolutionary rise of man "only the undirected play of such natural forces as had created the rest of the living world of plants and animals," Wallace, by contrast, "totally abandoned this point of view and turned instead toward a theory of a divinely directed control of the evolutionary process" (Eiseley 81). Only a few years after the publication of *The Origin of Species*, he challenged the Darwinian position on man by insisting that "artistic, mathematical, and musical abilities could not be explained on the basis of natural selection and the struggle for existence. Something else, he contended, some unknown spiritual element, must have been at work in the elaboration of the human brain" (Eiseley 84). Wallace believed that his position, *vis a vis* Darwin's, would be validated if human evolution should prove to have been comparatively rapid. "Today, with the solution of the Piltdown enigma," Eiseley concluded, "we must settle the question of the time involved in human evolution in favor of Wallace, not Darwin," though we need not "pursue the mystical aspects of Wallace's thought–since other factors yet to be examined may well account for the rise of man" (90).

Eiseley further left evolution open to spiritual explanation when he chose for his second epigraph for *The Immense Journey*, after that of Henry David Thoreau, the emphatic quotation from William Temple (1881-1944), Archbishop of York and then of Canterbury: "Unless all existence is a medium of revelation, no particular revelation is possible ... Either all occurrences are in some degree revelation of God, or else there is no such revelation at all" (Eiseley 2; Temple 306). The prominence of the word "revelation" in *The Immense Journey* carries over to *The Crying of Lot 49*, almost always in either a mystical or otherwise extraordinary context. A paragraph in the first chapter begins with "As things developed, she [Oedipa] was to have all manner of revelations" and ends with three sentences, each containing the word "magic" (*Crying* 20, 21, 22). In the second chapter, "a revelation also trembled just past the threshold of her understanding" and she "seemed parked at the centre of an odd, religious instant" (24). The third chapter begins with "revelation in progress all around her," much of it coming from Pierce's stamp collection, "thousands of little colored windows into deep vistas of space and time" that "might have something to tell her" (44, 45). Later in that same chapter there is the "miraculous[...] revelation of what really happened to the Lost Guard of Faggio" (74). The fourth chapter begins with "other revelations which now seemed to come crowding in exponentially, as if the more she collected the more would come to her, until everything she saw, smelled, dreamed, remembered, would somehow come to be woven into The Tristero" (81). Less than ten pages further Oedipa has come to The Scope "because of other revelations; because it seemed that a pattern was beginning to emerge, having to do with the mail and how it was delivered" (89). By the sixth chapter, Oedipa was "anxious that her revelation not expand beyond a certain point. Lest, possibly, it grow larger than she and assume her to itself" (166), It was for this reason that she did not want Bortz to "bring in D'Amico, who was at NYU" (166). D'Amico is a mysterious character in *The Crying of Lot 49*–perhaps the only character identified only by his surname–who, according to a footnote in the edition of plays Oedipa acquired from the Lectern Press in Oakland, had attributed the incorrect line in *The Courier's Tragedy* to "the printer, Inigo Barfstable" (102). This same D'Amico also thinks, we learn later, that "this edition was a Scurvhamite project" (155), which connects it, for the first time, to the non-God part of "Creation" (155). Because the fictional footnote is in the fifth chapter of *The Crying of Lot 49*, the word "revelation" resonates in all six of its chapters and ultimately connects to biblical Creation, which brings "revelation" into the religious context in which Archbishop Temple associated it. It is quite likely that SCURVHAMITE, the novel's "sect of most pure Puritans," which "ran off the will of God, its prime mover," is an anagram for, in what Italians call *latino maccheronico*, "AVE CHRISTUM" (155).

For Pynchon's Oedipa, as for Temple and Eiseley, revelations, even scientific revelations, had spiritual connotations. When she first drove into San Narciso, the "ordered swirl of houses which had grown up all together, like a well-tended crop from the dull brown earth" reminded her "of the time she'd opened a transistor radio to replace a battery and seen her first printed circuit" in all its "astonishing clarity" (*Crying* 24):

> Though she knew even less about radios than about Southern
> Californians, there were to both outward patterns a hieroglyphic sense of
> concealed meaning, of an attempt to communicate. There'd seemed no
> limit to what the printed circuit could have told her (if she had tried to
> find out). (24)

It was in that "first minute of San Narciso," that the second chapter's revelation "trembled just past the threshold of her understanding" (24). It resonates at the end of the novel with Oedipa "walking among matrices of a great digital computer, the zeroes and ones twinned above, hanging like balanced mobiles right and left, thick, maybe endless. Behind the hieroglyphic streets there would either be a transcendent meaning, or only the earth" (*Crying* 181). There is still the hieroglyphic image, but what had been "concealed meaning" now promised "transcendent meaning"–or only the same brown earth. Somewhere between this first and last "hieroglyphic," tucked under the iconic post horn, is "God, hieroglyphics" (52), one of the almost 30 repetitions in *The Crying of Lot 49* of that capitalized, three-letter, biblical word. Reading this novel verges at times on a religious experience. David Seed "pointed out that a main source of irony in *Lot 49* is that it constantly heads for a revelation which never comes" (*Labyrinth* 131). For Archbishop Temple, as for Eiseley, revelation at its most profound is spiritual, and it can come from anywhere, not just from religious scriptures written by God. The importance of revelation for *The Crying of Lot 49* may not be in its absence, as Seed argues, but in the plentitude of sources. We need *not* "be on the alert for anything that will undercut it [the revelation of spirituality]" (*Labyrinth* 131). It *can* come from Mucho's studio, which he sees "in a religious way," from "the walls of a ladies' toilet," from "the California smog"–as when "Smog hung all round the horizon, the sun on the bright beige countryside was painful; she and the Chevy seemed parked at the centre of an odd, religious instant"(*Crying* 24)– and from the ancient bones that Eiseley uncovered (*Labyrinth* 131). Although Seed's claim that *The Crying of Lot 49* sets "up a context inhospitable to the spiritual"(131) is well argued, I may prefer Mendelson's view that this novel "cross[es] the threshold between the profane and sacred worlds" (29). My steadfast faith in the polysemy of Pynchon's novel compels me to conclude that both interpretations are correct.

Literary Darwinism

One of the newest methodological approaches for interpreting novels is literary Darwinism. In the opinion of Joseph Carroll, its foremost advocate, the new approach was inspired by Edward O. Wilson's 1975 book, *Sociobiology: The New Synthesis*. Although it came out nine years after *The Crying of Lot 49* was published, Pynchon appears to have anticipated the relevance of Darwin's evolutionary theory for literary theory. Just as he identified Eiseley by his first name alone, so he may have subtly signified Charles Robert Darwin by his first and middle names in the line: "Robert Scurvham had founded, during the reign of Charles I, a sect of most pure Puritans" (*Crying* 155). Emory Bortz's son is named "Charles" (150), of whom the father later says: "I keep my Wharfingeriana locked in here so the kids can't get at it. Charles could ask no end of questions I'm too young to cope with yet" (*Crying* 156). This seems like an exaggeration on Bortz's part, but Darwin surely asked–and answered–more profound questions in his life than most men who've ever lived.

It follows from the Darwinian thesis, as expressed above by Eiseley (81), that life is "a constant struggle for existence" and only "the most cleverly adapted" species and individuals in those species "survive and leave offspring"; they "inherit, and in turn enhance, the genetic endowment they have received from their ancestors." Eiseley saw Darwinian evolution as an "unceasing process" that promoted "endless slow changes in bodily form, as living creatures [were] subjected to different natural environments, different enemies, and all the vicissitudes against which life has struggled down the ages" (81). What Eiseley failed to appreciate was the important role of genetic mutations that, together with the new field of molecular biology, would eventually stimulate a massive revival of Darwinism. The contemporary Darwin scholar Janet Browne noted that "the 'modern synthesis' was in place just in time for lavish centenary celebrations of the publication of the *Origin of Species* in Chicago in 1959," which was of course after *The Immense Journey* was published (138). An important first step in the transition to contemporary Darwinism, Browne continued,

> was the reconciliation of Darwin's original proposals with early twentieth-century genetics. In effect, it was necessary to turn the external process of animal and plant evolution into changes in the frequencies of genes. Repeated small mutations in the chromosomes were consequently reinterpreted as building up the fund of variability needed for the raw material of selection. Every trait, it was now realized, exhibited a continuous range of variation, so that in a large population there would be plenty of differences circulating through the gene pool on which selection could work. (Browne 138-39)

One such mutation that allowed for the growth of the pre-human brain, and there must have been numerous other such mutations circulating through the gene pool that added to that same effect, was the one noted in the previous section, discovered by Stedman *et al.* According to evolutionary psychologist Michelle Sugiyama, encephalization "began roughly 2 mya [million years ago] with the emergence of H. [Homo] habilis (mean endocranial volume 630 cc [cubic centimeters]), and continued with the emergence 1.8 mya of H. erectus (mean endocranial volume 1000 cc), the emergence around 400,000 bp [years before the present] of *archaic H. sapiens* (mean endocranial volume 1200 cc), and the emergence around 130,000 bp of anatomically modern humans (mean endocranial volume 1560 cc)" (256). Sugiyama's data suggest that there were two periods in which the hominin brain grew explosively: From 2.0 mya to 1.8 mya, it grew at an average rate of 1.85 cc per millennium, and from 0.40 mya to 0.13 mya at an average rate of 1.33 cc per millennium . In the intervening 1,400,000 years, it grew at an average rate of only 0.14 cc per millennium, more than an order of magnitude less than the two outlying periods. Because there were two spurts, and because the first and larger one happened so long before *homo sapiens* evolved– which is compatible with the 2004 discovery by Stedman *et al.* that the mutation that led to the "marked size reductions in [...] masticatory muscles" occurred approximately 2.4 million years ago (415)–undercuts Wallace's view of "some unknown spiritual element" at work "in the elaboration of the human brain"

(Eiseley 84). Rather, it supports Sugiyama's view that "Complex adaptations tend to evolve gradually [...] and the trend toward encephalization is no exception" (256).

Carroll credits Edward O. Wilson's 1975 book on sociobiology for opening an immense field of research in multiple disciplines, including literary criticism. It was this book, writes Browne, that "located animal and human behavioral patterns [...] in the genetic framework of each species. [...] All behavioral patterns could be linked more or less back to the gene's drive to survive" (Browne 146). Literary Darwinism began when Carroll and a few others endeavored to "connect the basic life history goals" enunciated by Wilson, "survival, growth and reproduction," with the "most detailed and subtle aspects of literary meaning in specific works." (Carroll *Literary* 189). To "a remarkable extent," Carroll claims, "literary authors represent human behavior in ways that correspond to our current understanding of evolutionary psychology" (*Literary* 38).

Carroll has not looked specifically at *The Crying of Lot 49*, but his writings suggest that this novel does foster basic life history goals. Pynchon's allusions to Eiseley's work on the growth in size of the pre-human brain over the past few millions years, demonstrates that he recognizes the important contribution of intelligence to human survival. In Carroll's words, "the adaptive value of high intelligence is that it provides the means for behavioral flexibility, for dealing with contingent circumstances and hypothetical situations. Such behavioral flexibility has made of the human species the most successful alpha predator of all time" (*Evolutionary* 122). However, Pynchon does much more than subtly allude to Eiseley's paleontology. Because of its complex polysemy, *The Crying of Lot 49* activates what Carroll calls the "need to create cognitive order," compelling readers in whom that need is implacable to sort out this Maxwell's box of a novel (*Literary* 159). Oedipa exemplifies the need to create cognitive order–motivated by "the scatter of business interests that had survived Inverarity. She would give them order, she would create constellations" (*Crying* 90). The need for cognitive order that Carroll postulates is anticipated in *The Crying of Lot 49*, where Oedipa struggles throughout the novel to make sense of "the forging of stamps and ancient books, constant surveillance of [her] movements, planting of post horn images all over San Francisco, bribing of librarians, hiring of professional actors and Pierce Inverarity only knows what-all besides" (*Crying* 170-71). If, indeed, Oedipa senses "fractions of brain current" tracing back some 450 million years to her gill-bearing progenitors, that is not only remarkable, but is in line with Carroll's claim that evolutionary psychologists were able to repudiate "the idea that the mind is a blank slate" on which "all particular cognitive structure is supplied by culture" (*Literary* 154).

Concluding Remarks

In this essay, there are two models based on the assumption that Pynchon had carefully read Loren Eiseley's *The Immense Journey*. The many references in the novel to bones, especially the bones at the bottom of three different lakes, the likely allusions to the Piltdown skull, and Nefastis's cry that "Communication is the key" affirm the assumed influence of *The Immense Journey* on *The Crying of Lot 49*. The first model has to do with the postmodern turn from secularism, identified by McClure. Pynchon's interest in "revelation" appears to have been inspired by the quotation from William Temple that Eiseley chose for an epigraph to *The Immense Journey*. This, combined with allusions to ancient Egyptian gods, the Greek and Roman goddess of love, Christianity, *The Tibetan Book of the Dead*, and the Jewish Kabbalah, bring Pynchon's novel away from modernist secularism into postmodern resacralization (see Kohn, *Seven Buddhist Themes* 76, 82).

The second model connects *The Crying of Lot 49* to literary Darwinism as it is enunciated by Joseph Carroll. When Pynchon included Darwin's first and middle name in the same sentence, he subtly anticipated the impact that the theory of evolution, in combination with molecular biology and the resultant discovery of DNA, would have on the arts as well as the natural and social sciences. *The Crying of Lot 49* has multiple allusions to evolutionary encephalization and the ability of early humans to intelligently communicate and strategize. One of the consequences of human intelligence, first recognized for its adaptive conditioning by Carroll, has been the need to create cognitive order. By virtue of its invitingly challenging complexity, *The Crying of Lot 49* appears to have been written in response to this mentally invigoratingly need. The final hypothesis of this essay, which I leave for future research, is that *The Crying of Lot 49* nurtured the idea of literary Darwinism almost ten years before Wilson wrote the enabling text and almost thirty years before Carroll followed through on Wilson's lead.

The Plate Tectonic Revolution

> What really keeps her [Oedipa] where she is is magic, anonymous
> and malignant, visited on her from outside and for no reason at
> all. Having no apparatus except gut fear and female cunning to
> examine this formless magic, to understand how it works, how to
> measure its field strength, count its lines of force, she may fall
> back on superstition, or take up a useful hobby like embroidery,
> or go mad, or marry a disk jockey. (*Crying* 21-22)

Grant has made Pynchon's "enthusiasm for scientific metaphors" well-known
(xi). Through such metaphors, Pynchon has pursued his enduring mission in
fiction, which in David Seed's words, is "to articulate the cultural implications of
modern scientific theory" (*Order in* 140). In general, these implications were
sobering compared to modernity's confidently utopian expectations for science
and technology. The latter fostered the "repudiation of modernism" which, in
Andreas Huyssen's words, would give it "the name of the postmodern" (49).
Despite the fact that *The Crying of Lot 49* was written during a time of great
ferment in the earth sciences—the long held theory of continental drift was being
soundly discredited—and that its action takes place from the San Francisco Bay
Region to Santa Barbara, which are extremely vulnerable to earthquakes, no one
has recognized that this intensively studied novel is laced with metaphors based
on the science of plate tectonics. "The plates" in these regions of California,
writes Berkeley geologist Doris Sloan, "are restless and in constant movement:
they separate and spread apart, they converge (collide), or they slide past each
other [, ... though it] is only in an earthquake that we are forcefully reminded that
the rocks beneath us are not as unmoving as they seem" (28). Even Sloan was
moved to articulate this science with metaphors when she wrote in her popular
layman's guide to the geology of the San Francisco Bay Region:

> The familiar hills and valleys, which to our 'rock of the ages' mindset
> seem to have been here forever, are mere geological infants. Get into the
> family time machine and visit the Bay Area of a million years ago and you
> will see a far different landscape. Take your time machine a million years
> into the future, and it is likely you will not recognize your homeland. The
> mountains that look so solid, so unchanging, are rising and eroding
> rapidly. [...] The present landscape is temporary, here today but gone
> from the geologic tomorrow. (Sloan 2)

To our "rock of the ages" mindset, the immediate reality of plate tectonic activity
is far more unsettling, literally and figuratively, than the far-off implications of
entropy that have monopolized the attention of Pynchon critics. The present
essay starts with the assumption that Pynchon was eminently aware of the

paradigm shift that was engulfing the earth sciences while he was writing *The Crying of Lot 49* and that he incorporated it in his Maxwell's box of a novel. If my assumption is correct, I should be able to develop a model in which *The Crying of Lot 49* is shown to contain numerous signifiers to plate tectonics. If the model is successful, I should also be able, in Seed's words, "to articulate [its] cultural implications" (140).

The Paradigm Shift from Continental Drift to Plate Tectonics

Since the beginning of the 20th century, scientists argued whether the unproven hypothesis of continental drift could explain why the continents have been sliding along the ocean floor for the past 200-million years, away from their assemblage known as Pangaea. Skeptics doubted that there was a force strong enough to overcome the immense friction that would impede such motion. In the late 1920s a British geologist, Arthur Holmes, proposed that the radioactive heat in the earth's interior creates a hot, viscous mantle whose convective rise to the surface could provide the as yet unexplained force to move continents. It has long been known that the lines of force of the earth's magnetic field everywhere point in the direction of the North Pole. Rocks typically contain small amounts of magnetic material, such as the iron oxide magnetite, whose magnetism when it is formed becomes aligned with the earth's magnetic field. Thus frozen in the rock are the direction to the pole and the latitude at which the rock formed. Researchers in the 1950s and early 60s found that the magnetism in rocks only a few million years old was consistent with the present magnetic field, whereas that in older rocks was not. Their magnetism often pointed in the opposite direction, to the geographic South Pole. Such reversals, every million or so years, as recorded in stone, confirmed that the various continents were all in motion with respect to the poles and with respect to one another.

In 1961, Robert Dietz discovered that the continents are not sliding along the sea floor but that the seafloor itself is spreading a few centimeters per year in response to the intrusion of molten mantle from below. In 1963, Frederick Vine and Drummond Matthews published the results of their study in which they mapped the varying magnetic field strengths across three mid-ocean ridges, reporting linear stripes of alternatively higher and lower field strengths parallel to the respective mid-ocean ridges. They explained this variation in magnetic field strength as they passed over areas of the ocean as follows: when the permanent magnetization of a crustal stripe is in the same direction as the Earth's present main field at that locality, the magnetic field caused by the stripe above itself is parallel to the direction of the main field and adds to its strength. On the other hand when the magnetization of such a stripe is in the opposite direction, the field which it causes above itself will reduce the strength of the main field.

The discoveries of Dietz and of Vine and Matthews provided a major boost to the developing theory of plate tectonics, which eventually accounted for many of the major features of the earth's surface as well as of the ocean basins. The extrusion of molten rock material spreads the seafloor, providing the force that moves tectonic plates. Plate collisions occur causing one plate to fold upward and form mountains while the other plate sinks downward, becomes molten, and to complete the circular flow, is subducted back into the partially-molten mantle from which it came. When two continents collide, there is commonly an ocean between them and a trench at the subduction zone. The uplift of sediments from such a trench created what is now the Coast Ranges and Transverse Ranges of California, which ultimately figure in *The Crying of Lot 49*.

The above is about where the plate tectonic paradigm stood when *The Crying of Lot 49* was published in 1966, although more convincing data supporting sea floor spreading were presented at the American Geophysical Union annual meetings in San Francisco in late 1966 and in New York in early 1967. Pynchon may have read the article by Arthur Raff in the January 1962 issue of the *Journal of Geophysical Research* and known that the Murray fracture zone off the coast of California near Santa Barbara is "an area of random anomalies within the large area of orderly lineation found off the west coast of North America" (417), though he would not yet have read the lead article by Roland Von Huene in the December 1969 issue of *Marine Biology*, because it was not yet published. However, he could have known about the contradictory "geophysical observations" that were being made from the eastern Murray fracture zone to the western Transverse Ranges on eight short cruises over a five-year period," which would have included some of the time in which he was writing the novel. These observations will be discussed later in the paper in the context of an episode in *The Crying of Lot 49*, where they may have been influential. It was much later that geologists discovered that reversals of polarity in the earth's magnetic field occur more frequently than once every million or so years. Based on studies of lava formations in Hawaii, it was deduced that the Earth's magnetic field reverses at random intervals, ranging from tens of thousands to many millions of years, with an average interval of approximately 250,000 years. The last such reversal occurred some 800,000 years ago. Nor is the theory that seafloor-spreading is caused by the upward push of molten rock material the preferred explanation now. Instead, the plates are moved by convection currents in the mantle and are pulled apart by the sinking of the oceanic plate into the subduction zone. Magma is then extruded at the spreading center.

Allusions to Plate Tectonics in *The Crying of Lot 49*

In the first paragraph of *The Crying of Lot 49*, Pynchon's protagonist, Oedipa Mass, appears to be alluding to earthquakes felt in San Narciso, a fictional city near Santa Barbara, when she remembers the "bust of Jay Gould that Pierce [Inverarity, her former lover, who lived in San Narciso] kept over the bed on a shelf so narrow for it she'd always had the hovering fear it would someday topple on them" (10). In the second paragraph, she recalls an intrusive telephone call "last year at three or so one morning" from Pierce, speaking in "his Lamont Cranston voice" (*Crying* 11). Although Lamont Cranston was "The Shadow" of

radio fame (Grant 17), Pynchon would have been aware of the Lamont
Geological Observatory, the branch of Columbia University which provided
much of the data that justified the transition in the mid-1960s from the old idea of
continental drift to the new idea of seafloor spreading and plate tectonics.

The allusions in the novel to plate tectonics continue in the oppressive
sadness that Oedipa remembers feeling when she saw the painting, "*Bordando el
Manto Terrestre*" ("Embroidering the Earth's Mantle"), of "frail girls with heart-
shaped faces" (21), prisoners in the top room of a circular tower,

> embroidering a kind of tapestry which spilled out of the slit windows and
> into a void, seeking hopelessly to fill the void: for all the other buildings
> and creatures, all the waves, ships and forests of the earth were contained
> in this tapestry, and the tapestry was the world. [...] She had looked down
> at her feet and known then, because of a painting, that what she stood on
> had only been woven together a couple thousand miles away in her own
> tower, was only by accident known as Mexico, and so Pierce had taken
> her away from nothing, there'd been no escape.
> [...] Having no apparatus except gut fear and female cunning to examine
> this formless magic, to understand how it works, how to measure its field
> strength, count its lines of force, [...] (*Crying* 21-22)

The tapestry, having to do with the "Earth's Mantle" spilling out of the thin
windows of the tower is surely a metaphor for molten magma flowing from a
volcano or seafloor fissure, filling voids along its way. The reference above to
where Oedipa stood, having been woven together a couple thousand miles away
in her own tower, which was only by accident known as Mexico, may reflect the
fact that the whole of Mexico was scrunched up closer to California before
Pangaea began coming apart as a consequence of plate tectonics. Oedipa's "tears,
those specific tears, as if indices as yet unfound varied in important ways from cry
to cry"(21), may have been occasioned by the terrible sadness of her realizing the
insubstantiality of familiar landscapes that we want to believe are everlasting. In
his best-selling book on plate tectonics, John McPhee quotes a prominent
geologist Anita Harris's plaint that

> we were taught all wrong. We were taught that changes on the face of the
> earth come in a slow steady march. But that isn't what happens. The slow
> steady march of geologic time is punctuated with catastrophes. [... They]
> happen in the hundred-year storm, the hundred-year flood, [..., the]
> earthquake. (43)

"There is no part of the face of the earth," McPhee laments, "that vertically and
laterally does not move" (174). Although, Dr. Harris told McPhee that plate
tectonics has "been misused terribly [, ...] has misrepresented facts [and] has
oversimplified the world," when he asked her if she believed "that ocean crust is
subducted into trenches, that it melts and then comes up behind trenches as
volcanoes and island arcs," she replied "That is straightforward. [...] And I have
no doubt that one edge of the Pacific Plate is grinding northwest through

California" (122). Surely that Pacific Plate "grinding northwest through California, will someday, millions and millions of year from now, drag what's left of its bridges and skyscrapers and freeways into deep subduction and molten magma.

Oedipa's allusion to "field strength" suggests that Pynchon had read Vine and Matthews' "Magnetic Anomalies over Oceanic Ridges" in the September 1963 issue of *Nature*, in which the measures of "field strength" confirmed long-term periodic reversals of the earth's magnetic polarity, as well as the "spreading sea-floor theory" that Dietz proposed in the 1961 issue of that same journal (854). When Pynchon writes that "Oedipa could carry the sadness of the moment with her that way forever," that sadness could have something to do with the "formless magic" of plate tectonics and "how it works" (*Crying* 21).

Arguably, the second-most multi-layered episode in *The Crying of Lot 49* takes place in the second chapter when Oedipa and Metzger are alone in her hotel room in San Narciso, and she snaps on the television set:

> Onto the screen bloomed the image of a child of indeterminate sex, its bare legs pressed awkward together, its shoulder-length curls mingling with the shorter hair of a St. Bernard, whose long tongue, as Oedipa watched, began to swipe at the child's rosy cheeks, making the child wrinkle up its nose appealingly and say, 'Aw, Murray, come on, now, you're getting me all wet. (29, 30)

This movie, entitled *Cashiered* and ostensibly culminating in the bloody rout in 1915 of British and allied forces in their failed attempt to occupy the Gallipoli Peninsula and defeat the Turks, contains a number of possible allusions to plate tectonics, starting with the dog named "Murray," who is licking the child "all wet" (*Crying* 30). A major study of the Murray Fracture Zone was underway off-shore near Santa Barbara when Pynchon was writing *The Crying of Lot 49*. For much of the 1960s, Pynchon was living in an apartment in Manhattan Beach, California, which would have been less than a hundred-mile drive to Santa Barbara, where he might have gotten wind of the research on the Murray, which seemed to promise a "clear demonstration that a feature of the oceanic crust extends across the continental margin into the continental crust" and would "help to clarify current geologic hypotheses of the origin of continents and ocean basins" (Von Huene 476). If Von Huene's references to "the submarine structures of the Murray" (476), the "Arguello Submarine Canyon (487), the "sea-floor physiography" (490), and even the "Rejuvenation of the ocean floor" (495) were being discussed on shore, they might explain Pynchon's elaborations on the "submarine" (*Crying* 30, 32, 40), its going "to the bottom" of "the Narrows"(32), and the choice of juvenile lead, Baby Igor, in this weird film. At the end of the film, the three are trapped in the perforated submarine, and Murray, the "dog was first to drown, in a great crowd of bubbles" (42). It would be like Pynchon to include "Fracture Zone" somewhere close to "Murray," but it is not until a sunny afternoon in Oakland, days later, that Oedipa, skimming through the book that she has gone to great trouble to acquire, reads something "in the leaf-fractured sunlight" that makes her freeze (*Crying* 101). Because "fractured" is used in such an arcane context here, there is reason to suspect that Pynchon hoped readers would eventually catch on. Indeed, every link–there are only three of them–in a computer search of "leaf-fractured sunlight" has to do with *The Crying of Lot 49*.

There is no mention *per se* of "plate tectonics," "sea-floor spreading" or "continental drift" in *The Crying of Lot 49*. However, they may be imbedded on consecutive pages referring to the "GalactrONICS Division of Yoyodyne" and to being kept "happy, coherent, proTECTed from pain" (25, 26). Then, further in the novel, Oedipa idiosyncratically "flung a babushka over her license PLATE" and drove toward another "freeway, heading irreversibly for the Bay Bridge" (*Crying* 108). On page 177, Oedipa "tried to face toward the SEA"; on page 180, "kids sat on the FLOOR planking"; and on page 181, "What would the probate judge have to say about SPREADING." Finally, there are "higher, more CONTINENTAL solemnities" on page 178) and "remembered DRIFTers she had listened to" on page 180. Coincidences? Perhaps. But all three key terms?

Allusions to plate tectonics continue with Oedipa on a wild automobile drive southeast from San Narciso to

> Fangoso Lagoons, one of Inverarity's last big projects. […] Somewhere beyond the battening, urged sweep of three-bedroom houses rushing by their thousands across all the dark beige hills, somewhat implicit in an arrogance or bite to the smog the more inland somnolence of San Narciso did lack, lurked the sea, the unimaginable Pacific, […] the hole left by the moon's tearing-free and monument to her exile [. …] Oedipa had believed, long before leaving Kinneret, in some principle of the sea as redemption for Southern California (not, of course, for her own [northern] section of the state, which seemed to need none), some unvoiced idea that no matter what you did to its edges the true Pacific stayed inviolate and integrated or assumed the ugliness at any edge into some more general truth. Perhaps it was only that notion, its arid hope, she sensed as this forenoon they made their seaward thrust, which would stop short of any sea. (*Crying* 55-56)

The above mentioned dark beige hills packed with new subdivisions are the southern slopes of the Transverse Ranges along the California coast running east from Government Point to Carpenteria. A "tectonic rotation of the western Transverse Ranges block," about 20 million years ago, explains this particular east-west diversion of the generally southeast-northwest inclination of the California coast (Nicholson *et al.* 491). Presumably, the new subdivisions are south of the freeway here, because the sea is further "beyond" them. The sentence beginning with "Somewhere beyond …" is convoluted, probably to blur Pynchon's disapprobation of the seeming "arrogance" of the denizens of the "battening, urged sweep" of new houses, whose long commutes eastward augment the "smog" in greater Los Angeles (*Crying* 55). The above description of California coastline suggests that San Narciso appears to have been Goleta, which is two

New Close Readings of *The Crying of Lot 49*

miles north of the coast, eight miles west of Santa Barbara, and 75 miles west of
Los Angeles. In 1965 it was an unincorporated Census-Designated-Place, not
unlike the fictional San Narciso, which "was less an identifiable city than a
grouping of concepts–census tracts, special purpose bond-issue districts," *et cetera*
(*Crying* 24). After World War II, residents of the district "supported the
construction of Cachuma Lake, which provided water enabling a housing boom
and the establishment of research and aerospace firms in the area. In 1954 the
University of California, Santa Barbara" located nearby (< *Goleta, California*, http:/
/en.wikipedia.org/wiki/Goleta,California >). Goleta's lake-engendered boom in
housing and high technology firms are suggestive of Fangoso Lagoons and its
research and aerospace firms, Galactronics and Yoyodyne. The University of
California, Santa Barbara corresponds to San Narciso College; it is more likely that
Professor Bortz would have transferred from UC-Berkeley to UC-Santa Barbara
than to a college in an unincorporated place like the fictional San Narciso.

The novel's allusion to "the hole" in the Pacific "left by the moon's
tearing-free and monument to her exile" goes back to 1892 when some geologist
argued that, in its early years, the earth spun so rapidly that the sun's gravity
yanked a chunk of earth under the ocean loose and flung it into the sky. *The Crying
of Lot 49* memorialized what was then still the leading theory of the origin of the
moon, which would become obsolete within three or four years after the novel
was published. That theory was rejected in 1969 when Neil Armstrong and Buzz
Aldrin started bringing rocks back from space that were different from rocks of
the earth's crust. It is now theorized that the moon was made of dry particles of
iron-depleted earth-crust, blown loose by the impact of an early planetary body
from space, that accreted to form the moon.

That Oedipa had once believed "in some principle of the sea as
redemption for Southern California" connotes the splitting of the Red Sea that
redeemed the early Hebrews, though in the case of Southern California, "no
matter what you did to its edges the true Pacific stayed inviolate and integrated,"
that is, it did not split or spread apart like the Red Sea is believed to have done
(*Crying* 55). Instead of the sea, it is the seafloor that spreads from mid-ocean
fractures, ridged and violated, anticipating the new geological paradigm, the "more
general truth" (55). Can Oedipa even hope that "the battening, urged sweep of
three-bedroom houses rushing by their thousands across all the dark beige hills"
will safely "stop short of any sea" (*Crying* 56).

The next reference to plate tectonics in *The Crying of Lot 49* occurs when
Driblette, showering after the play, tells Oedipa: "'If I were to dissolve in here,
[…] be washed down the drain into the Pacific,'" the only residue would be
whatever was true in tonight's script, and perhaps "'the other, also. The
Adversary. But they would be traces, fossils. Dead, mineral, without value or
potential'" (*Crying* 79-80). This allusion to fossils may signify their importance in
plate tectonics. It was not enough for Alfred Wegener that Africa and South
America appeared to fit together like jigsaw puzzle pieces; he was able to find

fossils and rock types along the western coast of Africa that matched those along the eastern coast of South America, confirming that, before Pangaea started breaking apart 200-million years ago, these organic forms and minerals were coexistent on that same super-continent. It was especially germane to plate tectonics that a half-century later it was found that the rate of seafloor spreading calculated from fossils is identical to that estimated from paleomagnetic data.

Driblette's allusion (*Crying* 80) to "the other" and to "The Adversary" is interesting because it puts the second law of thermodynamics in the context of plate tectonics. Later in the novel, we learn that it, the second law, is "the brute Other, that kept the non-Scurvhamite universe running like clockwork" (156) and still later, that "if Thurn and Taxis have no clear idea who their adversary is, or how far its influence extends, then many of them must come to believe in something very like the Scurvhamite's blind, automatic anti-God" (165). That the second law of thermodynamics is both the "brute Other" and the "adversary" is made clear in the explanation of the "two kinds" of "predestination":

> Nothing for a Scurvhamite ever happened by accident, Creation was a vast, intricate machine. But one part of it, the Scurvhamite part, ran off the will of God, its prime mover. The rest ran off some opposite Principle, something blind, soulless; a brute automatism that led to eternal death. (*Crying* 155)

What may be more interesting is that Pynchon goes further in connecting Driblette with the Scurvhamites when he has him tell Oedipa: "You guys, you're like Puritans are about the Bible. So hung up with words, words" (79), and then later calls the Scurvhamites "a sect of most pre Puritans" (*Crying* 155). Pynchon may have wanted to associate the "eternal death" of the second law with the melting and re-melting of earth's continents into molten magma, on and on, until the mantle and the outer core of the earth itself experiences its own heat death. Pynchon was prescient, for Charles Lineweaver would eventually apply the theory of "Maximum Entropy Production" to the dissipative process by which "Plate tectonics [...] slowly stirs and differentiates the crusts" (67, 68).

The Crying of Lot 49 reaches a denouement seven pages before it ends. Oedipa, at a telephone booth near the highway turn-off to San Narciso, has run out of change for the telephone and lost her connection to the fellow in the San Francisco bar who'd called her Arnold Snarb:

> She stood between the public booth and the rented car, in the night, her isolation complete, and tried to face toward the sea. But she'd lost her bearings. She turned, pivoting on one stacked heel, could find no mountains either. As if there could be no barriers between herself and the rest of the land. San Narciso at that moment lost [, ...] gave up its residue of uniqueness for her; became a name again, was assumed back into the American continuity of crust and mantle. (*Crying* 177)

The reference here to "crust and mantle" is the most unambiguous signifier of plate tectonics in *The Crying of Lot 49*. There are surely multiple interpretations of the sentences preceding it, to which Pynchon alludes in *Against the Day,* a novel he published in 2006, apparently to commemorate the fortieth anniversary of the 1966 novel and to revisit some of those sentences that critics had not yet understood. The allusions to earthquakes in the earlier novel, an aspect of the plate tectonic archetype apparently disregarded until the present essay, are re-signified in *Against the Day* in a brief reference to the 1925 "earthquake" in Santa Barbara, a 6.3 tremblor that struck Santa Barbara a little before 7 AM on June 29 of that year and leveled much of the commercial district (*Against* 1043). The above scene in *The Crying of Lot 49* in which Oedipa "lost her bearings" and "turned, pivoting on one stacked heel" (177) is evoked in the later novel in which, because "of the right-angled piece of local coastline known as the Rincón, the ocean lay to the south of town instead of west, so you had to rotate ninety degrees from everybody else in Southern California to catch the sunset" (*Against* 1043). Because Oedipa was at that part of the California coast below Santa Barbara that has run east and west since the tectonic rotation of the range some 20 million years ago, the mountains that she was looking for in the wrong direction must have been the Transverse Ranges. Oedipa appears to have been orienting herself by a north-south spur of the "stretch of railroad track" that she "walked down," thinking that the spur was actually the main track, running east and west along the horizontal coast (*Crying* 177). The mountains that she couldn't see because of her disorientation were the barriers between herself (and San Narciso) and the rest of the country. That she had "lost her bearings" and "could find no mountains" represented an illusionary compression of 20 million years of plate tectonic folding and faulting.

Concluding Remarks

The Crying of Lot 49 was an early example of "the kind of literature that critics and scholars would soon be calling postmodern" (Robert McLaughlin 55-6). By the 1970s there was a groundswell of disillusion that science, technology and disciplined rationality had not lived up to their utopian expectations. It was a measure of that groundswell that a humble rabbi in Long Island sermonized "his disappointment that so many idealistic goals he had worked for since he was ordained had failed to materialize" (Kohn *Unwitting Witness* 309). It is as though modernism itself had failed, and we were entering a new era, a postmodern era, as it came to be called. In a 1984 book review in *The New York Times,* Pynchon associated utopian modernity with "the cheerful army of technocrats" who claimed that by getting "the right data to those whom the data will do the most good" and with "the proper deployment of budget and computer time, we will cure cancer, save ourselves from nuclear extinction, grow food for everybody, detoxify the results of industrial greed gone berserk – realize all the wistful pipe dreams of our days" (*Is it O.K. To Be a Luddite* 41). However, the science that Pynchon depicted in *The Crying of Lot 49* is hardly utopian. Until the problem was recognized by Rachel Carson and corrected, the science of pest control did more harm than good. The second law of thermodynamics, which Pynchon perceived as "having to do with heat-engines" (*Crying* 105), envisages the dystopian running down of energy in the solar system. It is relevant to the present essay that Kevin Kilty likened Earth's plate tectonics to a Carnot heat engine:

> Hot material rises from the deep mantle to the base of the lithosphere in the upper mantle at a spreading ridge. Here it flows laterally rejecting heat all along the way. This heat gets conducted to the earth's surface. As it cools the lithosphere thickens. Eventually the lithosphere is forced, somehow, back into the mantle where it must melt [absorbing heat], mix back into the bulk material, and reappear millions of years later at a ridge again. (Kilty)

The amount of heat loss is relatively small, notes Kilty, "0.04 watts/m^2 averaged over the entire earth" and the efficiency is "much less [...] than a Carnot engine." Still, it is interesting that the earth itself, from a plate tectonic perspective, is a self-operating Maxwell's box. But it is unsettling that plate tectonic motion reveals itself in successions of devastating catastrophes–in 2010 there was the volcanic eruption in Iceland that grounded flights across Europe and the North Atlantic for nearly a week, the hundred-year flood in Pakistan that killed 17,000 people, and the earthquake in Port-au-Prince, that killed 220,000 Haitians. The last was the worse of 20 earthquakes of magnitude 7.0 or greater that year. In turn, it was dwarfed by the 9.0 magnitude quake that struck off the coast of Japan in March of 2011, setting off a tsunami that killed more than 10,000 people, damaged nuclear power plants and released toxic levels of radiation. The cultural consequence of the new skepticism toward science that *The Crying of Lot 49* epitomized was the 1960s shift from modernism to postmodernism.

Whereas Grant discerned Pynchon's "enthusiasm for scientific metaphors" in general, the new essays presented in the present book narrow that enthusiasm, if it can still be called that, to dystopian scientific metaphors (*1ˢᵗ Ed.*, xi). In *Against the Day*, Pynchon would later extrapolate the succession from postmodernism's skepticism of science and technology, as first recorded in *The Crying of Lot 49*, to hypermodernism's outright *fear* of what science and technology may have coming next.

Essay Six

Evans-Wentz and the Tibetan *Bardo*

> Her climax and Metzger's, when it came, coincided with every
> light in the place, including the TV tube, suddenly going out,
> dead, black. It was a curious experience. The Paranoids had
> blown a fuse. (*Crying* 21-22)

From February 1960 to September 1962, Pynchon lived in Seattle, where he was a
technical writer for the Boeing Company. Coincidently, it was in the city of
Seattle, when Pynchon was there, that the first official presence of Tibetan
Buddhism in America took place, in the person of Dezhung Rinpoche. "At dusk
on March 17, 1959, less than a year before Pynchon arrived in Seattle,

> Tendzin Gyatso , the Fourteenth Dalai Lama, disguised as a Tibetan
> peasant, slipped out a backdoor of the Norbu Lingka Summer Palace, and
> passed through the lines of the Chinese troops surrounding Lhasa. He
> was met on the banks of the Kyichu river by a party of Khampa (East
> Tibetan) horsemen, and two weeks later crossed the Himalayas into India.
> By the time the Chinese sealed the border close to a hundred thousand
> Tibetans had followed him into exile. (Rick Fields 273)

This mass exodus coincided with the beginning of the 1959 Tibetan revolt against
China. By the time the revolt was suppressed, "a half million people lost their
lives, and Tibetan culture had been nearly eradicated" (Fields 276).

"In the very early morning of March 19, 1959," a day and a half after the
Dalai Lama escaped, "Dezhung Rinpoche and the Sakya family (one of the
Tibetan Buddhist Schools) quietly set out from Lhasa, divided into small groups
[…] so as not to arouse suspicion" (David Jackson 228). Born in 1906, the future
lama had an ordinary name and life, until "his parents decided to dedicate the boy
to the Buddhist monkhood" (Jackson 3). He proved to be a superior student and,
because certain "auspicious events before and at his birth led some members of
his family to suspect that the boy was the rebirth […] of a lama," he was later
"recognized to be the third Dezhung Rinpoche" (7). Within months of the large
exodus of the Buddhist nobility, American professors sought to bring some of
their leading scholars to the United States. "One of the first of these was Dr.
Turrell Wylie of the University of Washington Inner Asia Program," which was
"endowed in part by the Rockefeller Fund and Department of Defense" (Fields
289). According to Jackson's account, Wylie travelled to Darjeeling in March 1960
in search of a prominent Tibetan scholar who would be "interested in coming to
the United States […] to collaborate for three years with American researchers at
[his] university" (243). On October 13, 1960, the much-sought-after Dezhung
Rinpoche and a "party of nine other Tibetans landed at the international airport

south of Seattle. Waiting to greet them were a delegation from the University of Washington and several people from the local news media" (249). "For the next few weeks, the Tibetans became local celebrities" and were the subject, well into December, of "at least ten or eleven articles" that "appeared in the *Seattle Times*" (Jackson 251, 252).

Presumably, Pynchon was aware of the well-publicized Tibetan presence in Seattle; he might also have known, in the spring of 1961, that "Wylie dropped a bombshell" by informing the visiting scholars

> that he wanted to do a seminar with them on the *Hevajra Tantra*, the basic text of their school's central esoteric tradition. They were to give him the initiation, he told them, and then they would all sit down and study the tantra together. [...] Dezhung Rinpoche and the others in the Sakya family were horrified. Their religion was not for sale to people who had no intention of practicing it. They flatly refused to go along if they had to divulge tantric secrets. (Jackson 274)

Though Wyle "reacted angrily," made remarks about "wanting to send them back to India," the Tibetans felt obliged, "[o]n religious grounds," to refuse his request; "they had definitely *not* come to Seattle under the agreement that they would make public their treasured esoteric traditions" (Jackson 274-75). The *Hevajra Tantra*, the basic text of the Sakya School, centers on the male deity Hevajra, who is typically depicted or visualized in sexual union with his consort, the goddess Nairatmya. This is typical of the iconic imagery exoterically referred to as "*Yab-Yum*," which is "Father-Mother" in Tibetan.

The "first tantric Buddhist text presented to the public without apology," wrote Fields, was *The Tibetan Book of the Dead*, the name given to the English translation of the *Bardo Thödol* by W.Y. Evans-Wentz, who edited it in collaboration with the translator, Kazi Dawa-Samdup (286). Originally published in 1927, Oxford Press introduced a paperback edition in 1960 in response to the surge of interest in Tibetan Buddhism in the West. The original Tibetan manuscript used by Evans-Wentz and Dawa-Sandup, which the translator at the time judged "to be from 150 to 200 years old" (*Tibetan Book* 69), contained illuminations "in color (now much faded) painted on the folios" (xxvii). Most interesting, in the context of the *Hevajra Tantra*, is Evans-Wentz's description of one of the illuminations, now depicted on the frontispiece of the Oxford editions, which features in the central circle the "Dhyani Buddha Vairochana, embraced by his *shakti*, or divine spouse, Mother of Infinite Space" (xxvii). It is appropriate that the *Bardo Thödol* has long been associated with the *Yab-Yum* because each has, according to Buddhist doctrine, a

> literal or exoteric interpretation, which is the popular interpretation; and the symbolic or esoteric interpretation, which is held by the initiated few, who claim not scriptural authority or belief, but [first-hand] knowledge. With respect to Tibet, these few are chiefly learned lamas who are said to have made successful applications of methods like those which the

Buddha expounded for remembering past incarnations, and for acquiring the yogic power of seeing what really takes place in the natural process of death and rebirth. (*Tibetan Book* 39-40)

A full understanding of Tibetan Buddhism would, in the words of Evans-Wentz, "involve the esoteric as well as the exoteric interpretation of an enormous mass of doctrines" (61). I assume in the present essay that Pynchon was aware and interested in the Sakya presence in Seattle, which began while he was living there, and that he became familiar with *The Tibetan Book of the Dead*, whose author claimed having "received instructions," such as Wylie had been denied, on its esoteric as well as its exoteric interpretations (*Tibetan Book* 42).

In my first published article on *The Crying of Lot 49*, I argued that this novel "can be better understood (or at least some of its ambiguity resolved) in the context of Tibetan Buddhism" (*Seven Buddhist Themes* 73). In that article, I also suggested that the fictional San Narciso professor Emory Bortz was a modern day version of the Stanford educated Evans-Wentz, who earned his doctorate at Oxford University and became a professor there. Both were editors of ancient manuscripts. The names, Emory and Evans, both begin with an E and have five letters. Bortz and Wentz both end with tz and have five letters. The absence of a hyphen and the cartoonish allusion to emery boards make the esoteric connection less obvious. Although Bortz is not entirely the serious scholar that Evans-Wentz was, the latter has not escaped criticism; Fields made a point of noting "certain inaccuracies" in *The Tibetan Book of the Dead*: "the diction, for example, with all its 'ye's' and 'thou's,' suffered from Biblical rhetoric, and Evans-Wentz had failed to adequately distinguish between Hindu and Buddhist terminology" (286). My own objection to Evans-Wentz's commentary, as opposed to the translated text, is that, having written it in 1927, when the modernist West was glorying in its science, he pandered to Anglo-American taste by asserting that "the *Bardo Thödol* seems to be based upon verifiable data of human physiological and psychological experiences; and it views the problem of the after-death state as being purely a psycho-physical problem; and is, therefore, in the main, scientific" (*Tibetan Book* 34). More flagrantly, Evans-Wentz insisted that "the Great Teacher," that is, The Buddha, has "made the corner-stone of Buddhism (as it is of Hinduism) the belief in a Supreme Power or Universal Law, called the Law of Cause and Effect by the Science of the West and, by the Science of the East, *Karma*" (*Tibetan Book* 236). Surely Dezhung Rinpoche would have scorned such simplistic exotericism of the *Bardo* and of *Karma*. To seal the connection between Evans-Wentz and Emory Bortz, the latter is married to a "wife named Grace" (*Crying* 148); Evans-Wentz's edition of *The Tibetan Book of the Dead* instructs the deceased, upon "enter[ing] into the womb" to "emit thy gift-waves [of grace, or good-will] upon the womb which thou art entering, [transforming it thereby] into a celestial mansion" (191, square brackets in the original). In the index, they are listed under "Grace-Waves" (245), rather than "gift-waves."

Bardo Rebirth

This essay is based on the hypothesis that *Bardo* rebirth, as Pynchon interpreted it from Evans-Wentz's *Tibetan Book of the Dead,* is an underlying theme of *The Crying of Lot 49.* While reading the original during the death ceremony for the recently deceased (who presumably has retained consciousness and is listening), the lama or monk advises him or her that the "Intermediate State," which is the English translation of *"Bardo,"* will last "either for one, two, three, four, five, six, or seven weeks, until the forty-ninth day" (*Tibetan Book* 161). He reminds the mourners that "perseverance in the reading of the Great *Bardo Thödol* for forty-nine days is of the utmost importance" (183), for only the deceased will actually know how many of the 49-days he or she will spend in the in-between state. In a footnote, the editor explains that through "a series of visions, the Knower will become aware of the lot or destiny associated with each womb or place of birth seen" (188n). Rebirth occurs in the particular womb which the deceased enters at the time of conception. Note that Evans-Wentz associates both "the lot" and the number "49" with rebirth, one of the many likely explanations for the title of Pynchon's novel. The *Bardo* is indirectly signified by the first three words of *The Crying of Lot 49,* as follows:

> One summer afternoon, Mrs. Oedipa Maas came home [...] to find that she, Oedipa, had been named executor, or she supposed executrix, of the estate of one Pierce Inverarity, a California real estate mogul who [...] had died back in the spring." (*Crying* 9, 10)

Presumably, the "summer afternoon" is within the prescribed 49-day period for the actions of Chapters 1 and 2 to play themselves out. The exact dates are not given, though we do know that Oedipa's affair with Pierce "ended a year before Mucho married her" (*Crying* 16), and that she has been married to Mucho for three years, that is, five years since he joined Station KCUF, minus "the two years at the station" (15, 14). When Oedipa learned that summer afternoon when the novel began that she "had been named [...] to execute the will in a codicil dated a year ago [, ...] and tried to think back to whether anything unusual had happened around then" (10), it

> took her till the middle of Huntley and Brinkley to remember that last year at three or so in the morning there had come this long-distance call, from [...] a voice beginning in heavy Slavic tones as second secretary at the Transylvanian Consulate, looking for an escaped bat; modulated to comic-Negro, and then on into hostile Pachuco dialect, full of chingas and maricones; then a Gestapo officer asking her in shrieks did she have relatives in Germany and finally his Lamont Cranston voice, the one he'd talked in all the way down to Mazatlán. (11)

For a novel that Seed "nudge[s] the reader not to expect too much certainty within" (*Fictional Labyrinths* 123), it is significant that the temporal dating, however non-linearly it is revealed, is as specific as it is. My hypothesis is that Pynchon is establishing a credible foundation on which to launch Pierce's *Bardo* rebirth. The latter, probably twice Oedipa's age, may have anticipated his own death, and because he sounds familiar with her husband's name—"I think it's time Wendell Maas had a little visit from The Shadow" –may have known about Mucho's conjugal problem and has plans to have his "shadow" impregnate Oedipa (11). Seed is in that ball-park when he speaks of Oedipa's being "penetrated" or "impregnated" (*Fictional Labyrinths* 118-19). Pierce (homonymous with penetrate) is perhaps practicing various voices in preparation for whatever body his consciousness-bearing *prahna* is destined to inhabit. It appears that Pierce goes to a lot of effort and expense to make this reincarnation happen, but why? The answer to that question is also in the first paragraph of the novel: "a California real estate mogul who had once lost two million dollars in his spare time," Inverarity "still had assets numerous and tangled enough to make the job of sorting it all out more than honorary" (9). If Pierce were reborn as the soul of a child in Oedipa's womb, he could inherit his own fortune. The tenth prayer for salvation in "the dangerous narrow passageway of the *Bardo*" reads accordingly:

> Obtaining for myself the body of a male [which is] the better,
> Let it come that I liberate all who see or hear me;
> Allowing not the evil *karma* to follow me,
> Let it come that whatever merits [be mine] follow me and be multiplied.
> (Evans-Wentz *Tibetan Book of the Dead* 207, square brackets in the original)

Pierce had good reason to pray that evil karma would not follow him. He had used Mafia connections to salvage and import soldiers' bones "to decorate the bottom" of Lake Inverarity for the enjoyment of "the scuba nuts" and to "develop [a] filter" for Beaconsfield cigarettes (*Crying* 61, 63). He had bribed government officials so that the "highway outfits in the area" that he "had bought into [...] got contracts" (61). Worst of all, for Arrabal, was that Pierce "played the rich, obnoxious gringo so perfectly that Oedipa had seen gooseflesh come up along the anarchist's forearms" (*Crying* 120). Your friend, he told Oedipa, "unless he's joking, is as terrifying to me as a Virgin appearing to an Indian" (120). At the same time that we learn about Inverarity's terrifying *karma*, we discover that Oedipa ended their affair when she learned that Arrabal had "seen that about Pierce and she hadn't" (120). With this epiphany, she finally realized that "Inverarity pose[d] a threat to [her] from the very beginning" (Seed *Fictional Labyrinth* 118).

The endless, sad cycle of human death and rebirth from which humans seek emancipation seems to be the subtext for Mucho's horror of the "endless rituals of trade-ins" (*Crying* 13). It was as if "the way each owner, each shadow, filed in only to exchange a dented, malfunctioning version of himself for another, just as futureless, automotive projection of somebody else's life" were the most natural thing. To Mucho it was horrible. Endless, convoluted incest" (13, 14). Such overtones of reincarnation are affirmed by the above reference to "each shadow," only three pages after Pierce threatens "Wendell Maas [with] a little visit from The Shadow" (11).

While he was still alive, Pierce appears to have set the stage for what Oedipa, even while it was happening, sensed was "all part of a plot, an elaborate, seduction, *plot*" (*Crying* 31). Pynchon gives us a hint that it is Pierce's *Bardo* plot, when he italicizes that second mention of plot (P-LOT) and follows it with an explicit reference to the "Book of the Dead…." (31). Significantly this mention of *plot* may be one of the few words in the novel that is italicized purely for emphasis! Oedipa's

> climax and Metzger's, when it came, coincided with every light in the place, including the TV tube, suddenly going out, dead, black. It was a curious experience. The Paranoids had blown a fuse. When the lights came on again, […] she and Metzger lay twined amid a wall-to-wall scatter of clothing and spilled bourbon. […] "What did Inverarity tell you about me," she asked finally. "That you wouldn't be easy." (*Crying* 42- 43)

Indeed, Oedipa had wondered if this was "really happening in the same way as, say, her first time in bed with Pierce, the dead man" (35). The climax that signals the ending of the *Bardo* is recorded by Evans-Wentz in *The Tibetan Book of the Dead*–"Enter upon the White Light-[Path] of the *devas*, or upon the Yellow Light-[Path] of human beings" (192, square brackets in the original)–whereas the reference to spilled liquor may be Pynchon's own twist on the *Bardo*. When Metzger showed up at Oedipa's motel room, "there was only himself and a debonair bottle of French Beaujolais, which he claimed to've smuggled last year into California, this rollicking lawbreaker, past the frontier guards" (*Crying* 28). Maybe Pierce's soul came in the motel room in that bottle of Beaujolais; or maybe it was in the fifth of Jack Daniels that the Paranoids left "[o]n the doorsill" of Oedipa's room; "As if the dead really do persist, even in a bottle of wine" (*Crying* 40, 99).

After the climax, the movie on the TV ended violently, "the father, dog and Baby Igor trapped inside the darkening "Justine," as the water level inexorably rose" (42). This may have something to do with Pierce's anguish at "closing the womb-door" (Evans-Wentz *Tibetan Book* 176), feeling distraught for "being of evil karma" (180), and experiencing his "sinking" in "the Ocean of Misery" (180), though actually, Baby Igor, who was played by Metzger when he was a child-actor, is "electrocuted, thrashing back and forth and screaming horribly" (*Crying* 42-43).

I would not have picked up on these subtle signifiers of *Bardo* phenomena in *The Crying of Lot 49* had I not, as I said under Essay Three of the *Introduction*, read Pynchon's *Vineland* first. In that novel, which was published in 1990, Weed Atman describes "the after-death state, the Bardo, with its time limits for finding a new body to be born into–seeking out men and women in the act of sex, looking for a just-fertilized egg, slipping to and fro with needful dim others in a space like a black smoke tarnished district of sex shows and porno theatres, looking for the magical exact film frame through which the dispossessed soul might reenter the world" (*Vineland* 364). Pynchon may in part have intended this light-hearted caricature of the *bardo* as a belated clue to Inverarity's scheme in *The Crying of Lot*

49. The term "Atman" is often related to self-attachment, which Buddhism considers the root of sangsaric ignorance. That a character named Atman would talk about an ego's quest for another life and body to recover his worldly wealth and power is contrary to the highest Buddhist values. It would have been much more in tune with "*bardo* logic," Kathryn Hume might say, if Pierce had considered "detachment from the world and giving up all desire" (434), rather than devote his final year on earth to reclaiming his fortune. "Within the Tibetan context, our goal should be enlightenment" (Hume 437).

Mike Fallopian may have had literary criticism in mind when he told Oedipa: "Write down what you can't deny. Your hard intelligence. But then write down what you've only speculated, assumed. See what you've got. At least that" (*Crying* 168). In this essay, the *bardo* plot in *The Crying of Lot 49* is affirmed by the key role in it played by Metzger, whose name signifies the 1964 manual, *The Psychedelic Experience: A Manual Based on The Tibetan Book of the Dead*, by Timothy Leary, Ralph Metzner, and Richard Alpert, because his name is so obviously a caricature of the second author's (Kohn *Seven Buddhist Themes* 84). Turning back to what I've "only speculated, assumed," a number of lines in *The Crying of Lot 49* can be read through the lens of *bardo* rebirth: "set up or sensitized [...] by her peculiar seduction" (45); "If it was really Pierce's attempt to leave an organized something behind after his own annihilation, then it was part of her [Oedipa's] duty, wasn't it, to bestow life on what had persisted" (*Crying* 81-82); "Oedipa, so hung up and interpenetrated with the dead man's estate" (109); "a child roaming the night who missed the death before birth" (123); a "Negro woman [...] who kept going through rituals of miscarriage each for a different reason, deliberately as others might the ritual of birth, dedicated not to continuity but to some kind of interregnum" (123); "another voyeur, who hung outside one of the city's still-lighted windows, searching for who knew what specific image" (123); "she's any number of people, all over the world, back through time" (143); "a transient, winged shape, needing to settle at once in the warm host. [...] she felt briefly penetrated, as if the bright winged thing had actually made it to the sanctuary of her heart. [...] She waited for the winged brightness to announce its safe arrival. But there was silence" (161-62). Note that, in the present set of essays, the bright winged thing represents vanishing songbirds, Driblette's essence, and Pierce's *prahna* consciousness. The above allusions to miscarriages not only have special significance for *bardo* rebirth in general, but for Inverarity in particular.

The plot that Inverarity hatched went much further than getting his soul into Oedipa's fertilized ovum. It was

> expensive and elaborate, involving items like the forging of stamps and ancient books, constant surveillance of [her] movements, planting of post horns all over San Francisco, bribing of librarians, hiring of professional actors and Pierce Inverarity only knows what-all besides. (*Crying* 170-71)

We know that Oedipa is pregnant:

There were headaches, nightmares, menstrual pains. One day she drove into L.A., picked a doctor at random from the phone book, went to her, told her she thought she was pregnant. They arranged for tests. Oedipa gave her name as Grace Bortz and didn't show up for her next appointment. (171)

Before his death, Inverarity appears to have conspired with "Bortz, along with Metzger, Cohen, Driblette, Koteks, the tattooed sailor in San Francisco, the W.A.S.T.E. carriers she'd seen" (*Crying* 170), to keep Oedipa so discombobulated by fantasies and hallucinations as to make her hope that "she was mentally ill" and perhaps, most importantly, distract her from even thinking about an abortion (171). That she gave her name at the doctor's office as Grace Bortz suggests that she, more than Pierce, is snared in "the dangers of the *Bardo*" (Evans-Wentz *Tibetan Book* 109n). Her gynecologist would have had "no test for what she was pregnant with" (175).

When Oedipa, in a phone booth by the side of the road, placed the station call to The Greek Way in San Francisco and was connected to the man who called her "Arnold Snarb," she told him

what she'd learned about The Tristero, what happened to Hilarius, Mucho, Driblette, Fallopian. "So you are," she said, "the only one I have. I don't know your name, don't want to. But I have to know whether they arranged it with you. To run into me by accident, and tell me your story about the post horn. Because it may be a practical joke for you, but it stopped being one for me a few hours ago. I got drunk and went driving on these freeways. Next time I may be more deliberate. For the love of God, human life, whatever you respect, please. Help me." (*Crying* 176-77)

"Arnold," he started to say, and then there was a long stretch of bar noise: "It's over," she said "they've saturated me" (177). For readers who miss the point, Pynchon's narrator subsequently refers to a "squall-line" and "storm-systems" (178). Taken in the *bardo* context in which "rituals of miscarriage" are balanced against "the ritual of birth" (*Crying* 123), it appears that Oedipa has had the kind of heavy menstrual period that follows a miscarriage. "Miscarriage" is not listed in Evans-Wentz's index, and its consequence for the re-embodied *prahna* may be an esoteric issue known only to lamas and their initiates. Pynchon appears to have concluded that it marks the ending of the re-birthing soul, for he concludes the paragraph that follows "they've saturated me" with "Pierce Inverarity was *really* dead" (177, italics added). Oedipa finally relaxed, felt "compassion for the cul-de-sac" that Pierce had "tried to find a way out of" (178). He had devised a plot "too elaborate for the dark Angel to hold at once, in his humorless vice-president's head, all the possibilities of," to slip through and [...] by that much beaten death" (179).

Earlier in the novel, Pynchon had introduced Hernando Joaquin de Tristero y Calavera, "founding figure" of the Tristero (159): Claiming that the Thurn and Taxis postal monopoly belonged to him "by right of blood," he "styled himself El Desheredado, The Disinherited," and began a guerilla war against the postal monopoly (160). Though Oedipa might have been the heiress to Pierce's estate–that could have "been in the will, in code, perhaps without Pierce really knowing" (178)–she viewed his legacy as America, and saw the poor around her as the disinherited:

> What would the probate judge have to say about spreading some kind of a legacy among them all, all those nameless, maybe as a first installment? Oboy. He'd be on her ass in a microsecond, revoke her letters testamentary, they'd call her names, proclaim her through all Orange County as a redistributionist and pinko. [...] Who knew? Perhaps she'd be hounded someday as far as joining Tristero itself, if it existed, in its twilight, its aloofness, its waiting. (*Crying* 181)

From the "Young Republican" she claimed to be, Oedipa has matured into one of "these lib, overeducated broads with the soft heads and bleeding hearts," that Metzger derided (76). From this perspective, *The Crying of Lot 49* has a traditional theme: the personal development, fostered by duress, of the hero or heroine.

Concluding Remarks

Resonating though the entire novel, from the first numbered page, 9, to the last,183, Pierce's death-avoiding *bardo* strategy comes close to being what might be called the novel's central plot. This is not to deny Grant's charge that it is practically impossible to tease out a "more or less comprehensive account of the novel's message" (xii), for plots such as this can, on their own, have unlimited numbers of meanings. Hume elucidates a rich variety of meanings in Pynchon's *Vineland* from the *bardo* plot in that novel. Had she based her philological essay on Evans-Wentz's *Tibetan Book of the Dead* rather than the later translation by Francesca Freemantle and Chögyam Trungpa, she would surely have recognized as many allusions to it in *The Crying of Lot 49* as she did in *Vineland* (Hume 417n; The reverse was true for me in Kohn *Merging of Tantric Buddhism,* which draws mostly on Freemantle and Trungpa). It is possible that I am wrong in attributing so much in *The Crying of Lot 49* to Evans-Wentz's interpretation of the *bardo* in *The Tibetan Book of the Dead,* but it has given me insights into aspects of the novel that I wouldn't have had otherwise. For example, the child actor, Baby Igor, in the TV movie is a project of the lawyer, Metzger. The horrors that the child experiences are imagined rather than real. "I know this part," Metzger told Oedipa as they watched the film on the television set, "For fifty yards out the sea was red with blood. They don't show that" (*Crying* 36). This horror is not real for the child or the adult Metzger, just as "there is no reality behind any of the phenomena of the Bardo plane, save the illusions stored up in one's own mind as accretions from *sangsaric* [worldly] experiences" (Evans-Wentz *Tibetan Book* 126n). It connects to the TV movie that one of the common scenes in the *bardo* is that of the male consort of Vajrayogini, "red of color, smiling and radiant" and "holding a crescent-knife and a skull [filled] with blood" (*Tibetan Book* 128, square brackets in the original). Hume was the first to build on the "awareness of the Tibetan bardo experience, where figures encountered on the bardo plane are in some sense projections of ourselves" (434). By identifying "the Tibetan belief that we project our world" (435) in early 1980s writings of Kathy Acker and William Burroughs and the 1990 *Vinelands*, Hume makes us aware that Oedipa's famous line, "*Shall I project a world*" (*Crying* 82, 87. italics in the original), also has Tibetan *bardo* inferences.

      The *bardo* interpretation greatly enriches the meaningfulness of *The Crying of Lot 49*. That Pynchon had it in mind is suggested in *Against the Day*, where affirmative hints about the earlier novel are dropped when Dr. Rao "abruptly vanished" in plain sight and then "reappeared." (*Against* 539). When one of the eye-witnesses asked him: "Can you do it backwards and return to who you were?"' which is what Pierce intended to do in *The Crying of Lot 49*, he replied: "'Some master Yogis are said to know the technique, but for me it remains noncommutative—mostly, I just like to hop about. Each time I become somebody else. It is like reincarnation on a budget" (539).

      One of the astonishing discoveries that awaits the western reader of Evans-Wentz's *Tibetan Book of the Dead* is that the Oedipal Complex did not originate with Freud, but 1200 years earlier with Padma Sambhava (liv). In the instructions on the closing of the womb-door, the deceased is warned that if he or she is "to born as a male," he will experience "attraction towards [his] mother and repulsion towards [his] father, and if " he or she is "to be born as a female, attraction towards the father and repulsion towards the mother [...] will dawn upon thee" (*Dead* 180). This too may be one of the reasons that the heroine is named "Oedipa." When Hume writes that "Freudian theory grants less literary significance to preoedipal literary fantasies than to oedipal ones," one wonders whether she dates the oedipal insight back only to Freud (423n). The *bardo* also provides another interpretation for the frequently mentioned (46-times) word "Tristero." It could be–an anagrammatic combination of "TRIT" and "EROS," the first part being the equivalent of a "bit" in the case of the excluded middle between zero (death) and one (life), the second part being the driving force for conception. In this anagrammatic sense, the Tristero symbolizes the *bardo*, "an accommodation reached, in some kind of dignity, with the Angel of Death" (*Crying* 182), who also could be the "descending angel" in the final paragraph of the novel (183).

Essay Seven

Diagnostic and Statistical Manual of Mental Disorders

> She was not sure what she'd do when the bidder revealed himself. She had only some vague idea about causing a scene violent enough to bring the cops into it and find out that way who the man really was. She stood in a patch of sun, among brilliant rising and falling points of dust, trying to get a little warm, wondering if she'd go through with it. (*Crying* 183)

World War II brought U.S. psychiatrists to prominence in the diagnosis and treatment of soldiers, moving the focus of treatment away from mental institutions and introducing new clinical perspectives. At the outset of the war, William C. Menninger, who with his father and older brother had, in 1925, established the Menninger Foundation in Topeka to treat psychiatric patients, train doctors and conduct research, became the Director of the Psychiatric Consultants Division in the office of the U.S. Surgeon General. Attaining the rank of Brigadier General, he chaired a committee which in 1943 significantly revised existing U.S. classifications of mental disorders. The new classifications, adopted by all the Armed Services, were to have a substantial influence on the first mental disorders section of the *International Statistical Classification of Diseases*, published by the World Health Organization in 1949, and especially on the first *Diagnostic and Statistical Manual of Mental Disorders*, published by the American Psychiatric Association in 1952. The structure and conceptual framework of the Manual, the first in a series of revisions and new editions of what would familiarly be called the *DSM*, were taken from the Menninger committee's 1943 document, many passages of which were reproduced verbatim.

Menninger's name and the *DSM-I*, which his work inspired, might have been known to Pynchon, especially because Menninger was a 1924 graduate of the Cornell University College of Medicine and his youngest son, William Walter Menninger, was a medical student at Cornell during some of the years that Pynchon was an undergraduate there. Pynchon's nostalgia for Cornell is reflected in the opening paragraph of *The Crying of Lot 49*, where Oedipa "thought of [...] a sunrise over the library slope at Cornell University that nobody out on it had seen because the slope faces west" (*Crying* 10). This, and the possibility that she subsequently recognized that the Yoyodyne hymn was sung to "the tune of Cornell's alma mater" (83), suggests that Oedipa, like Pynchon, was a graduate of Cornell–auspicious because Cornell in 1870 had been the first in what came to be known as the Ivy League to admit women–and possibly the author's alter-ego as well.

The hypothesis that motivates the present essay is that Pynchon had read the *DSM-I* and based Oedipa's intermittent dysfunctional behavior on that of mental patients who are "severely depressed and manifest gross misinterpretations of reality, including, at times, delusions and hallucinations," usually in the "presence of environmental precipitating factors" (*DSM-I,* 25). Such a "personality disorganization may result in aimless running or 'freezing'"(32); the involved "anxiety is associated with the persistence of unwanted ideas […] which may be considered morbid by the patient" (33). The "anxiety in this reaction is allayed, and hence partially relieved, by depression and self-depreciation" (33). The *DSM-I,* the volume that Pynchon could have been one of the first novelists to read, was outdated by the time he wrote *The Crying of Lot 49.* The *DSM-II* was published in 1968, but is rare, not in the library systems I frequent, and costs hundreds of dollars to buy used. The volume that I own, the *Diagnostic and Statistical Manual of Mental Disorders (Third Edition - Revised),* published in 1987 and commonly referred to as the *DSM-III-R,* had its roots in the first and second editions and designated the code numbers that psychiatrists currently use for insurance claims. According to the *Encyclopedia of Multicultural Psychology,* "hundreds of thousands of copies [of this volume were sold] at over $80 each" (G. Scott Sparrow 162), so it was clearly a very influential work. It is likely that some of its descriptions of mental disorders were either in the second edition or were circulating in the mid 1960s, when Pynchon was writing *The Crying of Lot 49.* Drawing on the *DSM-III-R,* which I own, I shall argue that Oedipa has the following mental disorders: "296.3x Major Depression, Recurrent," "300.30 Obsessive Compulsive Disorder [OCD]," and "300.02 Generalized Anxiety Disorder " (*DSM-III-R,* 228, 245, 251). I am hardly a psychiatrist, but I have been diagnosed with those particular disorders and recognize them in Oedipa. This enables me, in the previously cited words that Anderson used in his contribution to the cover-page article "Words About Words About Words" in the January 2, 2011 edition of *The New York Times Book Review,* "to imaginatively intermingle with [*The Crying of Lot 49*]–to somehow match or channel or negate the energy of the text." If, indeed, Pynchon intended Oedipa to be his alter ego, he too may have personal familiarity with the three closely related mental disorders.

Oedipa's Triad of *DSM* Disorders

Pynchon concludes the opening paragraph of the novel with Oedipa's thoughts of the

> whitewashed bust of Jay Gould that Pierce kept over the bed on a shelf so narrow for it she'd always had the hovering fear it would someday topple on them. Was that how he'd died, she wondered, among dreams, crushed by the only ikon in the house? That only made her laugh, out loud and helpless: You're so sick, Oedipa, she told herself, or the room, which knew. (*Crying* 10).

It was perfectly consistent with plate tectonic activity–see Essay Five–that an earthquake could someday cause this bust to topple. From the psychiatric perspective, Oedipa perceives this fear as unreasonable. It exemplifies the kind of obsessive "persistent ideas, thoughts, impulses, or images that are experienced [by OCD sufferers ...] as intrusive and senseless" (*DSM-III-R*, 245). In Oedipa's case, "she'd always had [this] hovering fear" and recognized that it was senseless (*Crying* 10). "You're so sick, Oedipa, she told herself" (10), echoing the "self-depreciation" identified in the *DSM-I* (33). All three of Oedipa's mental disorders are ego-dystonic, that is, they are recognized by her to be in conflict with a realistic perception of her environment, to be "the product of [...] her own mind," as the *DSM-III-R* puts it (245). This contrasts with disorders such as paranoia, which are ego-syntonic, having to do with fears that are seen by the patient as entirely realistic and somatically self-protective.

Oedipa's "mixing of the twilight's whiskey sours against the arrival of her husband" (*Crying* 11) represents one of the complications of OCD, namely "the abuse of alcohol and anxiolytics" (*DSM-III-R*, 246):

> Mucho Maas, home, bounded through the screen door. "Today was another defeat," he began. "Let me tell you," she also began. But let Mucho go first. [...] "I don't believe in any of it, Oed," he could usually get out. "I try, I truly can't," way down there, further down perhaps than she could reach, so that such times often brought her near panic. It might have been the sight of her so about to lose control that seemed to bring him back up. (*Crying* 12)

This is the first glimpse of Oedipa's "Generalized Anxiety Disorder [, t]he essential feature of [which] is unrealistic or excessive anxiety and worry (apprehensive expectation) about two or more life circumstances," the most relevant in Oedipa's case, because Mucho had been having trouble at work with his program director, being "worry about finances" (*DSM-III-R*, 251). Oedipa had hoped to put off her panic by interrupting him, but gave up and let him talk.

It is also in the first chapter of *The Crying of Lot 49* that we learn that, for help with her neuroses, Oedipa consults "Dr Hilarius, her shrink or psychotherapist" (16). Perhaps strategically, he has awakened her with a "three-in-the-morning phone call," hoping to coax her into an "experiment he was helping the community hospital run on effects of LSD-25, mescaline, psilocybin, and related drugs on a large sample of suburban housewives" (17). He had already given her the pills, but thinking, rightly, that they are mind-altering, hallucinatory and addictive, she "would be damned if she'd take the capsules he'd given her. Literally damned. She didn't want to get hooked in any way" (17-18). Oedipa's refusal is consistent with the *DSM-III-R's* warning, 21 years later, that complications of OCD include the abuse of anxiolytics, of which psilocybin–which is extracted from various genera of fungi–is an example. Presumably, Oedipa's rejection of psychedelic drugs mirrored Pynchon's views at the time, which were compatible with the view expressed by the *DSM-III-R* in 1987.

However, the general view of drugs was beginning to change. Buspirone, an anxiety-reducing anxiolytic drug was approved for marketing in 1986. Because it has virtually no side effects, it is still generously prescribed today. Prozac, which not only reduces anxiety in general but also OCD in particular, was introduced to the U.S. market in 1988. It continues to be sold not only as Prozac but also generically as fluoxetine. It should be noted that psilocybin, which Oedipa refused, activates serotonin, just as Prozac and fluoxetine do. However, the latter manufactured drugs are strictly controlled substances, sold only by prescription. Under the care of a psychiatrist who specializes in pharmacology and sees me only two or three times a year to adjust the dosages, I take both of these drugs, plus a third. They channel a lot of my anxiety away from unproductive thoughts and obsessions that squelch creativity and are in no way hallucinogenic. There are sexual side effects from fluoxetine, though in my case, these can also be the result of drugs I take to counteract various maladies of advancing age. As prescient as Pynchon was and is, I don't believe that he anticipated in *The Crying of Lot 49* the useful role that drugs would play a third of a century later.

A few pages later in Chapter 1, we learn that besides seeing Hilarius one-on-one, Oedipa "went to the same group therapy sessions" (*Crying* 19) as Roseman, "her trusted family lawyer" (18). But it is at the end of the chapter that we learn about the first of her major depressive episodes. If she had had only one such episode, the *DSM* code would be 296.2x. Because Oedipa's are recurrent, the code is 296.3x, where the x is the measure of severity as diagnosed by her psychiatrist; it can be "either mild, moderate, severe without psychotic features, or with psychotic features" (*DSM-III-R*, 228). The prevalence of Major Depression among adult populations in the United States and Europe is greater for women than for men, which could be one of the reasons that Pynchon chose a female as the protagonist in *The Crying of Lot 49*. The "range for females [who have or have had the disorder] is from 9% to 26%; that for males, 5% to 12%. Studies examining the proportion of the adult population, that at any given time has the disorder, report rates ranging from 4.5% to 9.3% for females and 2.3% to 3.2% for males" (*DSM-III-R*, 229). Oedipa's first recorded episode of Major Depression was precipitated in Mexico City by a painting of frail girls imprisoned in the top room of a circular tower, a well known phallic symbol:

> Oedipa, perverse, had stood in front of the painting and cried. No one had noticed; she wore dark green bubble shades. For a moment she'd wondered if the seal around her sockets were tight enough to allow the tears simply to go on and fill up the entire lens space and never dry. She could carry the sadness of the moment with her that way forever. (*Crying* 21)

Seed likewise connects Oedipa's mental illness to "an issue raised by a painting to which Pynchon refers enigmatically in this novel" (*Fictional Labyrinth* 136). The painting of the imprisoned girls brings a rush of despair for Oedipa, who perceives herself as a modern day Rapunzel, a "prisoner among the pines and salt fogs of Kinneret, looking for somebody to say hey, let down your hair"(20), and when it turned out to be Pierce, she'd happily pulled out the pins and curlers so that Pierce could climb the tower and rescue her. The tearful episode in Mexico City must have come after Oedipa saw Pierce through Jesus Arrabal's eyes on the beach in Mazatlán and realized that the oligarchist "pose[d] a threat to" her as well as to Arrabal (Seed *Fictional Labyrinth* 118). The imprisoning "tower is everywhere and the knight of deliverance no proof against its magic, what else?" (22) She could "take up a useful hobby like embroidery, or go mad, or marry a disk jockey," the latter of which is what she did, a year later (22).

Oedipa did not go mad, but in a subsequent major depression came close to committing suicide. To make the sorting out of the novel even more difficult, Pynchon sometimes purposely misleads his readers. Thus, he plants the impression that Oedipa's relationship with Pierce had nothing to do with the major depression that concludes the first chapter:

> As things developed, she was to have all manner of revelations. Hardly about Pierce Inverarity, or herself; but about what remained yet had somehow, before this, stayed away. There had hung the sense of buffering, insulation, she had noticed the absence of an intensity, as if watching a movie, just perceptibly out of focus, that the projectionist refused to fix. (*Crying* 20)

This is why, for Seed, "revelation [...] never comes" in *The Crying of Lot 49* (*Labyrinth* 131). Except for the faithful who experience revelation in God's own sacred writings, it is inevitably buffered, insulated and just perceptibly out of focus (See "Revelation and Religion" in Essay Four).

The Tristero as a Distraction for Neutralizing Major Depression

The first chapter of *The Crying of Lot 49* illuminates Oedipa's three mental disorders: obsessive fears, neurotic anxiety, and major depression. The second chapter exhibits her related alcoholism. While watching a single movie on TV, she and Metzger (mostly Oedipa) polish off a bottle of Beaujolais, then a bottle of tequila, though by the time they get to the fifth of Jack Daniels, it is clear that whenever Oedipa refills her own glass, Metzger simply takes "another snort from the bottle" (*Crying* 41). Near the end of the TV movie, she "may have fallen asleep once or twice," but "awoke at last to find herself getting laid," her own "sexual crescendo in progress, like a cut to a scene where the camera's already moving" (42). In the second sentence of the third chapter, "The Tristero" is mentioned for the first time in the novel (44). The importance of the Tristero or Trystero–the name appears more that eighty times in the novel–has to do with Oedipa's mental disorders. In a blocked-off section of the *DSM-III-R*, entitled "Diagnostic criteria for 300.30 Obsessive Compulsive Disorder," it is noted that "the person attempts to ignore or suppress such thoughts or impulses or to neutralize them with some other thought or action" whose context is unrelated to the one that causes the primary disorder, "*e.g.*, the ideas, thoughts, impulses, or images are not about food in the presence of an Eating Disorder, about drugs in the presence of a Psychoactive Substance Use Disorder, or guilty thoughts in the presence of a Major Depression" (*DSM-III-R*, 247). Presumably, unwanted or even repressed thoughts underlie Oedipa's obsessive compulsive disorder, her recurrent major depressions, and/or her generalized anxiety disorder. "Associated features" common to the obsessive compulsive disorder include "[d]epression and anxiety" (*DSM-III-R*, 245), suggesting that the three disorders often go together, as they do with me and may have done with Oedipa. In my case, I have attempted to suppress the tensions of my mental disorders by concentrating on my work; first it was the shoe business, then economics, and now, more intensely than ever, literary criticism. For over fifty years, my family has paid a price for my withdrawal into my work. Pynchon appears to have had this kind of intense neutralization in mind for Oedipa, when he began Chapter 3 as follows:

> Things did not delay in turning curious. If one object behind her discovery of what she was to label the Tristero System or often only The Tristero (as if it might be something's secret title) were to bring to an end her encapsulation in her tower, then that night's infidelity with Metzger would logically be the starting point for it; logically. That's what would come to haunt her most, perhaps: the way it fitted, logically together. (*Crying* 44)

Oedipa had not gotten past the pain that caused her major depression in Mexico. All we know about the etiology of her depression is that it was triggered by her sense of being encapsulated in a tower and the failure of the love affair that would have rescued her from it. The *DSM-I* does note that a depressive "reaction is precipitated by a current situation, frequently by some loss sustained by the patient, and is often associated with a feeling of guilt for past failures or deeds. The degree of the reaction in such cases is dependent upon the intensity of the patient's ambivalent feeling toward his loss (love, possession) as well as upon the realistic circumstances of the loss" (33-34). What was not known in 1952, when the *DSM-I* was written, was that genetics can be more important than the actual trigger in the case of major depression. According to the *DSM-III-R*, "Most family studies have shown that Major Depression is 1.5 to 3 times more common among first-degree biologic relatives of people with this disorder than among the general population" (229). Pynchon may have observed this familial pattern in depressives, suspected genetic links, and felt less obliged to provide specific nurture-related causes in Oedipa's case. Indeed, more and more evidence is being reported of populations with "higher rates of major depression" having "a genome-wide significant linkage signal at chromosome 3p26-3p25" (Michele L. Pergadia *et al.*, 1).

Oedipa may have subconsciously feared that feelings of guilt from her past and most recently from her infidelity with Metzger would drag her down and precipitate a major depression. To preempt this foreboding line of thought, she unconsciously endeavored "to neutralize it with some other thought or action"

(*DSM-III-R*, 247). Hence "for Oedipa, the languid, sinister blooming of The Tristero" (*Crying* 54), which started "in what may be the shortest line ever written in blank verse: 'T-t-t-t ...'" (73), and which developed into poetry as "Thurn" morphed into "Thorn" and "Taxis into Tacit":

> He that we last as Thurn and Taxis knew
> Now recks no lord but the stiletto's Thorn,
> And Tacit lies the gold once-knotted horn.
> No hallowed skein of stars can ward, I trow.
> Who's once been set his tryst with Trystero. (75)

Trystero! The "word hung in the [...] dark to puzzle Oedipa [...], but not yet to exert the power" that was needed to calm her agitated psyche (75). The novel even suggests that Pierce, who was with Oedipa when she had her breakdown, may have known about her disorder and set up the Tristero clues to distract her from the pregnancy and thoughts of terminating it. When she confronted Driblette in the shower, she still "didn't know what she was looking for [or why], exactly" (77). It is ironical that she is seeking clarification of *The Courier's Tragedy* from a director who acknowledges that "all the closed little universe visible in the circle of that stage is coming out of my mouth, eyes, sometimes other orifices also" (79), who also sees a "shrink" (80), and who may be improvising on the Tristero to neutralize his own suicidal thoughts of being "washed [...] into the Pacific" (79).

As Oedipa continued her compulsive depression-suppressing quest in the fourth chapter, the more information she "collected the more would come to her, until everything she saw, smelled, dreamed, remembered, would somehow come to be woven into The Tristero" (*Crying* 81). There is more evidence in the fourth chapter of her self-distraction, "what you might have to call, growing obsession, with 'bringing something of herself'–even if that something was just her presence–to the scatter of business interests that had survived Inverarity" (90). In the *DSM-I*, there is mention of "'idiopathic' epilepsy," the "most common disturbance of this group" being the "clouded state occurring in those epileptics who develop, preceding or following convulsive attacks, or as equivalents of attacks, dazed reactions with deep confusion, bewilderment, and anxiety" (17). Oedipa similarly fears she

> could at this stage of things, recognize signals like that, as the epileptic is
> said to–an odor, color, pure piercing grace note announcing his seizure.
> Afterward it is only this signal, really dross, this secular announcement,
> and never what is revealed during the attack, that he remembers. (*Crying*
> 95)

Conflating her fear of a recurrence of major depression and the anxiety of managing the estate with her search for the Tristero,

> Oedipa wondered whether, at the end of this (if it were supposed to end),
> she too might not be left with only compiled memories of clues,
> announcements, intimations, but never the central truth itself, which

must [...] always blaze out, destroying its own message irreversibly,
leaving an overexposed blank when the ordinary world came back. (95)
Oedipa suspects (as the *DSM-III-R* suggests) that she is suppressing deeper, less
manageable fears, that her strategy will blaze out, and the ordinary world and its
terrors come back.

Neutralization and Hallucination

To suppress the thoughts that give rise to her depressive episodes,
Oedipa not only sets out in Chapter 5 "to find where Richard Wharfinger got his
information about Trystero," but to "also take a look at how the inventor John
Nefastis picked up his mail" (*Crying* 100). Hopefully, for her, the latter would
connect Maxwell's box to W.A.S.T.E, and ultimately to "Silent Tristero's Empire"
(169, 174). Her efforts to neutralize depressive thoughts were reinforced when the
clerk at the famous "sprawling, many-leveled, German-baroque hotel" Claremont,
in Oakland "took her to a room with a reproduction of a Remedios Varo in it"
(*Crying* 101). This was the same artist that painted the "frail girls with heart-shaped
faces, huge eyes, spun-gold hair, prisoners in the top room of a circular tower,"
that had triggered Oedipa's first major depression in Mexico City (21). A "gross
personality disorganization" of "aimless running" (*DSM-I*, 32) was looming for
Oedipa in San Francisco as she started thinking about "hallucinations" (*Crying*
107), "something for her shrink to fix" (109), "decid[ing] to drift tonight" (110),
"trying not to suggest hysteria" (111), "going out of my head" (111), and hearing
that love's "the worse addiction of all" (112), about deprived "sixty-year-old men"
and "women even older, who wake up in the night screaming" (113), about
"suicides who had failed, either through clumsiness or last-minute cowardice,"
none of whom "could offer any compelling reasons for staying alive" (114), about
"a Buddhist monk in Viet Nam who had set himself on fire to protest
government policies" (114). Oedipa sat,

> feeling as alone as she ever had, now the only woman, she saw, in a room
> full of drunken male homosexuals. Story of my life, she thought, Mucho
> won't talk to me, Hilarius won't listen, Clerk Maxwell didn't even look at
> me, and this group, God knows. Despair came over her, as it will when
> nobody around has any sexual relevance to you. (*Crying* 116)

She left the homosexual bar "and entered the city again, the infected city" (117),
where she would "manifest evidence of gross misinterpretation of reality,
including, at times, delusions and hallucinations" (*DSM-I*, 25).

Having had so little sleep the night before and too much to drink in the
bar, it is understandable that Oedipa "spent the rest of the night finding the image
of the Trystero post horn," "getting off [buses] only now and then to walk so
she'd keep awake," and having "trouble sorting the night into real and dreamed"
(117). "In Golden Gate Park she came on a circle of children in their nightclothes,
who told her they were dreaming the gathering" (118). They played a jump-rope
game to the words: "Tristoe, Tristoe, one, two, three,/ Turning taxi from across

the sea ..." (119). When Oedipa protested–"Thurn and Taxis, you mean,"–they said "They'd never heard it that way" and went "on warming their hands at an invisible fire. Oedipa, to retaliate, stopped believing in them" (119). "Out at the airport, [... c]atching a TWA flight to Miami was an uncoordinated boy who planned to slip at night into aquariums and open negotiations with the dolphins, who would succeed man. He was kissing his mother passionately goodbye, using his tongue" (122, 123). Just before the morning rush hour, Oedipa

> began to walk toward the Embarcadero. She knew she looked terrible–knuckles black with eye-liner and mascara from where she'd rubbed, mouth tasting of old booze and coffee. Through an open doorway, on the stair leading up into the disinfectant-smelling twilight of a rooming house she saw an old man huddled, shaking with grief she couldn't hear [*sic.,* bear?]. Both hands, smoke-white, covered his face. On the back of the left hand she made out the post horn, tattooed in old ink now beginning to blur and spread. (*Crying* 125)

Though she was shaking and tired, Oedipa asked the old man if she could help him.

> "My wife's in Fresno" (125), he said. "I left her. So long ago, I don't remember. Now this is for her." He gave Oedipa a letter that looked like he'd been carrying it around for years. "Drop it in the," and he held up the tattoo and stared into her eyes, "you know. [...] Under the freeway." He waved her on in the direction she'd been going. "Always one. You'll see it." (125)

Oedipa "gave him goodbye" and walked in the direction he'd told her:

> For an hour she prowled along the sunless, concrete underpinnings of the freeway, finding drunks, bums, pedestrians, pederasts, hookers, walking psychotic, no secret mailbox. But at last in the shadows she did come on a can with a swinging trapezoidal top, the kind you throw trash in: old and green, nearly four feet high. On the swinging part were hand-painted the initials W.A.S.T.E. She had to look closely to see the periods between the letters. (129-30)

I don't for a minute believe that Oedipa, dozing off in the shadow of a column of the Embarcadero Freeway, actually "woke to see a kid dropping a bundle of letters into the [garbage] can" (*Crying* 130), or that, toward midday, "a rangy young wino showed up with a sack; unlocked a panel at the side of the box and took out all the letters," or that Oedipa "followed him for hours" as he delivered the letters, "One by one" (130). It is a metaphor for Oedipa's hallucinations, which Pynchon could not have anticipated, that the elevated Embarcadero Freeway–where I remember inching for half-an-hour along the bend from which it sloped down to empty all its traffic from the Bay Bridge onto congested Broadway–was demolished after being damaged by the 1989 Loma Prieta earthquake. It has been so completely eradicated that I am sometimes surprised when reminded that it once existed.

My interpretation, based on the *DSM-III-R*, of Oedipa throwing herself into the convoluted search for Tristero to "suppress" or "neutralize" unwanted "thoughts or impulses" (247), is the reverse of Seed's view of Oedipa "becom[ing] a nervous wreck under the pressure of the information which bombards her" (*Labyrinth* 142). Seed supports his interpretation (that Oedipa is overwhelmed by actual information) as well or better than I do mine (that Oedipa is hallucinating), but both can be correct. Nor do the two exhaust all the possibilities that Pynchon could have had in mind.

Paranoia: Real and Unreal

Oedipa finally made it back to the Claremont Hotel "where she'd started, and could not believe 24 hours had passed. Should it have been more or less?" she naively asked (*Crying* 131). It was "more," of course; she'd been gone a day, a night and another day. No wonder that she "was too weak," that her "legs ached, [and] her mouth tasted horrible" (131). Back in her room, she slept for twelve hours without dreaming and finally recovered. She "drove down the peninsula to Kinneret," having "decided on route, with time to think about the day preceding, to go see Dr Hilarius her shrink, and tell him all" about her Tristero and W.A.S.T.E. sightings (*Crying* 132). She might well be in the cold and sweatless meathooks of a psychosis:

> Yet she wanted it all to be fantasy—some clear result of her several wounds, needs, dark doubles. She wanted Hilarius to tell her she was some kind of a nut and needed a rest, and that there was no Trystero. She also wanted to know why the chance of its being real should menace her so. (132)

When Oedipa finally drove up to the Hilarius Psychiatric Clinic, rifle shots were being fired. It was a few years after Eichmann's execution, and Hilarius, who had done psychological experiments on Jews in Buchenwald, was sure that Israeli agents, masking as local cops, were coming to capture and bring him "back to Israel, to stand trial, like they did Eichmann" (137). It was ironic that Oedipa hoped that Hilarius would explain away what she wanted to be a fantasy, when he himself was in the throes of his own fantasy, in which he totally believed and probably could not have been convinced otherwise.

Seed recognizes Oedipa's "depression" and argues that "her fear that everything is connected takes [her] towards the psychotic state of paranoia, although Pynchon is clearly not interested in delving into her psychology" (*Labyrinth* 135). Seed is an excellent critic, and, except for his claim that Pynchon is not interested in delving into Oedipa's psychology," I accept all his interpretations as valid. The same goes for another great Pynchon scholar, Bill Millard, who argues "that Pynchon habitually eschews a close focus on individual psychology because of a fully serious conviction that it is simply not as interesting as broader social systems, either as an intellectual problem or as an aesthetic object" (21). Except for this one strong disagreement with Seed and Millard, it would be hard for me to find any well-argued interpretation by an admirer of the polysemous *Crying of Lot 49* that is not to some extent valid.

Hilarius was in total paranoia, treating even Oedipa as his enemy—who would not hesitate, if he let down his guard, to "karate-chop [him] in the spine, no thank you" (*Crying* 134)—even though he ludicrously claims that he "chose to remain in *relative* paranoia, where at least I know who I am and who the others are" (136, italics added: He does not know who the others really are!). It is significant that this is the first mention of "paranoia" in the novel. The word resonates six more times, so it is meant to be important.

A true paranoid cannot be argued out of his fear; medicated out of it perhaps, but not argued. Oedipa may have been "on the brink of nervous collapse," as Seed claims (135), but she was not paranoid. She wanted to be reassured that the Tristero was just a fantasy, and why, if it even was "real [, it] should menace her so" (*Crying* 132). Hilarius was certain who his adversaries were and what they wanted to do to him. Whereas Freudian psychoanalysis "emphasizes the destructiveness of paranoia and obsession on human contentment and identity," Charles Cullum, drawing on Jacques Lacan's work on schizophrenia, shows that "paranoia and obsession can be seen to perform constructive functions for their protagonists" (1, 13). In Cullum's Lacanian view, Oedipa's paranoia toward the Tristero System ultimately led to her "acceptance of the chaotic nature of the world" (15). Even though I don't believe that Oedipa devolved into paranoia, I like Cullum's thesis because it builds on the advantages of paranoia in Lacanian theory, which is parallel to my belief that the Tristero was constructively intended to neutralize the neurotic thoughts that were undermining Oedipa's well-being.

Sigmund Freud, Psychoanalysis in the 1960s, and Timothy Leary

The last dozen pages in Chapter 5 of *The Crying of Lot 49* relate to Freud, psychoanalysis, and Timothy Leary. Freud's teachings include some "idiocies and contradictions" (*Crying* 134) and are based on the belief that talk "therapy could tame" the unconscious, making it "like any other room, once the light was let in" (135) and, by extension, create a "world that had no Buchenwalds in it" (137). For "once the light was let in," Buchenwald, according to Freud, "would become a soccer field, [where] fat children would learn flower-arranging and solfeggio in the strangling rooms" (138). In this sarcastic repudiation of modernist utopianism, Pynchon—taking on the mantle of postmodernism—made it Freud's vision that the ovens at Auschwitz "would be converted over to petit fours and wedding cakes, and the V-2 missiles to public housing for the elves" (138). When Oedipa told Hilarius that she came "hoping you could talk me out of a fantasy," he fiercely replied: "Cherish it! [...] Hold it tightly by its little tentacle, don't let the Freudians coax it away or the pharmacists poison it out of you" (138). This may well have been the first time that post-war psychiatric pharmacology was acknowledged in fiction—in the 1960s it was hardly even acknowledged by the Freudians. Pynchon appears to have drawn here on Freud's observation in his "Creative Writers and Day-Dreaming" that the adult "cherishes his phantasies" (145), suggesting that he was well-read in Freud. Based on his general characterization of Hilarius, Pynchon did not think well of psychiatrists, and the fact that he refers to them as "shrinks" suggests an easy familiarity, from which the weightiness of transference and authority have till now barred me. According to Michael Quinion, the term "*Shrink* [...] became popular in the USA in the 1970s, though it had first appeared in one of Thomas Pynchon's books, *The Crying of Lot 49*." (The word actually appears nine times in the novel: *Crying* 16, 18, 80, 109, 112, 132, 134, 137, 153.) There is "anecdotal evidence," wrote Quinion, that "shrink" was "around earlier, which is only to be expected of a slang term that would have been mainly transmitted through the spoken word in its earliest days." I was astonished, in the midst of an internet search of "shrink," to encounter the gratuitous mention of the very novel that sent me on the search in the first place.

Oedipa referred to her shrink as "Hitler Hilarius," which may not be a totally undeserved characterization of those psychoanalysts in the 1960s who ruled their sessions with an iron hand. Overwhelmed to begin with and needful of her psychiatrist, Oedipa's robust response to the violent crisis that engulf her at the clinic—"'Bust it [his office door] down,' roared Oedipa [to the police], 'and Hitler Hilarius here will foot the bill'" (*Crying* 138)—reveal that she is a "healthy neurotic," responsive to the "reality principle" (136), which temporarily takes her mind off the Tristero, those "malign agencies," which, in Seed's words, "Oedipa has feared are at work isolating her," but in fact are only "hypothetical" (*Labyrinth* 136). Indeed, in his opinion, "the novel as a whole has constantly rendered any reference to the Tristero as problematic" (149). In Mendelson's view, Oedipa was realistically nagged by the possibility "that the Trystero has no independent existence, but is merely her own projection of the world outside" (31).

The appearance of her husband (and her real life) at this point is unfortunate, and it is not surprising that they "later drove downtown to a pizzeria and bar, and faced each other through the fluted gold lens of a beer pitcher" (141). Given Mucho's newfound expansiveness engendered by LSD—there was "a serenity about him she'd never seen" (141)—it was probably Oedipa who downed most of the golden brew. As Mucho reveals his profound new interests, Oedipa can't "figure the expression on his face" and is "feeling anxious" again (141). There is "an edge to her voice" (142), and when she realized how "amiable, at peace" (143) he was, "Panic started to climb out of a dark region in her head" (143). Suspecting that he will become addicted to LSD, she reaches for the reality principle, and readers are on her side as Pynchon wants us to be, but is this her own generalized anxiety disorder surfacing again? She appears to be exhibiting the clinical "signs of motor tension, autonomic hyperactivity, and vigilance and scanning" detailed in the *DSM-III-R* (251). When Mucho took on a "patient, motherly look [, ...] Oedipa wanted to hit him in the mouth" (144). When he tried to reassure her about his bad dreams, she reacts:

"Oh, goodo.' Flipping her hair a couple times, furious. 'No nightmares any more? Fine. So your latest little friend, whoever she is, she really made out. At that age, you know, they need all the sleep they can get.' 'There's no girl, Oed. Let me tell you. The bad dreams I used to have all the time, about the car lot, remember that? I could never even tell you about it. But I can now. It doesn't bother me any more.' (*Crying* 144) As might be expected, when Oedipa says goodbye to Mucho, she goes back to suppressing, neutralizing the bad thoughts again: "Oedipa sat with her forehead resting on the steering wheel and remembered that she hadn't asked him about the Trystero cancellation on his letter" (145).

I have no idea what Pynchon thought of Leary–though "hi-Leary-us" may be a clue–and his mind-altering drugs. The fact that he manage to use the adverb "leery" (160, 166) a couple of times after this scene, may suggest that Pynchon himself is ambiguous. I did find a 1995 interview by Marianne Schnall with Leary, in which he reminded her of his 1960-1963 project at Harvard, in collaboration with forty scientists and divinity professors, in which they were able to reduce prison recidivism with the careful administration of psychedelic drugs. Our national policy of illegalizing psychedelic drugs seems flawed, so that sounded promising. I had a different reaction when she asked him how he "felt about the wide-spread use of the new psychoactive drugs, such as Prozac, for treating conditions other than depression – just for a sort of pick-me-up." Leary's reply included the following:

In the Fifties and Sixties we took the power monopoly of psychoactive drugs away from the doctors. Yes, I totally deplore the notion of an MD giving pills to patients – a medical doctor giving psychological or psychoactive change agents to another person. This is almost mechanical, it's factory like. To say that there is a cure for something like depression – well, for instance – one of the things that has run through all my work, and is quite important and I think easy to understand, is that we don't categorize human beings or human behavior. We quantify or dimensionalize. See, what they say is you're a hysterical, you're a schizophrenic, you're a paranoid – these are labels, they're codes, which of course comes basically from religion. Instead, we develop methods of dimensionalizing. "On a rating scale of one to ten, how depressed are you?" "Well, Jesus, I'm nine right now, but last Tuesday night I was up there with a two." In other words, when you dimensionalize a human behavior it's no longer a branded label on your forehead that you're a Jew or a Christian or a hysteric or an anal – You see, we all have these categories or behaviors that we can change and we can compare with each other and they're not final products. I still oppose the MDs passing out psychoactive drugs to patients and treating them like helpless victims. "Here, open your mouth and let Big Daddy give you a pill." (Schnall)

From my personal perspective, I believe that the categorization of behavioral disorders puts a greater emphasis on diagnosis and enables patients to better confront their disorders. Where appropriate, the fifth unit of the *DSM* code is used for dimensionalizing. I don't believe that every human has OCD to some degree; one of the most painful obsessions in that disorder is "a parent's having repeated impulses to kill a loved child" (*DRM-III-R*, 247)–I had a variant of that kind of impulse and know how utterly excruciating it can be. Surely, everyone does not have some degree of OCD. If they did, biochemists could not have shown that "the brains of those suffering from OCD are anatomically different– small groups of cells in the brain stem called the basil ganglia (and especially the caudate nucleus) are smaller than usual, as shown on magnetic resonance imaging" (Caldwell 118-19). As late as 1995, Leary seemed unaware of the immense potential of medicinal psychiatry.   Pynchon was surely aware of Leary's *The Psychedelic Experience: A Manual Based on the Tibetan Book of the Dead*, published several years before *The Crying of Lot 49*. Elsewhere I have commented on Hilarius's Fu-Manchu face, "which involved slanting the eyes up with the index fingers, enlarging the nostrils with the middle fingers, pulling the mouth wide with the pinkies and protruding the tongue" (*Crying* 18), which I likened to "that of a Wrathful Deity in the *Bardo*" (Kohn *Seven Buddhist* 81. I like to think that Pynchon read my article and played with the idea of wrathful deities at my expense in his 2006 novel; see my *Pynchon Takes* 161-62. For an image of a wrathful deity, see Figure 1 in my *Ambivalence in Kotzwinkle's* 123). I had overlooked the connection of wrathful and peaceful deities to Leary, who shared Pynchon's interest in Tibetan Buddhism. Perhaps, Pynchon saw two different sides of Leary. As obnoxious as he painted Hilarius, he also on the same page 18 in the novel acknowledged that the psychoanalyst's "faces" were "full of these delightful lapses from orthodoxy" (*Crying* 18), suggesting his own mixed feelings about Leary.

Post-Traumatic Stress Disorder

Chapter 5 ended with Oedipa remembering that she hadn't asked Mucho about the Trystero cancellation on his letter, although "by then it was too late to make any difference" (*Crying* 145). The "too late to make any difference" suggests that she may be losing interest in the Trystero, which Seed invites us to suspect is a ploy of her own making. The cancellation could have been a misprint, as Metzger suggested, and it was she who in the first place imagined that it had something to do with "what *she* was to label the Tristero System" (*Crying* 44, italics added). Given that the Tristero played a useful role in keeping her depression at bay, the search fortunately got more engrossing as it went along. In Chapter 6, it took her past what had been Zapf's Used Books, where she "was alarmed to find a pile of charred rubble where the bookstore only a week ago had been" (149), and a store selling rifles–"Fella was in just this forenoon, bought two hundred for his drill team. I could've sold him two hundred of the swastika armbands too, only I was short, dammit" (149)–and SS uniforms, which got Oedipa so angry "She left wondering if she should've called him something, or tried to hit him" (150), though by "the time she'd pulled into Bortz's subdivision [...], she was only shaking and a little nauseous in the stomach" (150). The Professor and three of his graduate students, "all sodden with drink," were "surrounded by [...] an astounding accumulation of beer bottles," and, despite her nausea, "Oedipa located a full one" for herself (150). When she learned that Randy had committed suicide, she took it as a personal loss, along with the loss of Hilarius to madness, of Mucho to LSD, and of her "one extra-marital fella" to "a depraved 15-year-old" (153). "[F]eeling like a fluttering curtain in a very high window," she asked "Where am I?" (152, 153). "Again with the light, vertiginous sense of fluttering out over an abyss, she asked [Bortz] what she'd come there to ask. 'What was Trystero?'" (156) From Bortz's copy of Blobb's Pergrinations, obscure philatelic material from Genghis Cohen, and other dubious sources, Oedipa learned the history of the Tristero back to its founder, Tristero y Calavera in 1577, who claimed he was being unlawfully denied his share of the ownership of the Thurn and Taxis mail monopoly, began a guerilla war against it, and ultimately set up his own system. The more Oedipa learned about the historic Tristero, the more she imagined that it was her present day enemy. "She feared a little for their [Bortz's and Cohen's] security [they were helping her with her research] in view of what was happening to everyone she knew" (*Crying* 160-61), wondered "whether, as Driblette had suggested that night from the shower, some version of herself hadn't vanished with him" and that "her mind would go on flexing psychic muscles that no longer existed [, ...] betrayed and mocked by a phantom self as the amputee is by a phantom limb" (161). Oedipa tried to reach out to Driblette, prayed for him to bring his memories of that last night:

> so I'll know if your walk into the sea had anything to do with Tristero. If they got rid of Hilarius and Mucho and Metzger–maybe because they thought I no longer needed you. They were wrong. I needed you. [...] Driblette, she called. The signal echoing down twisted miles of brain circuitry. Driblette! (161-62)

For Emory Bortz, who egged her on, "it seemed to turn into a species of cute game" (162). With "the Thurn and Taxis ass in a sling," he tells Oedipa,

> the paranoia recedes, as they come to discover the secular Tristero. Power, omniscience, implacable malice [...] are carried over to the now human enemy. So much that, by 1795, it is even suggested that Tristero has staged the entire French Revolution, [...].
> "Suggested by who, though," said Oedipa. "Did you read that someplace?"
> "Wouldn't somebody have brought it up?" Bortz said. "Maybe not."
> She didn't press the argument. Having begun to feel reluctant about following up anything. (*Crying* 165-66)

Oedipa finally got to the point where her mind was made up, and she wanted no more information about the Tristero; it made her more anxious, and she "began, reflexively, to grind together her back molars" (167). When Fallopian asked if it had ever occurred to her "that somebody's putting you on? That this is all a hoax, maybe something Inverarity set up before he died?" she said "No" and "that's ridiculous" (167). She must have become irritable, because Fallopian, "nothing if not compassionate," told her "Please, don't be mad" (*Crying* 168).

Some of my neurotic behavior, I was told early in my relationship with my present psychotherapist, was suggestive of "Post-traumatic Stress Disorder," which is designated by code number 309.89 in the *DSM-III-R* (247). Given that it immediately follows Obsessive Compulsive Disorder in the *Manual* and immediately precedes Generalized Anxiety Disorder, it is not surprising that "[s]ymptoms of depression and anxiety" lead the list of its "Associated features" (*DSM-III-R*, 249). Although neither my therapist nor I can identify the specific cause of my post-traumatic stress disorder, which is typically "a psychologically distressing event that is outside the range of usual human experience" (247), I definitely exhibit the telltale "exaggerated startle response" (248, 250). I cannot determine from Pynchon's text that Oedipa has that same response, but she does appear to have "recurrent distressing dreams during which the [traumatic] event is experienced" (248). In her restless night at the hotel in the Berkeley hills, she "kept waking from a nightmare about something in the mirror, across from her bed. Nothing specific, only a possibility, nothing she could see" (*Crying* 101). Other behavioral features of post-traumatic stress disorder identified in the *DSM-III-R* (248) are "a numbing of general responsiveness [...] referred to as 'psychic numbing,'" as in Oedipa's "Where am I?" (*Crying* 153); "feeling detached or estranged from other people," *e.g.*, Mucho, Metzger, Hilarius, Driblette; "hypervigilance," as in Oedipa's obsession that the Tristero has intentionally punished her by taking away these people whom she most needed; and a "reduced capacity for modulation [which] may express itself in unpredictable explosions of aggressive behavior or an inability to express angry feelings," the former exhibited when Oedipa "roared" to the cops about "Hitler Hilarius" paying the bill, and the latter when she called herself a "chicken" for not calling the swastika merchant "something" (150), for failing to "press the argument" with Bortz (166), and for not following up on the valuable stamps that Cohen had taken the liberty of releasing to his so-called "Expert Committee" for their evaluation (166). Finally, there may be "irritability with fears of losing control" (DSM-III-R, 248), that Oedipa exhibited when Fallopian gently urged her to consider whether this was "all a hoax" (*Crying* 167).

The Second Major Depression

When, back at The Scope, "a couple weeks into raising a beard, wearing button-down olive shirt, creased fatigue pants minus cuffs and belt loops, two-button fatigue jacket, no hat" (166), Fallopian entreated Oedipa not to be mad, then "didn't say anymore," she appears to have become more angry:

> She stood up, wondering if her hair was in place, if she looked rejected or hysterical, if they'd been causing a scene. "I knew you'd be different," she said, "Mike, because everybody's been changing on me. But it hadn't gone as far as hating me."
>
> "Hating you." He shook his head and laughed.
>
> "If you need any armbands or more weapons, do try Winthrop Tremaine, over by the freeway. Tremaine's Swastika Shoppe. Mention my name." (*Crying* 168)

Oedipa was so distraught and angry that she associated Fallopian's "modified Cuban ensemble" with the Nazis (168). Just as the anxiety in a depressive reaction is "allayed, and hence partially relieved, by [...] self-depreciation" (*DSM-I*, 33), she told herself: "you are a nut, Oedipa, out of your skull" (171). Succumbing to her second major depression in the novel, she

> hoped that she was mentally ill; that that's all it was. That night she sat for hours, too numb even to drink [, ...] this, oh God, was the void. There was nobody who could help her. Nobody in the world. [...] Old fillings in her teeth began to bother her. She would spend nights staring at a ceiling lit by the pink glow of San Narciso's sky. Other nights she could sleep for eighteen drugged hours and wake, enervated, hardly able to stand. (*Crying* 171)

At conferences with the lawyer who replaced Metzger, "her attention span could often be measured in seconds, and she laughed nervously more than she spoke" (171). Perhaps intentionally, "Genghis Cohen, once so shy, now seemed to come up with new goodies every other day" (171): more Tristero stamps, historical accounts of a reformed Tristero now seeking to support rather than destroy Thurn and Taxis, of the subsequent loss of "nearly all the noble patronage that had sustained" the Tristero, of their being "reduced to handling anarchist correspondence" (172), which, for Oedipa, might have been admirable, of their coming to America during 1849-50, of their befriending native American tribes. Oedipa shared the historical material with Bortz, who tried to spark her former enthusiasm. "Well, it's interesting [...] if the article's legitimate" was about all she could say (175). "'That ought to be easy enough to check out.' Bortz gazing straight into her eyes. 'Why don't you?'" (175) Instead of responding positively to his encouragement, her "toothaches got worse, she dreamed of disembodied voices from whose malignance there was no appeal, the soft dusk of mirrors out of which something was about to walk, and empty rooms that waited for her" (175). Cohen didn't help matters when he

> called to tell her that the final arrangements had been made to auction off Inverarity's stamp collection. The Tristero "forgeries" were to be sold as lot 49. "And something rather disturbing, Miz Maas. A new book bidder

has appeared on the scene, whom neither I nor any of the firms in the area have heard of before. That hardly every happens." […]

"What do you think?" said Oedipa, already knowing pretty much.

"That our mysterious bidder may be from Tristero," Cohen said. "And saw the description of the lot in the auction catalogue. And wants to keep evidence that Tristero exists out of unauthorized hands." (*Crying* 176) Oedipa thereupon went back to Echo Courts "to drink bourbon until the sun went down and it was as dark as it would ever get. Then she went out and drove on the freeway for a while with her lights out, to see what would happen. But angels were watching" (176). Instead of taking her mind off of whatever was at the bottom of her depression, thoughts of Tristero was making her feel more despondent. When she finally reached the fellow at The Greek Way bar in San Francisco, she was desperate: "a few hours ago," she told him, "I got drunk and went driving on these freeways. Next time I may be more deliberate. For the love of God, human life, whatever you respect, please. Help me" (177). Surely, the most serious symptom of a major depressive episode is "recurrent suicidal ideation without a specific plan, or a suicide attempt or a specific plan for committing suicide" (*DSM-III-R*, 222).

Obsessive Compulsive Disorder

In the penultimate paragraph of the novel, Oedipa stands at the door of the auction room with Cohen:

She was not sure what she'd do when the bidder revealed himself. She had only some vague idea about causing a scene violent enough to bring the cops into it and find out that way who the man really was. She stood in a patch of sun, among brilliant rising and falling points of dust, trying to get a little warm, wondering if she'd go through with it. (*Crying* 183)

In the obsessive compulsive reaction, according to the 1952 *Diagnostic and Statistical Manual of Mental Disorders,*

the anxiety is associated with the persistence of unwanted ideas and of repetitive impulses to perform acts which may be considered morbid by the patient. The patient himself may regard his ideas and behavior as unreasonable, but nevertheless is compelled to carry out his rituals. (*DSM-I*, 33).

Before I understood what it was, I used to have this kind of feeling when, sitting near the front of, say, a concert hall, I was attracted by a performer, especially if she was wearing a formal low-cut blouse. Talk about "causing a scene violent enough to bring the cops into it" (*Crying* 183), I imagined myself suddenly jumping up on to the stage and groping her. I was afraid that once I made the slightest move, I would feel compelled to go through with it, despite knowing how shocked my friends in the audience would be, what they would tell their friends, how I would be physically restrained and turned over to the police. It was as though nothing could save me from ruining my life and casting a pall on my wife's. I wish I could say that this was the most painful of the obsessions I used to have, for there were much worse. Fortunately I was finally diagnosed with OCD, assured that I was not psychotic and would therefore not actually follow through on these obsessive fantasies, and learned that the corollary behavior was my compulsive photocopying of hand-written drafts in case they were accidentally demolished, checking locks, *etcetera*.

I read the above excerpt from the last page of *The Crying of Lot 49* a dozen times over the last dozen years without associating them with my own disorder. The only reason that I finally made the connection is that Pynchon portrayed a more obvious example of OCD in his 2006 novel *Against the Day*, in which Dally Rideout sees a woman in a department store, who she almost thinks is her mother. She has

> to get an immediate grip on herself, because if she didn't, the next thing she knew, she'd be running over there screaming, to embrace some woman who would of course turn out to be a stranger, and all the embarrassment, maybe even legal action, that was sure to go with that, and the word she'd be screaming would be "Mamma." (*Against* 347)

I discuss this example in Kohn *Pynchon Takes* 163-64, where I also suggest that Dally's half-sister Bria likewise has OCD, which would be in keeping with this being a "genetic disorder" (*ibid.*, 173). The fact that "Oedipa settled back, to await the crying of lot 49," suggests that she may have gotten past "wondering if she'd go through with it" and knew that she wouldn't (183).

Concluding Remarks

This essay is based on the assumption that Oedipa has the same mental disorders that I have, which is a strong assumption given that the "lifetime prevalence" of, say, OCD, is only "2.5 to 3 percent," though that is equivalent to "between four to six million people in the United States" (Caldwell 108). I then closely read Oedipa's behavior in the context of a model in which all of her behavior in the novel is tested according to that assumption. Though it may be, to use Milton Friedman's words (14), a "wildly inaccurate descriptive" representation of the reality that Pynchon intended, the assumption has predictive power for me because it explains passages in *The Crying of Lot 49* that I never understood before. I am emboldened to the point of thinking that I now find some meaning in at least half the text of this extraordinarily complex novel.

It may be surprising, in the light of Peter Brooks's "worry about the legitimacy and force that psychoanalysis may claim when imported into the study of literary texts" (1), that psychoanalytic criticism appears to be effective in interpreting Oedipa's behavior. I suggest that my focus on the *DSM* and mental disorders is something different from the conventional psychoanalytic criticism which, in Brooks's view "deserves the bad name it has largely made for itself" (1). That hermeneutic, according to Charles Bressler, was founded on the "theories and practice of Sigmund Freud" pertaining to "patients diagnosed as hysterics," the root of whose problems, "was psychological, not physical" and which, he claimed, were related to "suppressed incestuous desires with which [these patients] had unconsciously refused to deal" (89).

    The fact that Pynchon gave Oedipa a name that connotes incestuous desires, but then gave no clues as to what childhood desires she might be repressing, suggests that he had a new approach to literary criticism in mind that could be more generally called "psychiatric literary criticism." Just as the "[t]raditional psychoanalytic criticism tend[ed] to fall into three general categories, depending on the object of analysis: the author, the reader, or the fictive persons of the text," the new psychiatric criticism, in part because it is more exoterically based on written material, especially the *DSM*, can be directed toward all three general categories (Brooks 2). To the extent that I have wondered whether Pynchon endowed Oedipa with some of his own psychological qualities, my psychiatric literary criticism embraces all three categories encompassed by Brooks. Whereas Wilde presents a well-argued philosophical case that Oedipa's unremitting pursuit of the Tristero confirms that she has "opt[ed] for madness" (96), my psychiatric model explains her pursuit of the Tristero as a strategy for counteracting the slide into madness. That both interpretations, as well as others, may be correct is compatible with Pynchon's "willingness," as Wilde sees it, "to accept randomness, contingency, and uncertainty as part of the very nature of things—of what is desired as much as of what is" (94).

    (This is one of the three essays in this volume that have not had the benefit of external, anonymous readings. As I proofed it, I recognized a flaw to which readers have called my attention, which is my failure to explain how particular quotations reinforce my thesis. In such cases in Essay Seven, the quotations from *The Crying of Lot 49* are meant as evidence of Oedipa's depressive, anxiety, obsessive or post-traumatic stress disorders.)

Pynchon's Typo and Barthes' Oversight

> Just before the morning rush hour, she got out of a
> jitney whose ancient driver ended each day in the red, downtown
> on Howard Street, began to walk toward the Embarcadero. She
> knew she looked terrible–knuckles black with eye-liner and
> mascara from where she'd rubbed, mouth tasting of old booze
> and coffee. Through an open doorway, on the stair leading up
> into the disinfectant-smelling twilight of a rooming house she
> saw an old man huddled, shaking with grief she couldn't hear.
> (*Crying* 125)

There appears to be a typo at the end of the above epigraph, which could
readily be explained by the close similarity in print of the words "hear"
and "bear." The grief with which the old man was shaking would more
likely have been something that Oedipa couldn't bear than something she
couldn't hear. But even if the wrong word had gotten though in the first
edition, Pynchon would probably have corrected it in subsequent
editions. But was it really a typo? The last two sentences of the epigraph
appear to have been intentionally crafted to include all five senses: touch,
taste, smell, sight, and hearing, so Pynchon must have had hearing in
mind when he wrote these sentences. No less a Pynchon scholar than
Duyfhuizen quoted this particular line, " […] shaking with grief she
couldn't hear" without a qualm" (241)! But what useful information was
he providing by "grief she couldn't hear," or was that perhaps meant to
be an example of noise in communication theory? (I cover that subject in
Essay Eleven.) Given that the old man was "shaking with fear," it is more
likely that she would have heard it, rather than *not* heard it. We will
probably never know what Pynchon was thinking here, which may be
another example of what Wilde referred to as his "willingness to accept
randomness, contingency and uncertainty as part of the very nature of
things" (94). I don't understand what Duyfhuizen meant when he wrote
that "Pynchon in *The Crying of Lot 49* asks his readers to look for texts
beyond those sanctioned and visible, to listen for the sounds of 'silence'"
(236). Is the "grief" that Oedipa "couldn't hear" a sound of silence? It is
certainly different from what Duyfhuizen calls "the incessant
textualization of privileged representations" (236).

It is significant that this faux typo, if that's what it is, was
important to Pynchon, for he appears to have alluded to it again in
Against the Day, which I have argued was written not only to
commemorate the 40th anniversary of *The Crying of Lot 49* but also to

identify anomalies in it that critics had overlooked. Early in the later novel, he used the word "bear" in the same sense in which it would have been appropriate in the above epigraph. Lew Basnight, the detective, had an atypical epiphany: "He understood that things were exactly what they were. It seemed more than he could bear" (*Against* 42). In my essay, *Pynchon's Transition*, I related Basnight's epiphany to the final line in *Against the Day*, of this novel and that final line, I went on to claim that: "Never has Pynchon written a more enigmatic novel nor ended one with a more enigmatic sentence than 'They fly toward grace'" (*Against* 1085; Kohn *Pynchon's Transition* 210). What had seemed more than Basnight "could bear" was a "luminosity [...]" which he later came to think of as grace," that was "new to him," *i.e.*, his understanding "that things were exactly what they were" (*Against* 42).

Just as there is this inscrutable typo in *The Crying of Lot 49*, so also is there an incredible oversight in Barthes' celebrated *S/Z*. The latter was first published in 1970, and its focus on the last lines of particular novels could have been inspired by *The Crying of Lot 49*. Alternatively, Pynchon's emphasis on the last line of *Against the Day*, which may have been a reprise of his emphasis on the last line of the 1966 novel, may also have been influenced by the final paragraph of S/Z, which is entitled "The Pensive Text." I recently discovered the oversight in S/Z and describe it in the following section of this essay.

The Incredible Oversight in Barthes' S/Z

There was great intellectual ferment in literary criticism in Paris in the late 1960s and early 1970s. Roland Barthes' *S/Z*, which Catherine Belsey calls his "anarchic, infinitely suggestive, and still unsurpassed close reading of Honoré de Balzac's short story, *Sarrasine*," was part of that ferment (43). Richard Harland sees it as "a scientific vision" to which "all Semioticians aspire" (61). Though it "disowned all pretensions to scientific objectivity," Terry Eagleton calls *S/Z* the "work of the break" (137). This break, from the structuralism of Claude Lévi-Strauss to the new poststructuralism of Samuel Beckett and on to postmodernism is memorialized in Luciano Berio's 1968/69 *Sinfonia*, the highly complex choral orchestration that features French text from *The Raw and the Cooked*, English text from *The Unnameable*, and musical pastiche from works such as those of the twelve-tone masters, Alban Berg, Pierre Boulez, Arnold Schoenberg, Karlheinz Stockhausen, Igor Stravinsky, and Anton Webern (See Goldford, Irvine and Kohn *Berio's Sinfonia*). Stockhausen, his "Radio Cologne sound," and his "audio oscillators, gunshot machines, [and] contact mikes" are alluded to by Pynchon (*Crying* 48), as is the kind of "twelve-tone" music that Berg, Berio, Boulez, Schoenberg, Stockhausen, Stravinsky and Webern composed, which Mucho may have whistled (*Crying* 145).

Barthes' *S/Z* differentiates classic (pre-1905) novels that are replete from modern (post-1905) novels that are "writable," *i.e.*, those that "make the reader no longer a consumer, but a producer of the text" (4). In Leona Toker's words, the latter novels "do not satisfy the reader's wish for what is deemed sufficient information about story events" (130). Barthes took Balzac's novel *Sarrasine* to the latter level in the final paragraph (before the appendices), as the result of an oversight, in which he violated his own hermeneutic code. Given Robert Scholes' assessment, expressed while Barthes was still alive, that "*S/Z* is a satisfying work in many ways though exasperating in others" (149), that its author is "an essentially unsystematic writer who loves system, a structuralist who dislikes structure," and a "literary man who [...] loves to take up the outrageous position on any question and defend it until it becomes plausible" (148), we can forgive his oversight and honor him for the contribution to literary criticism that resulted from that oversight.

In Appendix II of *S/Z*, entitled "Sequence of Actions (Act.)," Barthes lists those actions "which form the main armature" of Balzac's *Sarrasine* and remain invariant across several lexias. Surprisingly, this five-page appendix does not include "to remain pensive," although the French original, "*resta pensive*," appears on pages 64 *and* 77 of Balzac's 1830 text. It is not as though remaining pensive was less than an "Action," for the almost synonymous "to meditate" *is* properly listed in that same Appendix II (255). Not only are "*resta pensive*" the final words of *Sarrasine*, but the *Et* that begins the last sentence, "*Et la marquise resta pensive*" (Balzac 77), weakly implies its parallel to the earlier sentence, which is "*Au milieu de ce désordre, la Zambinella, comme frappe de terreur, resta pensive*" (64). Although Barthes justifies the omission of "this final lexia from any classification" by "the infinite openness of the pensive (and this is precisely its structural function)," he did not similarly omit the 364th lexia from classification (though it is labeled "ACT," which denotes the Action code), even though it too includes "*resta pensive*" (151). Richard Miller's English translation of Balzac's French text likewise ignored the pivotal repetition of "remained pensive" beginning in the sentence, "In the midst of this disorder, La Zambinella remained thoughtful, as though terror-struck," using "thoughtful" here rather than the "pensive," that would have resonated in the second: "And the Marquise remained pensive" (*S/Z* 245, 254). There is no indication that Barthes picked up in the least on the significance of Balzac's presumably intended repetition. If he had been aware of the glaring repetition, his interpretations in Sections LXIV and XCIII of *S/Z* would surely have contained some constructive cross-references (151-52, 216-17). It is all the more surprising that Barthes and Miller disregarded the repeated "*resta pensive*" because Barthes' title for his final section, XCIII, is "The Pensive Text" (*S/Z* 216). Nor do critics appear to have noted this loss in translation, even though the contiguous phrase "as though thunder-struck" has received prominent attention from critics (see Hugh Silverman 79 and Laurent Stern 71).

Barthes could have written a strong interpretation of the concluding lexia, totally in keeping with structuralism and semiotics, rather than the *non-sequiter* with which he concludes *S/Z* on pages 216-17. Readers know that La Zambinella "remained thoughtful [pensive], as though terror-struck" (245) and that the most recent cause of such terror was her "hearing Sarrasine describe a trait which revealed the excessive violence of his character" (*S/Z* 244). In Section LXIV of the text, significantly entitled "The Voice of the Reader," Barthes acknowledges "that La Zambinella really is terrified" but strangely adds that her/his terror

> expresses the interests of only one character, who is neither Sarrasine nor the narrator, but the reader: it is the reader who is concerned that the truth be simultaneously named and evaded, an ambiguity which the discourse nicely creates by *as though*, which indicates the truth and yet reduces it declaratively to a mere appearance. What we hear, therefore, is the *displaced* voice which the reader lends, by proxy, to the discourse: the discourse is speaking according to the reader's interests. Whereby we see that writing is not the communication of a message which starts from the author and proceeds to the reader; it is specifically the voice of reading itself: *in the text, only the reader speaks.* (*S/Z* 151)

It is reasonable to assume that Balzac intended that both characters that remained pensive perceived their aggressive masculine partner as threatening. In the marquise's case, she appears to have made an implicit promise to have sex with the narrator—who, by his own admission, could be, like Sarrasine, an "angry, pouting, admiring, loving, jealous" young man—if he would tell her the story of the richly bejeweled centenarian they had met at the de Lanty's sumptuous ball the preceding evening (*S/Z* 234). Barthes astutely read into Balzac's text that "the conditions are met for a narrative contract," that is, for a "bargain struck between the narrator and the young woman," namely, "if you give yourself to me, I will tell you the story: tit for tat: a moment of love in exchange for a good story" (*S/Z* 84, 86). When the Marquise peremptorily "demand[s] delivery of the goods (narration of the story)," she is hoping "to scant the other half of the bargain, since the narrator's desire cannot be fulfilled in the Lantys' salon" (87). Barthes calls this a "seesaw of proposals and refusals," through which "a very precise economy of exchange is established" (87). From the young narrator's perspective, the comfortable décor in which the pair settles down that evening "is as propitious for the telling of a good story as it is for a night of love" (88), suggesting his eager anticipation of the promised tit for tat.

The story that the narrator tells the marquise is that of a castrato, La Zambinella, renowned on the Italian stage, who is seen as a beautiful woman by an impetuous young French sculptor, Sarrasine, who pursues her and pleads with her to marry him. Fearing the youth's patent impetuosity, the castrato fends off his passionate advances, until Sarrasine finally discovers that La Zambinella is actually a male and is so enraged that he draws his sword to kill the dissembling youth. Alerted by the latter's piercing screams, the castrato's hidden protectors, storm the room and stab the young sculptor to death. La Zambinella has fearfully anticipated the tragedy that the deception, foisted on the castrato by the stagehands for a joke, is fostering. However, the singer is not without blame, for in the same paragraph that "*la Zambinella, comme frappée de terreur, resta pensive,*" she had, minutes earlier, "*commencé la première à lui presser le pied et à l'agacer avec la malice d'une femme libre et amoureuse,*" i.e., " begun by pressing his foot and teasing him with the flirtatiousness of a woman in love and free to show it" (Balzac 63; *S/Z* 244).

The final sentence of the novel, "*Et la marquise resta pensive,*" with which the earlier but parallel sentence resonates, again conveys guilt and fear. The marquise recognizes that the castrato had sold sexual favors to the cardinal, a *quid pro quo* not unlike her own implicit arrangement with the ardent narrator. Like the castrato, she is not the pure soul that she had claimed to be. When the guilty consciences and comparable fears associated with the two mentions of "*resta pensive*" are interrelated, *Sarrasine* the novel should properly be seen as structurally "replete: like a cupboard where meanings are shelved, stacked, safeguarded (in this text nothing is ever lost: meaning recuperates everything); like a pregnant female, replete with signifieds which criticism will not fail to deliver" (Barthes 200-01).

Barthes' argument for the crucial *quid pro quo* is symbolically reinforced in the light of the repetition, itself a kind of *quid pro quo*, of "*resta pensive.*" At the end of the narrator's tale of deceit and violence, after he and the marquise had "sat for a moment plunged in the deepest silence," the whole truth having been divulged–that the old man at the ball was not married to any young woman, that he had become enormously wealthy as la Zambinella, and that he was showering his wealth on the Lantys, whose uncle he is–the narrator alludes to the promised reward by simply saying "Well?" Instead, she looked at him "and spoke in an altered voice. 'You have given me a disgust for life and for passions that will last a long time. […] I would become a nun tomorrow did I not know that I can remain unmoved as a rock amid the storms of life. […] Leave me.' 'Ah,'" the narrator replied, "you know how to punish" (*S/Z* 253). The marquise remained pensive because of guilt for encouraging the narrator and of fear that her too eager, pouting suitor will respond to her hostile outburst with violence. The pivotal repetition in the original French text of the "*resta pensive,*" unfortunately lost in the English translation, is an essential element of *Sarrasine's* shelved and stacked classic repleteness.

Why Barthes Might Have Contradicted His Central Thesis

Despite an entire book of argument that "any classic" text "is replete" (S/Z 200), Barthes contradicts this thesis, allegedly on the basis of Sarrasine's final lexia–"And the Marquise remained pensive"–which lexia he pointedly removes "from any classification" (254). On the basis of this final lexia, he argues that the classic text

> still seems to be keeping in reserve some ultimate meaning, one it does not express but whose place it keeps free and signifying; this zero degree of meaning (which is not its annulment, but on the contrary its

recognition), this supplementary, unexpected meaning which is the theatrical sign of the implicit, is pensiveness: the pensive (in faces, in texts) is the signifier of the inexpressible, not of the unexpressed. [...] At its discreet urging, we want to ask the classic text: *What are you thinking about?* But the text, wilier than all those who try to escape by answering: *about nothing,* does not reply, giving meaning its last closure: suspension. (*S/Z* 216-17)

Well before this *resta pensive* concludes *Sarrasine,* it has already sounded, and its meaning "shelved, stacked,[and presumably] safeguarded (in this text nothing is lost)" 200-01). There are ample similarities in the two soundings; their common meaning is neither unexpressed nor inexpressible. Surely, this inconsistency alone would explain why Scholes, though he found *S/Z* to be a "satisfying work in many ways" was nevertheless "exasperating in others" (149). That there should be such a flagrant inconsistency in what Belsey (43) calls Barthes "unsurpassed close reading" is no less incredible than Pynchon's "typo" is inscrutable.

The questions asked me by the editor who reviewed and rejected the penultimate version of this essay helped me understand why Barthes, probably on purpose, ignored the repetition of *"resta pensive."* "Are we supposed to infer that the Marquise recognizes this similarity," *i.e.,* between her vulnerability at the end of the story and that of La Zambinella earlier? My answer to this question is yes. Does Balzac's "text only invite [this question] without answering [it]?"" My answer is no; Balzac's text answers the question, but Barthes chose to ignore the Marquise's recognition of that similarity. His grounds for that were that "La Zambinella remained thoughtful (*i.e,* pensive), as though terror-struck" (*S/Z* 151). The qualifying *"as though* [...] reduce[... her being terror-struck] to a mere appearance. What we hear, therefore [...] is not the communication of a message which starts from the author and proceeds to the reader; it is specifically the voice of reading itself: *in the text, only the reader speaks"* (151). Barthes seems to be telling us that the first *"resta pensive"* has to do with being terror-struck only if the reader chooses to give it that interpretation, so we have no hard information to connect the two mentions of the repeated phrase. It is after the first mention of the equivalent of *"resta pensive"* that Barthes' obeisance to the reader's primacy is sounded, and poststructuralism invoked, explaining why, in Eagleton's view, *S/Z* is "the work of the break" (137). But I am skeptical of Barthes' tenebrous argument. He even contradicts it when he states that *"as though* [...] indicates the truth," that "the narrator [...] knows that La Zambinella really is terrified," and, despite the *as though,* that the code for this lexia is "*ACT. 'Danger': 2: the victim's fear" (151). There is no good reason that Barthes could not have given that same exact code to the final lexia in *Sarrasine,* which is my response to the editor's suggestion that I "say something about which of the Barthesian codes the action belongs to." It follows that I agree with the journal editor that "the '*resta pensive*' conveys an action" However I disagree with him that Barthes is right "in saying that the text [*Sarrasine*] holds some larger meaning in reserve." He derives that result by suppressing the classical repleteness conveyed by the double mention of *"resta pensive"* in Balzac's text. It may have been when Barthes pondered the 364th lexia, that he realized that his essay "The Death of the Author," which he had published in 1968, could be relevant to *S/Z*, which was due to be published in 1970, whereupon he compromised his otherwise brilliant structuralist analysis of Balzac's text. The editor's question to me as to whether, at the end of the novel, the Marquise's "recognition extend[s] to thoughts about what she will be like when she is older" seems to be of less importance than the other question regarding her immediate danger.

Contrasting Barthes' Oversight with Pynchon's Typo

Pynchon must have realized when he came upon his typo, if that's what it was, that it was interesting and decided to retain it. It could even have been a faux typo to begin with. There appears to have been no effort on his part to trick his readers, only to intrigue them. Alternatively, Barthes' oversight of the first *"resta pensive"* was almost underhanded, and the "as though" explanation appears to have been contrived to establish his poststructuralist thesis empowering the reader. I have no quarrel with poststructuralism; as I said earlier in this book, it is the ideal hermeneutic for relating to Carter's *Infernal Desire Machines of Dr. Hoffman* and to Beckett's *The Unnameable* (see Goldford *et. al.*). The paintings of St. Louis artist Bessie Lowenhaupt best reveal their meaning in the context of the book, *The Truth in Painting*, by the great poststructuralist writer, Jacques Derrida (see Kohn *A Derridean Look*). Alternatively, I view *The Crying of Lot 49* as tightly as what Eagleton called "a closed entity, equipped with definite meanings which it is the critic's task to decipher" (158). These meanings, which in the case of Pynchon's novel, can number in the dozens for a single signifier, were put there by the author. If Pynchon would come forth and disagree with any of my conclusions on his novels that I disclose in these essays, I would renounce them. If he took issue with any assumption I made, but agreed with the results I obtained with that disputed assumption, I would readily acknowledge that the assumption is wrong, but still worthwhile, because it had enabled me to obtain results that Pynchon was willing to validate. Still, writes Umberto Eco, paraphrasing Geofrey Hartman, "it is legitimate for a sensitive reader to find what he finds in the text, because these associations are, at least potentially, evoked by the text; and because the poet might, perhaps unconsciously, have created some 'harmonics' to the main theme" (Eco 62; Hartman, 149-50). Following Hartman's and Eco's conditionality with respect to any conclusions or results which Pynchon denied consciously thinking, I would ask him, if I could, if it were possible that he might have had them subconsciously in mind. Only if he said no would I then renounce them. This is the version of Lévi-Straussian structuralism to which I hold my criticism of Pynchon's novels accountable. It is the exact opposite of Barthes' poststructuralist view of a modernist novel having "no determinate meaning, no settled signifieds, but is […] an inexhaustible tissue or galaxy of signifiers, a seamless weave of codes and fragments of codes, through which the critic may cut his own errant path, " in short, "a free space in which [he or she] can sport" (Eagleton 138). In the case of poststructuralist novels, perhaps only in that case, would I attribute meaning to a novel predicated on "what the text said independently of the intention of its author" (Eco 63-64). Thinking back to my September 21st, 2003 telephone conversation with Sukenick, I strongly believe that he would have acknowledged–or inferred as much–having unconscious thoughts about Tibetan Buddhism when he wrote *Out*, however, I did not put the question to him, and in respect for his wife's priority in the matter, I do not draw on any of his presumed Buddhist references in the following essay in this book, Essay Nine.

In the previous draft of this essay, I concluded that Barthes put the emphasis on the last line of *Sarrasine*– "And the Marquis remained pensive" (S/R 254)–to make the point that the final sentence in a novel is likely to continue resonating in readers' minds, "giving meaning its last closure: suspension" (217). The editor found fault with my discussion of "Barthes' putting 'an unexpected but seminal focus on the last line of all fictional works'" (inner quotation from my penultimate draft). When I reread the final section of *S/Z*, entitled "The Pensive Text," I realized that Barthes made no such claim. He was simply wrapping up his discussion, begun in "The Voice of the Reader" (*S/Z* 151-52), freeing the poststructuralist reader/critic to supplement the fictional text "with an *et cetera* of plentitudes" of his or her own making (217).

Stressing the Ending of Novels

Contrary to my original reading, it turns out that there is no evidence that Barthes meant to imply that the last line of every fictional work is especially significant. But, in the case of *Sarrasine*, he did claim that that the "Marquise's remain[ing] pensive" seems to be "keeping in reserve some ultimate meaning" (*S/Z* 216). Although Barthes was able to infuse special meaning into "*resta pensive*" by ignoring its earlier, information-rich appearance in *Sarrasine*, he may have laid the groundwork for what Peter Rabinowitz and Michael Smith refer to as the "rule governing most modern western narratives" that "stresses the ending" (55). Likewise, John Knapp stressed the importance of "completing texts and making sense of their endings" (72). It is especially relevant to this essay that Rabinowitz and Smith went on to suggest another "general rule that in most serious works of fiction, titles are stressed, and we know to pay special attention when they are repeated in the text" (55). In the case of *The Crying of Lot 49*, its last line also includes the title! Is this not another example of the "randomness, contingency, and uncertainty" that for Pynchon is "part of the very nature of things" (Wilde 94)?

Pynchon's "refusal to satisfy [...] the desire for a final resolution" of *The Crying of Lot 49*, writes Seed,

> is made abundantly clear in the last lines of the novel where Oedipa
> settles back in her seat at an auction to await the crying of Lot 49. Instead

of resolving the narrative Pynchon places Oedipa in an audience and by repeating the novel's title throws the reader back into the text. By this stage in the novel it has become abundantly clear that Oedipa's [frustrated] search for a text, [...] is a comically exaggerated imitation of the reader's own potential anxieties in making sense of the novel. (*Fictional Labyrinth* 123-24)

Seed's reading of the last line of *The Crying of Lot 49* is an impressive demonstration of last-line importance. Another such demonstration, one that comes from an opposite reading of the text, is the following:

Pynchon's work is notoriously complicated and concerned with issues of order and disorder [, ... but a]re there ways, too, in which Pynchon reins in the disorder? I am thinking in particular of the end of *Crying*, where the last sentence seems to resolve, in a rather game-like way, the reader's confusion as far as what the title can possibly mean ... Pynchon seems to almost string the reader along by taking an arbitrary set of words and then eventually allowing them to settle into sense in the final moments, sort of like taking a jet plane and landing it on a dime. Indeed, he lands it at the end, and yet is this an ironic gesture, where one level of order is re-established while others remain in disarray? Are there evolutionary advantages to cognitive disorder, toward the sort of scrambling that Pynchon galvanizes in the reader?

This is, of course, the work of the anonymous reader who prompted me to exclaim in the Introduction to this book, under *On Essay Four*: "What a wondrous field this literary criticism, where a scholar is willing to anonymously spill out original, eminently publishable ideas for someone else to take credit?" For all I know this anonymous reader could be the scholar I just cited, David Seed, for he obviously subscribes to the last-line rule.

Another interpretation of the final sentence of *The Crying of Lot 49* is based on Grausam's fascinating 2008 interpretation of Pynchon's quirky "potsmaster" reference as signifying a "total nuclear war" (234-35). Grausam extends John Dugdale's idea "that there are 49 states in the continental USA, and that it is bounded by the 49th parallel, so that (using 'lot' in the sense of 'unit of real estate,' as at *Lot* 49) the nation can be thought of as 'Lot 49' (Dugdale 9), so that Oedipa's "await[ing] the crying of lot 49" signifies "the lament of a population assigned a common lot, a common destiny as the target of a total war that [will] instantaneously destroy us all. (Grausam 234-35). Another interpretation of Oedipa's "settl[ing] back, to await the crying of lot 49" (183) metafictionally glosses "lot 49" as the title of the novel in which she is starring, and has her waiting for her next major depression, a reprise of the last in which she "stood in front of the painting and cried," except that this next time she would not only go "from cry to cry" but probably "go mad" (*Crying* 21, 22).

A final interpretation of the last line of *The Crying of Lot 49* was suggested by south-Arizonan Pynchon-enthusiast Jeffrey Chimene, who liked my idea that

Pierce Inverarity plotted to be reborn as Oedipa's baby but apparently dismissed my suspicion that the pregnancy ended because she had her period. In an email to me dated February 9, 2011, Jeff wrote

Not to put too fine a point on it: what is the Crying of Lot 49? The sound Inverarity makes as he's re-born.

Essay Nine

Zen, Tibetan Buddhism and Postmodernism

Or he might even have tried to survive death, as a paranoia; as a pure conspiracy against someone he loved. Would that breed of perversity prove at last too keen to be stunned even by death, had a plot been devised too elaborate for the dark Angel to hold at once, in his humorless vice-president's head, all the possibilities of? Had something slipped through and Inverarity by that much beaten death? (*Crying* 179)

One of the earliest, if not the earliest literary critic, to use the term postmodernism was Ihab Hassan in a 1971 article in which he asked the question, "When will Modernism cease and what comes thereafter," to which he memorably replied several pages later: "The change in Modernism may be called Postmodernism" (*POSTmodernISM* 7, 11). Subsequently Hassan authored *The Postmodern Turn*, from which the epigraph for the present volume is taken. It speaks to Pynchon's prescience that he wrote *The Crying of Lot 49* five years before Hassan modestly acknowledged: "I have not defined Modernism; I can define Postmodernism less; and the parallels and contrasts between these movements are least obvious to me" ((*POSTmodernISM* 24). However, he then provided a list of possible postmodernisms which include the following: "sporadic artistic reactions against Technologies" (25), "anti-elitism" (25), "post-existential ethos, psychedelics (Leary)" (27), "counter Western 'ways' or metaphysics, Zen, Buddhism, Hinduism" (28) and a "tend(ancy) toward Anarchy" (29). Some of these postmodernisms have parallels in *The Crying of Lot* 49, some anticipate Andreas Huyssen's definition of postmodernism, and the one having to do with Zen and Buddhism informs the essay at hand, in which I associate modernism with Zen Buddhism and postmodernism with Tibetan Buddhism, which was indeed derived from Hinduism. My antithetic interpretations of Zen and Tibetan Buddhism, based on rationalization, optimization, secularization and utopian progress, may no longer be up-to-date; however, my principal focus in this essay is on the differentiation of modernism and postmodernism that was current in the heyday of postmodernism.

The interest of postmodern American writers in Tibetan Buddhism was reflected in novels by Thomas Pynchon, Don DeLillo, William Kotzwinkle, John Hawkes, William Gaddis and possibly Ronald Sukenick (Given the related controversy on Sukenick discussed in Essay Six of the Introduction to this book, I am not pushing his novel as an example here). Although there were occasional allusions to Zen Buddhism by these five writers, they were in a less serious, sometimes mocking vein. It may be that Tibetan Buddhism got more attention from them because postmodernism took root at the same time that large numbers of Tibetan monks and lamas, fleeing for safety in the wake of the Chinese invasion of their country, were entering the United States and attracting followings. Looking "for breaks, for events rather than new worlds, for the telltale instant after which it is no longer the same," postmodern writers would surely have picked up on the "shifts and irrevocable changes" that the spreading influence of Tibetan Buddhism was fostering here (Jameson, ix).

However, there was considerably more to it than that. I suggest that these writers sensed that Tibetan Buddhism was congruous with the ethos that fostered postmodernism. This was a time, in Huyssen's view, when "the historical limits of modernism" were coming "into sharp focus" (49). What had "become obsolete" were "those codifications of modernism in critical discourse which, however subliminally," were "based on a teleological view of progress and modernization" (Huyssen 49). The motivating forces behind "progress and modernization" since the middle of the nineteenth century have been science and technology, each of whose advances nourished the other's. As science successfully explained sequences of causes and effects, it reinforced humans' confidence in their ability to reason correctly. The progression of science and technology was compatible with, and fostered, optimizational processes. Humanity's growing capability to explain phenomena and improve its own well-being lessened the need for a provident, personal God. That and the faith in human reason fostered expectations of life-sustaining plentitude and humanistic morality that verged on the utopian. At their most optimistic, the narrow teleological projections for human betterment and utopian moral behavior inspired elitism, and were increasingly recognized as exaggerated, especially in the turbulent 1960s, when they precipitated a backlash that would last for several decades (see Kohn *Unwitting Witness*). The terms, "rationalization," "optimization," "secularization" and "progress" were among the reductive codifications of which, in Jameson's words, "modernization [...] stands accused" (378, 379). "Intellectualization" was another of the code names that Jameson associated with modernist dogma, though in this essay it is equated with rationalization (379). Likewise, the postmodern incredulity toward progress is conflated here with the "end [...] of Utopia" (Jameson 159). These codifications, Huyssen famously declared, "prepared the ground for that repudiation of modernism which goes by the name of the postmodern" (49). What was being rejected, Huyssen made clear, was "not modernism as such" but "only that trend within modernism which had been codified into a narrow dogma" (49).

The turn to Buddhism was part of the post-secular attraction to new spiritualities that McClure indelibly identified with postmodernism. The main reason, I believe, that novelists like Pynchon and DeLillo were attracted to Tibetan rather than Zen Buddhism is that the postmodern ethos and Tibetan Buddhism are complementary, whereas Zen is complementary, or was generally believed to be complementary, with the codifications of modernity that postmodernism repudiated. If the respective pairs were not absolutely complementary or anti-complementary, they were at least *relatively* so. Again, these code words of modernism are rationalization/intellectualization, optimization, secularization and utopianism. With its irrational focus on remaining conscious beyond death, its acceptance of the suboptimal, its non-secular reverence for arcane deities, and its belief in the duality or oneness of good and evil, which is hardly utopian, Tibetan Buddhism tends toward complementarity with postmodernism and anti-complementarity with modernity, with which, of course, Zen Buddhism tends to be complementary. This hypothesis is based on the view of Zen Buddhism as it was explained by Hyman Kublin, Philip Kapleau and Eugen Herrigel in the early 70s and Robert Aitken in the early 80s; and on the view of Tibetan Buddhism as fostered by the writings of W. Y. Evans-Wentz, all of which were republished as popular paperbacks during the 1960s, and those of Chögyam Trungpa and Francesca Fremantle, and Robert Thurman. Subsequent writers on Zen, such as Dale S. Wright, and on Tibetan Buddhism, such as Geoffrey Samuel, though more scholarly, were too late to assert their broadening influences on the postmodern novelists discussed here.

The following four sections of this essay associates each of the four modernistic attributes with Zen Buddhism and each of the four corresponding anti-modernist attributes with Tibetan Buddhism. The latter are referred to as anti-rational/anti-intellectual, non-optimizational, anti-secular and anti-utopian, the latter of which has precedence in the term "anti-Utopianism," which Jameson introduced on page 340. The sixth section identifies each of the postmodern qualities of Tibetan Buddhism in specific postmodern novels, while the seventh section identifies cases in which some of these same postmodern novels are dismissive of Zen. Again, the reader is cautioned that this analysis is based on popular views of the two Buddhisms in the 1960s, 70s and 80s. The latest, published in 1995, is the work of a distinguished convert to Tibetan Buddhism.

Rationalization and Intellectualization

Kublin affirmed Zen's rationalization on negative grounds, such as its "rejecting scriptures" and "scorning rituals" and on positive grounds, for the "perceptive powers" it requires for interpreting the Zen koāns and for the fact that it has "attracted intellectuals and artists" (761). Zen went so far intellectually, wrote Kublin, as to stir "the suspicion and even opposition of the more popular Buddhist sects" (761). Even Trungpa acknowledged "that the utmost essence of Zen, [...] the principle of prajna [, ...] is a state of mind in which we have complete clarity, complete certainty" (80). Kapleau affirmed that Zen Buddhism is "a rational religion" and that it is an "entirely erroneous notion that Zen is alien or 'mystical'" (59, 85). It is engendered by personal doubt, which "implies not skepticism but a state of perplexity, of probing inquiry, of intense self-questioning" (59n). Zen meditation quickly becomes intellectually demanding, Aitken explained: "we begin with breath counting and then, if appropriate, go on to *koān* study" (58). The pedagogic statements or questions called *koāns*, such as,

Do "dogs have the Buddha-nature?", "What is the sound of one hand clapping?" and "slay the Buddha should you meet him" are "so phrased that they deliberately throw sand into our eyes to force us to open our Mind's eye and see the world and everything in it without distortion (Kapleau 63, 65, 64, 81). Ranging "over the vast area of Mahayana teachings," the *koāns* "compel us, in ingenious and often dramatic fashion, to learn these doctrines not simply with our head but with our whole being" (Kapleau 64, 65). The rigorous attitude of Zen toward intellect is exemplified by its skepticism of "mysterious visions" (*makyo* in Japanese), which "are spontaneous and cannot be summoned up" (46). Aitken told students to "please be careful" of *makyo* and "do not try to cultivate them," and when "they do occur, let them go as you would any other delusion (46). For Aitken, the traditional Buddhist aspiration of gaining enlightenment through the accumulation of good *karma* over multiple lifetimes was irrational; he dismissed the believer in *karmic* punishments and in rewards as "some kind of automaton" and explained that in Zen, "everything is enlightened from the beginning" (70, 76).

The essence of Tibetan Buddhism, Thurman asserted, is the "total awareness" gained by the Buddha during his enlightenment "of everything— hence by definition inconceivable, incomprehensible to finite, ignorant, egocentric consciousness" (9). Such awareness, Evans-Wentz explained "cannot be intellectually realized because it is beyond intellect" (*Liberation* 5). It is an "evolutionary process" (*Liberation* 6), likely to take myriads of lifetimes before the aspirant has the "first faint glimpses of the state of mind unmodified by thought processes. In the Occident this ecstatic condition is known as Illumination" (*Doctrines* 132n). The Tibetan lamas "maintain that, while mere goodness and book knowledge are desirable in devotees seeking Liberation, spiritual wisdom coupled with unshakeable faith, and the setting aside of all intellectualisms, are indispensible" (*Dead* 135n).

Optimization

Kublin recognized that Zen's "capacity to sharpen" perceptive powers conveyed the fine-tuning attribute of optimization (761). Aitken used the imagery of modern quantitative optimization when he spoke of Zen Buddhism as "one path among many" that "lead to the top of the same mountain" (13). The path of Zen, he explained, is called *zazen*, meaning seated meditation, which is the only way to success in Zen. The many variables in *zazen* include positioning of the legs, arms, hands, head and eyelids, floor cushioning, breathing algorithms, session scheduling, responsiveness to monitoring, and various thought exercises. Presumably there is for each Zen Buddhist some fine-tunable, optimal combination of all of these variables that will eventually bring the adept to the "top of the mountain."

Likewise, Herrigel's *Zen in the Art of Archery* read like exercises in optimization. Because it is easier to define success in mastering archery than success in mastering Zen, it is useful that the skills needed for success in archery—positioning the body, rhythmic breathing, pacing, responsiveness to the teacher, and concentration—correspond to those needed in *zazen*. If one develops these skills, he or she will attain success in archery and, in the process, in Zen as well. "So understood," wrote Herrigel, "the art of archery is rather like a preparatory school for Zen, for it enables the beginner to gain a clearer view, through work of his own hands, of events which are not in themselves intelligible" (12). The *zazen* thought-processes are often *koān*-like; in this case, "one knows [Zen] by not knowing it," that is, by knowing archery instead (7). Finding the optimal path to the top of the mountain is the consequence of "a profound and far-reaching contest of the archer with himself" (74).

Tibetan anti-optimization is evident in Evans-Wentz's edition of the biography of Tibet's 11th century Buddhist, Milarepa, who famously "came to the conclusion that there was no permanent benefit to be obtained in any state of *sangsaric* [worldly] existence" and decided to:

> go away to the Dragkar-Taso Cave and there pass my whole time in constant meditation. I determined to sit there night and day, till death should put an end to my life. I vowed that if any thought of worldly ambition should allure me, I would commit suicide rather than allow myself to be overcome by it. (*Tibet's Great* 175)

In his sole focus on meditation, Milarepa lived "on nettle broth alone," had "no clothes on the outside" of his body, which "became shrunken to a mere skeleton [. . .] greenish in hue, just like the nettles" (196). Having given "up all worldly aims and prospects" and spent most of his "life in meditation," Milarepa attained enlightenment at his death as he "sank in a trance into the Clear Light" (213, 286). This kind of optimization, if it can even be called that, is based not on fine-tuning but on sacrificial renunciation. Trungpa saw room in Tibetan Buddhism for "a sophistication of intelligence," but it had to be raised to the "point of limitlessness," at which "point, ordinary logical conclusions and logical debates become meaningless," which is as contrary to the process of optimization as it is to rationalization (Trungpa 78).

Secularization

Kublin wrote of Zen's "disdain" for "the worship of deities" (761). Whereas, the "Christian and the Jew put faith in God in this lonely place," Aitken contended, "Zen students feel even more alone and must plod along with trust in the *zazen* process," that is, in meditation and *koān* study (51). Kapleau wrote that the famous *koān*, "Slay the Buddha should you meet him," is the Zen way of emotionally and intellectually "ridding oneself of the idea that Shakyamuni Buddha is God or a super-being" (212n). Although pictures of the meditating Buddha are common in Zen meeting halls, Aitken acknowledged that some practitioners see them as "a threat to their rational spirit" (35). Kapleau insisted that "Zen is the only teaching which is not to one degree or another tainted with elements of the supernatural—thus Zen alone can truly be called the supreme teaching" (78).

In his description of Tibetan anti-secularization, Thurman took a middle road when he acknowledged that:

> While the Buddha did, on numerous occasions, calmly mention His attainment of Godlike omniscience, He [...] does not mean that He disbelieved the existence of gods–the Buddha was not an atheist. [...] He found them to be just as real as any other living beings. He simply discovered that no one of them had created the universe, no one of them possessed the key to salvation or liberation, no one of them had attained omniscient awareness. (Thurman 10)

At first there appears to be a contradiction here, but Thurman goes on to explain that these other gods "all needed the teachings of perfected Buddhas who have evolved the omniscient awareness of enlightenment. Among a Buddha's most important names are God Beyond Gods and teacher of Gods and Humans" (10). Previously, Evans-Wentz explained that some saints, having attained enlightenment, renounce Nirvana for themselves "and continue to reincarnate in order that their Divine Wisdom and Experience shall not be lost to the world, but employed to the divine end of leading all unenlightened beings to the same State of Emancipation" (*Doctrines* 95n). The most revered of these saints called *bodhisattvas* is Avalokiteshvara, who "is often depicted with eleven heads and a thousand arms, each with an eye in the palm [. . .] appropriately representing him as ever on the lookout to discover distress and to succor the troubled" (*the Dead* 113n). The famous mantra, *Om Mani Padme Hum*, is intoned by Tibetan Buddhists to summon Avalokiteshvara. (134n). The reverent intonation of this mantra, typically repeated 108 times in succession in Tibetan prayer services, conveys the deep spirituality and anti-secularity that pervades Tibetan Buddhism.

Utopian Progress

Kublin wrote of Zen's confidence that its "simplicity of technique" would overcome this world's "sense of insecurity" (761). Although the course of "*zazen* is a zigzag path," Aitken assured his students: "You can be confident that you are ripening all the while" (52). He added that Zen holds to its faith that "this very world of gain and loss, birth and death, cause and effect" is "the essential world of perfection" (63).

The "ancient teachings underlying all Tantric Schools," according to Evans-Wentz, held "that good and evil are inseparably one; that good cannot be conceived apart from evil; [and] that there is neither good *per se* nor evil *per se*" (*Liberation* 37). "So long as men are held in the bondages of appearances," he goes on to say, "so long will they use such terms as moral and immoral, right and wrong, good and evil, and enact laws to preserve virtue and to destroy vice" (38-39). The utopian moral progress that modernity anticipated can hardly be defined if good and evil are inseparably one. The closest that Tibetan Buddhism comes to utopia is "emptiness" (Fremantle and Trungpa xvi).

The Preference of Postmodern Writers for Tibetan Buddhism

Such novels as Pynchon's *Crying of Lot 49*, DeLillo's *Great Jones Street*, Kotzwinkle's *Fan Man*, Hawkes' *Passion Artist* and Gaddis's *Carpenter's Gothic* reveal their authors' attraction to the attributes of Tibetan Buddhism. Although one can find anti-rationalism, anti-optimization, anti-secularization and anti-utopianism in all five novels, some of the most representative examples are as follows:

Anti-rationalism is exemplified in Tibetan Buddhism by *bardo* rebirth, which, as noted above, Zen Buddhism summarily dismisses. The *bardo* is so irrational for western readers that in the 45 years since *The Crying of Lot 49* was published, it has never occurred to critics that Pierce Inverarity appears to have planned for Metzger's seduction of Oedipa within 49 days after his death, so that his *prahna* (consciousness) could be at the scene to enter her womb at the time of conception and become the soul of the child who would inherit the vast fortune he had left in trust to Oedipa. If so, it was this *prahna* that "slipped through and Inverarity by that much beaten death" (*Crying* 179; see also Kohn *Seven* 78-80). This reinforces Brian McHale's "claim of affinity between postmodern fiction and the fantastic" as well as its being "*about* death in a way that other writing, of other periods is not" (74, 231). The 49-day intermediate stage between death and rebirth parallels the "excluded middle" between zero and one in *The Crying of Lot 49*, zero being "only death and the daily, tedious preparations for it" and one, the "accommodation reached, in some kind of dignity, with the Angel of Death" (*Crying* 181, 182). How better to explain Oedipa's hints that Inverarity had "tried to survive death" and that a "plot [had] finally been devised too elaborate for the dark Angel to hold at once, in his humorless vice-president's head, all the possibilities of" (179)? With his extensive knowledge of mathematics, Pynchon would certainly have realized that this third possibility between zero and one, that mathematicians call a T-R-I-T instead of a "bit," when combined with E-R-O-S yields an intriguing anagram for the novel's mysteriously named T-R-I-S-T-E-R-O. Pynchon's arcane description of the profile of Clerk Maxwell with the "curious bump at the back of his head, covered by curling hair" may also relate to the Tibetan *bardo* (*Crying* 106). Evans-Wentz refers to the "Aperture of Brahma," from which the Tibetan lama pulls out a few hairs during the after-death ceremony to determine whether the deceased's spirit has departed thence (*Dead* 18).

The Passion Artist by Hawkes continues the anti-rational imagery of the *bardo*. Just as the novel's protagonist, Conrad Vost, "would discover complete illumination in blinding light" (69), so the Fremantle and Trungpa translation of *The Tibetan Book of the Dead* refers to the "dazzling white, luminous" light "that your eyes cannot bear to look at" (43). As Vost is "led like an animal on a length of rope [. . .] tied to his neck" (Hawkes 121, 122), so "the Lord of Death will drag you by a rope tied round your neck" (Fremantle 77). Fremantle and Trungpa's translation came out four years before *The Passion Artist* was completed, in time for Hawkes to have read it before publishing *The Passion Artist*. Margo Anand, already famous for her books on the art of passion, knew Trungpa and appears to have interested Hawkes in Tantric Buddhism and perhaps to have recommended Trungpa and Freemantle's *Tibetan Book of the Dead* to him (Kohn *Merging of Tantric* 160-62).

The example of Tibetan Buddhist anti-optimization given earlier is that of Milarepa's renunciation of worldly rewards. DeLillo's *Great Jones Street* can be taken as a modernized parody of the life of that self-punishing saintly seeker. Bucky Wunderlick, the protagonist of the novel, abandons his successful career as "a hero of rock'n'roll" to hole up in a "room in Great Jones Street," where the "refrigerator was unplugged," the water taps drew only "an intermittent trickle" and rags "had been stuffed into places where the window frame was warped and cold air entered" (1, 5). "Least is best" is the anti-optimization algorithm that Bucky adopts, to "become the least of what I was" (5, 87). Just as Milarepa, emaciated and greenish, survived on nettle broth, Bucky, also "a morbid sight," had "soup to eat when the old stove worked" (*Great* 8, 25). Each was demeaned by his closest woman companion, each used his musical talent as a lethal weapon, both attracted disciples from great distances, and both willingly assented to take poison, from which they both recovered (Kohn *Parody, Heteroglossia* 207-09). Just as Milarepa set an example by attaining enlightenment in a single lifetime, so the novel concludes with the self-negating Bucky "living among beggars and syphilitics, performing good works, patron saint of all those men who hear the river-whistles sing the mysteries and who return to sleep in wine by the south wheel of the city" (265). The final words evoke Evans-Wentz's description of the "countless multitude of sentient beings, for whose sake, he [Milarepa] continued setting the peerless Wheel of the Truth in motion, thereby redeeming them from the unutterable anguish and woe of [. . .] the City" (*Milarepa* 39). If there is any doubt about DeLillo's fascination with Tibetan Buddhism, it is confirmed by the stanza from Bucky's "American War Sutra," that enigmatically reads "East the vanished mountains / West the barren fields / Soccer-playing bodhisattvas / Flowing through the grass" (*Great* 97, 98, 99).

Although it is a comic novel, anti-secularization is pervasive in the emanation of Tibetan deities in Kotzwinkle's *The Fan Man*. The protagonist's first name "Horse" connotes the deity Hayagriva, which is Tibetan for the "Horse-Necked One," while his last name "Badorties," by the shift of one letter, rearranges to "*Bardo* ties," which allude to Horse's enumerable rebirths (Kohn *Ambivalence in Kotzwinkle's* 123). His "fifty fingers, all over the strings" denote his five sets of divine arms (124). Among the other deities represented in Kotzwinkle's novel are Padmasambhava (Hayagriva is Padmasambhava's wrathful emanation) and Avalokiteshvara, the compassionate *bodhisattva* who is summoned by the famous mantra, *Om Mani Padme Hum*, which is signified in *The Fan Man* by the hundreds of idiosyncratic repetitions of the hippie appellation, "man." One senses the presence of the golden, eleven-headed Avalokiteshvara waving his thousand arms when Horse steps "out of the subway car," climbs "[u]p the subway steps, man " and sees where he is: "I am on Brooklyn Heights, man, there is the sea below. A wild wind is blowing and the sun is dropping toward the ocean. The water is gold and the tugboat goes through the gold. I am with you again on the Heights, man" (117). Near the end of the novel, we have the sense that Horse himself is Avalokiteshvara, and that the newly enlightened saxophone player, Frank, having directed the Love Concert in Tompkins Square, feels himself, "risin up through the trees, man, out over the park and I am flappin my wings, man, takin off into the sky, lookin for Horse, man, where are you, man? If Frank has not yet attained enlightenment he has at least become a yogin (187).

Tibetan Buddhist anti-utopianism is signified by the Tibetan duality of good and evil in Gaddis's *Carpenter's Gothic*. The evil characters in this novel have redeeming qualities, and the good characters have their dark side. This blurring of good and evil is a textbook example of what McHale calls "postmodernist allegory" in which a "series of polar opposites proves to contain elements or traces of its opposed term" (142, 144). Whereas the traditional Manichaean allegory goes back to Prudentius's 4th century *Psychomachia* that famously "pitted personified Good against personified Evil," the "polar opposites" of the postmodern version are "allowed to 'bleed' into one another" (McHale 142, 144). The character in the novel most representative of Gaddis is McCandless; a reader can perceive him as either exploitative or as self-sacrificial. Nowhere else do Tibetan Buddhism and postmodernist fiction come together so nicely as in the correspondence of the duality of good and evil in the former with postmodernist Manichaean allegory in the latter (Kohn *Buddhist Duality* 423-24; Kohn *Postmodernist Manichaean Allegory*).

The Slighting of Zen by Postmodern Writers

After mentioning to DeLillo that there "are references to Zen in most of your books," Thomas LeClair asked him: "Would you consider it an influence on your work?" (26). "I may have used the word several times," DeLillo replied, "but I think only in *Americana* is there any kind of extended reference and it has more to do with people playing at Eastern religion than anything else. I know very little about Zen" (Le Clair 26). The notion of "playing" at Eastern religion" is something of a slight. Surely the narrator's comments in *Americana* on the Zen master's "messageless message," the mind being "an empty box within an empty box," and seeing "the stone as other stones see it" are sarcastic (184, 185). For a contrasting, enthusiastically affirmative interpretation of Zen in *Americana*, see Benjamin Bird (191-192, 198).

DeLillo's remarks in *Great Jones Street* (16, 59, 17, 169, 192) about the "Happy Valley Farm Commune" having "two distinct factions," the eagerness of its emissary, Skippy, to please Bucky—"I can come back later if you want. Whatever you want, Bucky, I can bring my friend Maeve. Or I can come all by myself. Or I can just send Maeve"–Happy Valley's "leadership is not to be trusted" and its "life-style of privacy, isolation and so forth has spawned [an] outbreak in half its members" suggest that the fictional Happy Valley Farm Commune is a New York displacement of the San Francisco Zen Center's Green Gulch Farm, where reports of a sex scandal involving the director of the Center were becoming known when the novel was written. While the setting of the novel is New York City rather than San Francisco, DeLillo appears to have taken that into account when Skippy "seemed confused, apparently thinking this was San Francisco" (*Great* 260). The sex scandal at the San Francisco Zen Center is thoroughly documented in a book on the subject by Michael Downing and to a lesser extent by Rick Fields (362-64). Given the ill-will raised by this scandal, DeLillo's reference in *Great Jones Street* to "childish Zenlike spite" is an intentional slur (222).

Pynchon's latest novel, *Against the Day*, contains a large number of respectful references to Tibetan Buddhism. In contrast, the references to Zen in this same novel tend to be whimsical. Zen *koāns* are dismissed as "unsolvable riddles" (*Against* 783), and a dog named Pugnax confounds "a Zennist monastery, by answering the classic *koān*, 'Does a dog possess the Buddha-nature?' not with 'Mu!' but with "Yes, obviously—was there anything else?'" (412). Because *all* sentient creatures, *by definition*, have the Buddha-nature. "*Mu*" properly registers the wise student's disapprobation at being asked such a patronizing question. However, Pugnax being a dog feels entitled to give the naive answer that would elicit a rebuke if he were human. Lew Basnight, the detective, remembers being struck "repeatedly with a 'remembrance stick,'" prompting him to continue "to perform chores assigned him" (*Against* 40). In a later scene, Kit Traverse reacts "'Hey! What are you—You just *hit* me with, with that stick?'" and is told that this was an "ancient technique, borrowed from the Zennists of Japan" (624). This "flat, narrow stick," called a *kyosaku*, explains Aitken, was carried by monitors during periods of *zazen* (meditation) and "used to awaken students who [were] asleep and to punish others for wandering thoughts" (37).

Like those in *Against the Day*, the Zen references in Hawkes' *The Passion Artist* also tend to be whimsical. In the darkness Vost imagines that he sees "a dog emerging from an egg, a dancing man with the face of a pig, and a solitary pilgrim with the head of a fox" (176). The dog emerging from an egg connotes the Fu dogs, mythical flat-faced, lion-like dogs often portrayed in pairs guarding the Buddha. In her book, *The Lion-Dog of Buddhist Asia*, Elsie Mitchell includes an illustration of a mid-nineteenth-century Japanese netsuke Fu dog "being born from an egg," its "head and front paws [. . .] emerging from the broken shell" (12, 95, 172, 173). After taking instructions in Zen practice in the 1950s, Mitchell also wrote *The Way of Zen*, which went to several editions (Fields 207, 208). Hawkes' references to a "man with the face of a pig" and the "solitary pilgrim" suggest "Pigsy," the Zen Buddhist pilgrim with "short bristles on his swarthy cheeks, a long snout, and huge ears," who is one of the comic pilgrims in Wu Ch'eng-en's medieval novel *Monkey,* who travel to India to receive from the Buddha the ancient scriptures known as the *Tripitaka* (173).

Concluding Remarks

This essay builds on Huyssen's interpretation of postmodernism, Jameson's corresponding nomenclature, and on my hypotheses that Zen Buddhism is complementary with modernism, that Tibetan Buddhism is complementary with Postmodernism, and that Pynchon, DeLillo, Kotzwinkle, Hawkes, and Gaddis reflected the corresponding anticomplementarity and complementarity in selected postmodern novels. This is the kind of opening up of literature to an historical sense of "what has been" and "what is now" that Pankaj Mishra called for in his contribution to the 2011 *New York Times Book Review* sextet (10). That other postmodern writers as well as Pynchon had similar, contradictory reactions to Zen and Tibetan Buddhism illustrates why, in the same *Times* sextet, Batuman argued that, at least in some cases, the "role of the critic is then less to exhaustively explain any single work than to identify, in a group of works, a reflection of some conditional aspect of reality" (11).

Whether Zen was or is modernistic in the sense of dedication to intellectualism, rationalization, optimization, secularization , and utopian progress as compared to the way in which Postmodernism was not, is not as important for me as whether this differentiation of tendencies helps to explain why postmodernism repudiated modernism. The dominant weltanschauung of modernism was its exaltation of science and technology, which in turn stimulated intellectual values, encouraged optimization, engendered secularization , and fostered expectations of utopian progress. With postmodernism came skepticism of science and technology and the slaking of ebullient expectations. This tie to science and technology is only one interpretation of the postmodern turn; it's special advantage for me is that it predicts a sequel to postmodern, that Paul Virilio famously called hypermodernism, which is the outright fear of what science and technology may have in store. Hassan anticipated that next turn when he acknowledged:

> I am possessed by the feeling that in the next few decades, certainly within half a century, the earth and all that inhabits it may be wholly other, perhaps ravaged, perhaps on the way to some strange utopia indistinguishable from nightmare. I have no language to articulate this feeling with conviction, nor imagination to conceive this special destiny. (*POSTmodernISM* 22)

Essay Ten

Paul Virilio's Hypermodernism and Jerry Wilkerson's Pointillism

They return to Earth–unless it is to Counter-Earth–with a form of *mnemonic frostbite*, retaining only awed impressions of a ship exceeding the usual three dimensions, docking, each time precariously, at a series or remote stations high in unmeasured outer space, which together form a road to a destination–both ship and dockage hurtling at speeds that no one wishes to imagine, invisible sources of gravity rolling through like storms, making it possible to fall for distances only astronomers are comfortable with–yet, each time, the *Inconvenience* is brought to safety, in the bright, flowerlike heart of a perfect hyper-hyperboloid that only Miles can see in its entirety. (*Against the Day* 1084-85)

The cultural sequel to postmodernism, which Paul Virilio called "hypermodernism" (See John Armitage), surfaces in *Against the Day*. Pynchon appears to be signifying the term in the penultimate paragraph of the novel with a series of metaphorical scientific extremes followed by the reference to a "perfect hyper-hyperboloid" (*Against* 1085). As an ethos, hypermodernism is a pejorative description of science and technology in a world which has come to fear them. Just as modernism was associated with the exaltation of science and technology, and postmodernism with skepticism toward science and technology, so hypermodernism, the third phase of modernization, is associated with fearfulness of science and technology. Pynchon covers all three phases of modernization in *Against the Day*. The novel opens in 1893 at the World's Columbian Exposition in Chicago, where modernism in America is said to have begun. It featured "the fabled 'White City,' [with its] alabaster temples of commerce and industry, sparkling lagoons, and the thousand more such wonders, of both a scientific and an artistic nature" (*Against* 3). Andrea Tancredi, the fictional painter in *Against the Day*, who "sympathized with Marinetti and those around him who were beginning to describe themselves as 'Futurists,'" marks the beginning of Italian modernism in the novel (*Against* 584). According to H.H. Arnason, Futurism began in 1908

> as a rebellion of young intellectuals against the cultural torpor into which Italy had sunk during the nineteenth century; and, as so frequently happens in such movements, its manifestations were initially intent on what they had to destroy. The first manifesto demanded the destruction of the libraries, the museums, the academies, and the cities of the past that were themselves mausoleums. It extolled the beauties of revolution, of war, of the speed and dynamism of modern technology. (212)

It is consistent with Marinetti's first manifesto that Tancredi wanted to tear Venice "down, and use the rubble to fill in those canals" (*Against* 585). Tancredi's artist friend Hunter Penhallow's "chill, comfortless faith in science and rationality" presaged the turning point from modernist utopianism to postmodernism's repudiation of it, while Tancredi's "palette of fire and explosion," signaling "Hell in a small bounded space," evokes the later hypermodernism and the fears to which it would give rise (*Against* 585, 586). Whereas, the Futurists with whom Tancredi associated extolled the beauties of the speed and dynamism of modern technology, it was the more extreme versions of that technology that Virilio would fear a century later.

Jerry O. Wilkerson's artistic style builds on the pointillism that the Futurists loved and that Virilio wrote about. While Wilkerson's technique seems reminiscent of the late 19th century work of Georges Seurat, "his pointillism was much more influenced by the technology of the print industry where the size and intensity of dots of color increased or lessened the intensity of an image" (David Suwalsky 3). Accordingly, Wilkerson provides a bridge between modernist pointillism and hypermodern pointillism, which Pynchon may have had in mind when he described Tancredi's "Preliminary Studies Toward an Infernal Machine" (*Against* 585). Suwalsky's insinuation that Wilkerson's dots are relatively un-uniform in size compared to those of the French pointillists may be especially significant for the present essay because, as will be noted below, Pynchon emphasized that Tancredi "stabb[ed] tiny dots among larger ones" (587).

Hypermodernism and Fear

The fear that made Virilio famous is based on his predictions of the potentially ruinous consequences of hypermodern science and technology. Some of these consequences may seem or actually be far-fetched, but they are at least intellectually conceived. They differ greatly from fears of science and technology that are otherwise irrational. "Anti-intellectualism has a long history" among religious fundamentalists, wrote Nancy Schaefer, many of whom "feared that society's increased dependence on technology" and the globalization accelerated by it "might usher in worldwide domination by the Antichrist" (93, 98). Felicia Wu Song described a "significant shift [...] to *fatalist* ideologies of Progress," in which "the organizational and personal experience of technological adoption and use has often been driven by a fear of being left behind" (41-42). In his public lectures, physicist Lawrence Krauss attributes the widespread rejection of evolutionary biology and the dismissal of scientific evidence for global warming to the irrational fear of science and technology, rooted in religious and economic fundamentalism. When "[t]elevangelists such as Jerry Falwell and Pat Robertson, among other evangelical elites, warned that the Y2K computer problem was a likely omen that foreshadowed impending disaster," they triggered "pre-exiting fears about computer technology (Schaefer 82, 98).

The intellectual fear of science and technology burst on America in 1970 when Alvin Toffler warned of "future shock" from "the shattering stress and disorientation that we induce in individuals by subjecting them to too much change in too short a time" (4). When computerization had become widespread, Franco Berardi reasoned that "the insertion of the electronic into the organic, the proliferation of artificial devices in the organic universe" and the "digitization of communication processes" is causing "a mutation of the conscious organism" which we read "through the categories of psychopathology: dyslexia, anxiety and apathy, panic, depression and a sort of epidemic of suicide" (*(T)error* 42). Virilio's long sustained "perception of technology [...] is largely," he himself acknowledged, "catastrophic" (Armitage 26). A recent metaphor for hypermodern anxiety, though for a small minority of scholars, has been the expansive Hadron Collider in Switzerland, that will accelerate protons to energies of seven trillion volts and smash them together, generating temperatures a hundred-thousand-times hotter than the center of the sun and simulating for a split second, in a space a billion times smaller than a speck of dust, the forces and particles created during the first second of the birth of the universe known as the Big Bang. Among the debris thrown off by the collisions, scientists hope to find the elusive Higgs-Boson, which gives particles their mass, and a graviton, which, if it disappears into another dimension, would support the arcane assumptions of "String Theory." While most scientists believe that the collider will not be producing anything more dangerous than routine cosmic rays, some fear that the terrible forces will create a black hole that will swallow the earth. In Europe and America, they urgently sought court injunctions to shut down the experiment (Richard Gray). Their fears evoked Virilio's dread of an "integral accident" and the consequent "total destruction of the world" (Armitage 36-37).

Not everyone in the age of modernism carried his or her admiration for science and technology to utopian extremes; not everyone in the postmodern interval reacted to that utopianism with the "incredulity" that Jean-François Lyotard registered (xxiv), and not everyone in the age of hypermodernism fears calamitous consequences from "*extreme sciences*" and technologies as Virilio (*Art & Fear* 51) and Berardi do. But this cycle of exaggerated emotions instilled by science and technology—adoration, skepticism, then terror—put its stamp on cultural history in the late 20th and early 21st centuries. "Without endorsing some general view that a 'culture of fear' has become a general condition of contemporary societies" David Lyon argues "that fear, in a multiplicity of manifestations, has risen to a prominent position on the cultural radar" (82). It is relevant that the issue of *The Hedgehog Review* that contains Lyon's article is entitled "Fear Itself" and that its cover illustration shows six terrified faces, in the pointillist cartoon style of Roy Lichtenstein that Wilkerson emulated. It speaks to the climate of apprehensiveness that Berardi called this, not once but twice, "the century with no future" (*(T)error* 39, 43). He made that more explicit a decade later, in 2009, when he warned readers of "the final collapse of the global economy which is now unfolding under the eyes of an astonished mankind [, …] the final collapse of a system that has lasted five hundred years" (*Soul at Work* 210). "Chaos (*i.e.* a degree of complexity which is beyond the ability of human understanding) now rules the world [; …] the speed and complexity of the surrounding flow of information exceed the ability of the social brain to decode and predict" (*Soul at Work* 212, 217). This extreme complexity is characterized in a musical composition by Luciano Berio (See Goldford *et al. Berio's* Sinfonia) and in an art video "Liquid Crystal" by Van McElwee (Search < "Liquid Crystal" and "Van McElwee" > on the internet).   Many of the effects in McElwee's video conform to the insights of Virilio and Berardi (See Kohn *Motorization of Video Art*).

Virilio has written over twenty-five books since 1977 and four books have been written about him by other scholars in the last decade; he has achieved a significant following, and it is likely that Pynchon has read some of his books. In addition to the few arcane parallels between his 1984 *Negative Horizon* and *The Crying of Lot 49* that were noted in the introductory section of this book, there are more parallels between his later works, starting with *The Vision Machine,* which was originally published (in French) in 1988, and Pynchon's 2006 *Against the Day.* One of the leading themes, "bilocation," in *Against the Day* can be traced back to Virilio. Bilocation, "which enables those with the gift literally to be in two or more places, often widely separated, at the same time" (*Against* 143), may have been suggested by Virilio's arcane reference to "leav[ing] one's body, to become one's own double" (*Art of the Motor* 28). The shadowed doubling of the title on the cover of Virilio's *Art of the Motor* may have sparked Pynchon's interest in Iceland spar and inspired the corresponding shadowing of the print on the dust jacket of *Against the Day.* William Logan's insightful hypothesis that "Pynchon writes neither counterfactual history nor historical fiction" (227) in *Against the Day,* allows Pynchon to fabricate all kinds of historical falsehoods that trick the reader into believing they are factual (see Kohn *Pynchon Takes the Fork* 174-75). Consider the following example in which Viridian explains to her husband, Chick Counterfly, how the wives' airship flies on Æther waves. Like Virilio, Viridian thinks in terms of space-time: "The Æther," she

> explained, "like the atmosphere around a skyship, may produce lift and drag on the Earth as it moves through space. As long ago as the Michelson-Morley Experiment there's been speculation about a boundary layer."
> "Which the planet's irregular surface" Chick began to see then, "mountains and so forth, creates vortices to keep from separating—"
> "And we also know that its thickness is proportional to kinematic viscosity, expressed as area per second—making Time inversely proportional to viscosity, and so to the boundary-layer thickness as well."
> "But the viscosity of the Æther, like its density must be negligible. Meaning a very thin boundary layer, accompanied by a considerable dilation of Time." (*Against* 1031)

Not understanding this technical exchange, I sent Dr. John Stachel—Founding Editor of the *Collected Papers of Albert Einstein* (as well as my daughter-in-law's father), who has worked extensively on general relativity and the foundations of quantum mechanics—a copy of the above conversation between Viridian and her husband Chick for his assessment. His email reply to me was as follows:

> Pynchon's conversation is a mixture of sense and nonsense. The failure of the M-M experiment to detect the expected motion of the earth with respect to the ether did lead to a revival of earlier speculative theories, according to which the earth dragged along a layer of ether surrounding it, so that there was no relative motion to detect. But the rest of the conversation seems to be gobbledegook, using a lot of scientific terms in a nonsensical mixture. (Email, January 2, 2010)

The historical reference to Michelson-Morley in the first two sentences above is apparently accurate—Pynchon never writes counterfactual history—but taken in the context of the second exchange between the couple, which is gobbledegook, it becomes tainted—this demonstrates that Pynchon never writes historical fiction, though in this case it took an Einsteinian physicist to convince me that it was a hoax.

Pynchon's interest in a person being two people at once and in tricking readers into believing that something false is true and *vice versa* may have something to do with Virilio's observation that the process of "strategically concealing information by a process of disinformation" (*Vision Machine* 66), is "part of the stage show of a regime of perverted temporality, where TRUE and FALSE are no longer relevant. The actual and the virtual have gradually taken their place" (68). This obliteration of truth is the second major theme in *Against the Day* that coincides with an idea of Virilio. A third reason for Pynchon's interest in Virilio may have been that the latter's books were spearheading a possible sequel to the postmodern ethos, of which he had become emblematic. In the three following sections of this essay, a position taken by Virilio is first stated, then filtered through one or two artworks by Wilkerson, and finally responded to through the art and persona of the fictional Tancredi and other of Pynchon's characters in *Against the Day*.

Wilkerson and Pointillism

Inspired by the strong interest in modern art that he developed at Cornell, Pynchon could have made periodic visits to Manhattan art galleries, on the watch for new directions in aesthetic media that might carry over into literature. If any one artist symbolized the hypermodern ethos for Pynchon, it might have been Jerry O. Wilkerson (1943-2007), whose paintings he would have encountered at the OK Harris Gallery in SOHO. Its owner, Ivan Karp, who had been instrumental in launching the careers of Andy Warhol, Roy Lichtenstein and Robert Rauschenberg, always had a selection of Wilkerson's paintings on the premises. It has already been noted that Wilkerson's forte was pointillism, as was that of Pynchon's fictional artist Andrea Tancredi in *Against the Day*. Pointillism connects to hypermodernism when Virilio observes that "the decomposition of figures in Pointillism or Divisionism leads today, thanks to fractal geometry, to another type of deconstruction: the dismantling of the space-time of the work" (*Information Bomb* 130). "Contamination has in fact spread," writes an apprehensive Virilio, "as far as the space-time of our planet" (*Open Sky* 22). "Pretty much like in a pointillism masterpiece of say Georges Seurat or Paul Signac," explains physicist M.S. El Naschie, "quantum space-time, which is in reality a collection of [a] transfinite discrete set of points, appears [...] to be a nowhere disjoined continuum" when observed from a distance (1377). This one sentence of El Naschie links Pynchon's interest in science and art, Virilio's premonitions about hypermodernism, and Wilkerson's pointillism.

Wilkerson's death in 2007 inspired a major retrospective of his work at the St. Louis University Museum of Art in 2008. In a brochure prepared for the exhibition, art scholar Carlo Lamagna noted that Wilkerson applied "separate strokes of bright color, slightly overlapping or placed in close proximity, that made the viewer's eye do the work of pulling the image together" (12). In her article in the brochure, Petruta Lipan, the Museum's curator, remarked that Wilkerson's artworks were "closer to the mechanically reproduced and mass produc[ed]" works described by Walter Benjamin "than to Seurat" (5). His commercial "felt-tip pens" and colors "the same as in commercial printing: magenta, yellow and blue" bring him close to the scope of hypermodern technology (5).

It is conceivable that Pynchon had Wilkerson in mind when he fleshed-out his early-twentieth century Italian painter, Andrea Tancredi, in *Against the Day*. By giving Tancredi the first name of "Andrea," which is unique in Italian for being gender neutral—in almost every case, the first names of Italian males end in either an o or an i—he provided a tie-in with "Jerry," which is a common gender-neutral first name in the U.S. This would not be unusual for Pynchon because his characters' names more often than not have extraneous significance. Most intriguingly, as noted earlier, one of the five wives of *Against the Day's* "Chums of Chance" is named "Viridian" (3, 1030). If "Virilio" were a word in *Webster's New Collegiate Dictionary (1980)*, it would follow only two entries after "Viridian," a chrome green color. Given Pynchon's fascination with the letter V, which goes back to his first novel, could his interest in a writer whose name begins with a V and an artist whose name begins with a double-V be more than coincidental?

After "having been to Paris and seen the works of Seurat and Signac, the fictional Tancredi had converted to Divisionism," which is the Italian equivalent of pointillism (*Against* 584). "[W]ith an impossibly narrow brush, no more than a bristle or two, stabbing tiny dots among larger ones," Tancredi defined the "smallest picture element, a dot of color which becomes the basic unit of reality" (586-87). Pynchon could be responding through Tancredi's imagery to Virilio's writing, as when the fictional painter explains that his art has "to do with Time"; that

> everything that we imagine is real, living and still, thought and hallucinated, is all on the way from being one thing to being another, [that] from past to Future, the challenge to us is to show as much of the passage as we can, given the *damnable stillness* of paint. (*Against* 586)

Because of Wilkerson's early experimentation with advanced printing technologies, because of his use of pointillism, which is a bridge between art and science, and because the themes of some of his paintings relate to themes that Virilio elaborates, Wilkerson's art could have characterized for Pynchon the transition from postmodern to hypermodern stylistics. In the following three sections of this essay, we compare the treatment of three themes by Virilio, Wilkerson and Pynchon.

Theme 1. The Information Bomb

Virilio's Obsession with the Information Bomb

Virilio sees "the atomic bomb" as the "weapon of the apocalypse," but believes that nuclear deterrence has spawned a more likely threat: "a technoscientific explosion," which has reached "the dimension of the integral accident" (Armitage 36):

> The metaphor of nuclear catastrophe and fallout is no longer a stylistic trope, but in the end an accurate enough image of the damage to human *activity* caused by this sudden implosion-explosion of computerized *interactivity* which Albert Einstein predicted in the 1950s would probably constitute a second bomb, after the purpose-built atomic one. (*Open Sky* 86)

Virilio's warnings of computerized interactivity are more explicit in his subsequent book, *The Information Bomb*:

> After the first bomb, the *atom bomb*, which was capable of using the energy of radioactivity to smash matter, the specter of a second bomb is looming at the end of this millennium. This is the information bomb, capable of using the interactivity of information to wreck the peace between nations. (*Information Bomb* 63)

This new bomb, which threatens the world with "an unutterable technical contamination" (39), is as easy to set off, using commercial bulk-mailing software, as "submerge[ing] a particular server in a veritable 'mail-bombing' campaign" (63). Whatever is launched "is then succeeded by the immaterial and electronic volume of information; acoustic and visual information, but also tactile information, through the virtual reality gauntlet, and olfactory information with the recent invention of digitized chemical sensors" (119). The threat that Virilio described in *The Information Bomb* now seems tame compared to the Stuxnet Worm that allegedly invaded Iran's nuclear facilities. "After the disasters of technocracy," wrote Virilio, are we going to go from the frying pan into the fire by yielding to the social cybernetics so dreaded by the inventors of automation? Are we going to cede the administration of life to inanimate but ultra-rapid devices which are capable of scaling the heights of technical progress? [...] In fact, with the acquisition of the *global speed* of telecommunications, as opposed to the *local speed* of our previous 'means of communication,' we are moving towards inertia, towards the sterility of movement. (*Information Bomb* 122)

By propounding the process of change in which the potential for catastrophe is just as bad, if not worse than what it bypassed, Virilio is posing the Hegelian "dialectical argument" that Pynchon may be alluding to in *Against the Day* (586, see below). Virilio is less fearful that civilization will be degraded or destroyed by nuclear weaponry than that it will be ultimately degraded by hyper-scientific developments in the offing. He believes that "information is indeed the third dimension of matter, after mass and energy" (*Information Bomb* 140). Whereas Toffler saw ways of ameliorating future shock from the beginning, and Berardi, in 2009, made a turnaround from his fear of digital technology when he realized that "high tech workers," instead of being alienated, now "tend to consider labor as the most essential part in their lives" (*Soul at Work* 76), Virilio sees no "future [for] twenty-first-century technoscience," only the "tendency to chaos" (*Art of the Motor* 71-72).

Wilkerson's Vision of the Atomic Bomb

Gail Wilkerson recalled for me how she and Jerry "hunted for the perfect blueberry" muffin six-pack in Schnuck's Markets, which he intended to use for "recreating Monet's" painting, "Haystacks at Chailly at Sunrise." A haystack and especially a muffin are a far cry from an atom bomb, but the pointillism in this giclee print (a high resolution image printed with professional 8- to 12-color inkjet printer) does suggest the mushroom shaped debris of an atomic explosion. A book review by William Broad, science writer for *The New York Times*, published in 1987 and entitled "The Men Who Made the Sun Rise," was about the making of the atom bomb. More than once, the explosion of an atomic bomb has been compared to the sunrise, a connection which Wilkerson may have had in mind when he entitled this print. Virilio's claim that the "metaphor of nuclear catastrophe and fallout is no longer a stylistic trope" was premature, for it appeared again recently in the painting *Pumpkin Cloud* by Wayne Thiebaud on the November 23, 2009 cover of the modish *New Yorker* magazine (*Open Sky* 86).

Figure 1. Jerry Wilkerson, "Sunrise" 2006, Giclee print, A/P,
6.5" x 5.25", Estate of Jerry O. Wilkerson.

Pynchon's Ambiguous Bomb

Part Three of *Against the Day*, entitled "Bilocations," includes two sections
of text, totaling a little more than three pages, in which Hunter Penhallow
introduces Dahlia (Dally) Rideout to artist Andrea Tancredi and subsequently
takes her to his studio. The narrator amplifies on the conversation there:

> Tancredi's paintings were like explosions. He favored the palette of fire
> and explosion. He worked quickly. *Preliminary Studies Toward an Infernal
> Machine.*
> 'It would actually work?' Dally wanted to know.
> 'Of course,' Tancredi a bit impatiently.
> 'He's a sort of infernal-machine specialist,' Hunter pointed out. But
> Tancredi showed a curious reluctance to speak of what the design might
> actually do. What chain of events could lead to the 'effect.' (*Against* 585,
> 586)

It is not clear from Pynchon's text whether the infernal machine is a painting or a
bomb. The reference to a chain suggests the atomic chain reaction, though the

149

year in the novel, approximately 1910, was 35 years before the first such reaction was set off.

'You're talking about an explosive device, *vero?*'

'Not in Venice, never. Fire would be suicidal insanity. I would not bring fire. But I would bring Hell in a small bounded space.'

'And ... that would be ...'

'[...] the finite space would rapidly expand. To reveal the Future, we must get around the inertia of paint. We desire transformation. So this is not so much a painting as a dialectical argument.' (*Against* 586)

The dialectical argument suggests the explosive flow of information that Virilio fears (*supra*), especially when Tancredi adds "Of course it's to do with Time" (586). "'It isn't Seurat,' it seemed to Hunter, 'none of that cool static calm, somehow you've got those dots behaving dynamically, violent ensembles of energy states, Brownian movement...'" (*Against* 587).

Theme 2. Telesexual Interactivity

Virilio's Telesexual Obsession

Extrapolating the "general speeding-up of phenomena in our hypermodern world" (*Fear and Art* 51), Virilio foresees "the demiurgic pretensions of a eugenics that no longer has any limits" (54). Earlier, he expressed his obsession that what

was till now still 'vital,' copulation, suddenly becomes optional, turning into the practice of remote-control masturbation. At a time when innovations are occurring in artificial fertilization and genetic engineering, they have actually managed also to interrupt coitus, to short-circuit conjugal relations between opposite sexes, with the aid of biocybernetic (teledildonic) accoutrements using sensor-effectors distributed over the genital organs. [...] In donning the DataSuit, *the individual slips into information*; his body is suddenly endowed with a second skin, with a muscle and nerve interface that fits over his own cutaneous layer. For him, for both of them, information becomes the sole 'relief' of corporeal reality, its unique 'volume'" (*Open Sky* 104, 105).

Virilio foresees not only "the *test tube baby* of in-vitro fertilization but in fact, and sooner than you think, *love experienced at a distance*, thanks to telesexual interactivity" (107). "*Sex no longer exists; it has been replaced by fear.* Fear of the other, of the dissimilar, has won out over sexual attraction. [...] Fear of catching AIDS or other fears, other, disavowable, terrors" (113). "[C]ybernetics will *virtually* achieve the 'metaphysics of love'—to the detriment of the species and its sexual reproduction" (115). "Thanks to the force-feedback control glove (DataGlove), and, especially to the DataSuit, *everything is ruled by lightning* (Virilio 117).

Wilkerson's Transmogrification of Sex

"One of the most significant features or practices in postmodernism today," wrote Fredric Jameson, "is pastiche" (113). Wilkerson's serigraph, *Starry Night with Banana*, is a pastiche of Van Gogh's *Starry Night*, in which the yellow awning hanging above the terrace of the Arles café in Van Gogh's *Café Terrace at Night* has becomes the yellow banana floating in the air or sitting on the frame of Wilkerson's serigraph. Although the conceptual model of modernism, postmodernism and hypermodernism used in this essay is an abstraction based on changing attitudes toward science and technology, the repudiation of modernity's utopianism generalizes to the repudiation of modernity's rationalistic metanarratives and, in the case of pastiche, its repudiation of modernism's cultural elitism that would have withheld Van Gogh's *Starry Night* from mass culture. The postmodern artist's strategy, to use the words of Virilio, was "to divine the pop potential of the masterworks of past art" (*Ground Zero* 58). The top of the banana in Figure 2 is "lit up like [the] birthday cake" in Tancredi's painting, and we can imagine the stars above as sparkling candlewicks (*Against* 586). This painting could have inspired the fictional one in *Against the Day*, when Tancredi, "[u]sing his thumb against a brushful of orpiment yellow, [...] aimed a controlled spatter of paint at his canvas, followed by another brushful of scarlet vermillion and a third of Nürnberg violet," causing the patch of canvas "to light up like a birthday cake" (586). Indeed, the front tip of Wilkerson's banana is Nürnberg violet; the flecks and upper-stem are scarlet vermilion; and the skin is orpiment yellow.

The starry night banana can be taken as a phallic symbol. This is confirmed by another painting of two fortune cookies, which is reproduced in Figure 3. One of them, set in the same pose as the banana in Figure 2, shows the opening slit of the upper cookie which is couched within the lower cookie, whose arch-shaped bottom clasps the first cookie where it begins its upward rise. The warmth and eroticism of this painting are sadly missing in the telesexuality that Virilio foresees. (For a cooler, less subtle eroticism, see Pablo Picasso's 1944 still life, "The Coffee Pot," owned by the San Francisco Museum of Modern Art, which is displayed on a number of image-only websites.)

Figure 2. Jerry O. Wilkerson, *Starry Night with Banana* 1991, serigraph 28/45, 19.25" x 19.25", Estate of Jerry O. Wilkerson

Figure 3. Jerry O. Wilkerson, *Fortune Cookies on Red,* 1998, Acrylic on Board,
8.5" x 7", Estate of Jerry O. Wilkerson

Pynchon's Vision of Electronic Sexuality

In *Against the Day*, there are parallels to Virilio's futuristic teledildonics. A "long cylinder with a knob of a certain size on one end and a wire coming out of the other" is "inserted in the rectum" and in combination with a second electrode "rolled about on the abdominal surface" causes "the current flowing between to simulate a peristaltic wave," a procedure "valued by some [...] on its own merits [; ...] for everything, you know, including "the élan vital itself, will soon be proven electrical in nature" (*Against* 714). Though Pynchon may have been responding here to Virilio's electronification of sexuality, he had written this kind of thing twenty-five years before any of Virilio's books were translated into English. In his 1963 novel, *V.*, he envisaged

> an automaton, constructed, only quaintly, of human flesh [, ...] an
> inanimate object of desire. Stencil even departed from his usual ploddings

153

> to daydream a vision of her [The lady V.] now, at seventy-six: skin radiant
> with the bloom of some new plastic; both eyes glass but now containing
> photoelectric cells, connected by silver electrodes to optic nerves of
> purest copper wire and leading to a brain exquisitely wrought as a diode
> matrix could ever be. Solenoid relays would be her ganglia, servo-
> actuators move her flawless nylon limbs, hydraulic fluid be sent by a
> platinum heat-pump through butyrate veins and arteries. Perhaps–Stencil
> on occasion could have as vile a mind as any of the Crew–even a complex
> system of pressure transducers located in a marvelous vagina of
> polyethylene. (*V.*, 14.II, 386-387)

Although Pynchon shares interests with Virilio, his tender account of the
relationship between Dally and Tancredi suggests that there is much more to the
mating process than Virilio allows in *Open Sky*.

The next time that Dally visited Andrea's studio, she looked again at his
paintings, and

> thought she could see emerging from the glowing field of particles, like
> towers from the *foschetta*, a city, a contra-Venezia, the almost previsual
> reality behind what everyone else was agreeing to define as 'Venice.'
> 'Not like Marinetti and his circle,' Tancredi [finally] confessed. I really
> love the old dump. Here.' He led her to a stack of canvases in a corner
> she hadn't noticed before. They were all nocturnes, saturated with fog.
> [He asked Dally: ']What are you thinking?' It was her first visit here
> without Hunter. What she was thinking was that Tancredi had better kiss
> her, and soon. (*Against* 587)

The young painter must not have kissed Dally when they were alone in his studio,
for she doesn't see him again until the next chapter, when she meets him by
chance in a caffè. "Tancredi, known as reluctant to touch anyone, gave her an
appreciative squeeze" (*Against* 739). A few days later, after he is dead, she sadly
reflects: "They might never have become lovers, but shouldn't they have been
allowed some time to find out? (744). Not yet able to cry, she remembers how
virtuous he was, "like all these fucking artists, too much for the world, even the
seen world they were trying to redeem one little rectangle of canvas at a time"
(744). Tancredi's relationship with Dally demonstrates the close relationship
between love and sex that is absent in what Virilio imagines will "become the
implacable imaginary of cybersex" (*Open Sky* 116).

I'd like to think that Pynchon was reacting to Virilio's fantasy of solitary
telesexual interactivity when Yashmeen arranges the transfer of Reef's semen,

> all of it, out of [Cyprian Latewood's] mouth and inside [...] the muscular
> enclosure of her thighs, [... as] Reef, ready to roll once again [...] entered
> him ... But here let us reluctantly leave them, for biomechanics is one
> thing but intimacy quite another, isn't it, yes and by now Reef and
> Yashmeen were smiling too directly at one another, with Cyprian feeling
> too absurdly grateful here held between them so securely as to make the

vigorous seeing-to he was now receiving seem almost—though only almost—incidental. (*Against* 882-83)

"You are both my ... my .... ," murmured the penetrated Yashmeen, unable to quite pursue her thoughts" of this wonderful merging of heterosexuality and homosexuality that, according to Heinz Ickstadt's imaginative reading, "results in a pregnancy of which Cyprian, in a complex way, has also been an agent" (*Against* 882; Ickstadt 230). This reading would explain why Cyprian will have such a special feeling for Yashmeen and Reef's infant daughter Ljubica. Perhaps Pynchon, when he wrote that "biomechanics is one thing but intimacy quite another" (*supra*), is pointedly contrasting Virilio's sterile sexual biomechanics with the ineffable richness of human "intimacy.

Theme 3. Passion in Art

Virilio's Passion for Art

Virilio began his foreword to *Negative Horizon* with the revelation that "These days I have taken up painting, and in particular the still life" (26). Although this was one of his early books, it was the latest to be translated and the one that I most recently read—I was astonished to discover in it that Virilio had artistic interests in common with Wilkerson. This should not have been surprising because, as late as 1999, Virilio was the Director of the Ecole Speciale d' Architecture in Paris, and fine art is often taught in architectural schools. Both men liked painting still lifes; as noted earlier, Lamagna specifically noted that Wilkerson's food paintings "recall the opulence of 17th century Dutch still life's teeming with abundance (14). This accords with Virilio's view that the proper focus of the artist are the

> origins of the beautiful, of the good, entail[ing] the attainment of a means of orienting oneself within the surrounding landscape, in the midst of what is good to see and good to consume. Why wouldn't we expect this to be associated with the invention of alimentary customs, the selection of edible plants? (*Negative* 35)

What Virilio said of his own paintings—"Figures always spoke to me, the inanimate was clear to me, perimeters descriptive. I found shapes all around me expressive" (26)—also apply to Wilkerson's artistry. The glass figures on the front cover of this book invite us to caress their cool shapes. The banana in Figure 2 may be inanimate but it almost seems to know how privileged it is. The rims around the perimeter of the plate in Figure 3 fairly dance as they circle round, and the rectangular shapes in the foreground of the cover painting paradoxically go both downward *and* upward from left to right. When Virilio writes that

> The inanimate is merely a derogatory term used by those who read only appearances; those who perceive transparence know well that nothing is immobile, that everything is always moving, that SENSE circulates among things like blood in the veins, in the form of the frozen object, (26)

he appears to be referring to pointillist art. The same may also be true when he asks whether

> the value of the void actually precede[s] that of plentitude? My drawings, my paintings were above all exercises for interrogating the interstices of vision, a mode of *vision* that I could no longer take for granted. […] These sites, where simultaneously something ends and something begins, literally fascinated me. (*Negative* 35)

The interstices of vision correspond to the spaces between dots in Wilkerson's paintings. The perimeters where simultaneously something ends and something begins are aesthetically fascinating in Figures 1, 2 and 3. In Figure 4, the self-portrait, they are not only aesthetically charged but transcendently meaningful. It is true that once in his later books, Virilio mentioned "figures in Pointillism" (*Information* 130), and he did refer to "the pop potential of the masterworks of past art" (*Ground* 58), which, according to the brochure was Wilkerson's forte (Suwalsky 2, 3; Lipan 4, 5; Lamagna 12, 15), but I never imagined that I would learn more about Wilkerson's painting from Virilio's foreword than any other source. What had been a pair of intertextual readings, "Pynchon with Virilio" and "Pynchon with Wilkerson," characterized by an upward pointed, two-sided arrow, defined by three equidistant dots, representing Virilio at the left-hand extremity, Wilkerson at the right-hand extremity and Pynchon at the top, has become a three-sided equilateral triangle, with a line now directly connecting Virilio to Wilkerson.

I am struck by the coincidence that *The Truth in Painting*, a book by another French philosopher Jacques Derrida, provided the insights I needed to appreciate the art of another St. Louis painter, Bessie Lowenhaupt (See Kohn, *A Derridean Look*). But maybe it's not a coincidence? Virilio was quoted in 1999 as saying that he had always "felt close to" Derrida, that Derrida was one of his "very intimate friends," and that he himself "remain[ed] an art critic" (Armitage 34). The third assertion may explain why Virilio then said of Derrida that "There are parallels in our work" (35).

Wilkerson's Passion in Art

The most passionate painting in Wilkerson's retrospective was his "Self Portrait with Candles." Nancy Newman Rice, former chair of the art department at Maryville University, concluded her essay in the brochure for the Wilkerson exhibition by noting that:

> Jerry was a prolific artist. After his death, his wife and best friend, Gail, found rolls of completed canvases, suites of prints and drawings stored in various places throughout their home in South St. Louis. The one painting that she was most unprepared to find was a self-portrait Jerry had painted before he became ill. He told the only other person who knew of its existence that he painted it for Gail, and she would find it when she needed it most. (17)

In his foreword on art, Virilio distinguished between "the evident of the explicit and the evident of the implicit" (31), both of which are exemplified in Wilkerson's self-portrait. "[I]rresistibly attracted to the latter" and intrigued by the extreme fragility of "the vision of the between-world," Virilio knew that "the image of transparence could only be maintained by an effort of perception" (31). For me that effort of perception manifested itself in a series of questions. Does the evolving candle on the right express Wilkerson's faith in a second life after the first? Or is its evanescence a metaphor for life's fading away? If the dots on the bottom of that candle are disappearing, does this give new meaning to pointillism, presaging the dissolution of the body? In the cropping of the forehead, which brings the face closer to the viewer, is Wilkerson resisting his departure from this world or seeking to be remembered a little longer? Surely this "Self-Portrait with Candles" expresses Wilkerson's "will to represent the non-representable" (*Negative* 27). Does the fact that I ask the above questions of the self-portrait—the same questions I asked in the penultimate draft of this essay, well before I read the foreword to *Negative Horizon*—demonstrate what Virilio calls the "art of painting the pictorial as *questioning* and not as representation, just as writing is questioning before being a discourse or a novel" (27 italics added)? Does this portrait represent Wilkerson's attempt to envisage "the void, the null, nothingness," and, if so, has he not "produced [something] that is more original, more specific, than this idea of nothingness, of absence?" (*Negative* 28). Has Wilkerson created what Virilio calls "an external dynamic that induce[s ...] transparence" and gives "form and value to absence" (33)? Has he "taken on the goal of making visible the invisible" (33), which is what he will be when the painting is finally discovered by his wife? Surely, this self-portrait is Wilkerson's most meaningful painting. The fact that he set it aside and may never have shown it to the public, attests to his passion for his beloved wife.

Figure 4. Jerry Wilkerson. "Self Portrait with Candles." 1993. 14" x 17.5". Estate of Jerry O. Wilkerson

Wilkerson's passion for art extended to the special feeling he had for his artist friends in St. Louis. One of them, Jerry Weber, recalls the opening day of Tom's Bar and Grill,

> when Jerry introduced himself to one of the owners, Tom Dimitriades [, ... who] told Jerry of his wishes to bring real art work from St. Louis artists to hang in his restaurant. [...] Little did any of us realize, except maybe Jerry, that Tom would be one of our strongest supports. Jerry truly

defined the Central West End as "The Artist Community" in St. Louis. (Weber 19)

Pynchon's Passion in Art

When Tancredi, the "fierce young man" (*Against* 584), appears again in *Against the Day*, he is venting his anger: "What Mr. Vibe needs [...] is trouble he cannot pray himself out of" (739). "*'La machina infernale,'* Dally ventured. *'Appunto!'* Tancredi" agrees (739). A few pages later, we see him as "this skinny kid in a borrowed suit, shirt-collar too big," who is "immediately read as out of place and therefore in disguise and therefore a threat" (*Against* 584, 742). Pynchon is now describing himself as he famously appeared in his high school yearbook. This photograph, which can be readily downloaded as an internet image, shows Pynchon with flying shirt collars, overhanging shoulder pads and pushed-up jacket sleeves, matching the novel's description of Tancredi just before he was shot. Scarsdale Vibe's henchmen warned the kid off the dock. "*Via, via!* [...] but he kept approaching. He was doing the one thing authority cannot abide, will never allow to pass, he was refusing to do as he was told" (742). "[B]ody guards in black were rising up from everywhere, long-annealed teppisti newly arrived in town from strike-breaking duties in Rome and the factories of the North, armed, silent, masked, and on the move" (742). In the middle of it all stood the "Tancredi kid" holding an object "in his hand, carefully, as if it might explode at the slightest jar" (742). "Flame stabbed out of the muzzles of brand-new Glisentis, [...] as he slipped and fell in his own blood" (742-43). When Tancredi's friends learned that "nobody found a weapon," that his hands had been empty, they recalled him saying that

> he had an infernal machine, which would bring down Vibe and, some
> distant day, the order Vibe expresses most completely and hatefully. This
> was his precious instrument of destruction. It gave off a light and heat
> Tancredi alone could sense, it blinded him, it burned fiercely in his hands,
> like the glowing coal in the Buddhist parable, he could not let it go. (742)

If his infernal machine was not a weapon, it was an "offering, the masterwork he thought would change any who beheld it, even this corrupted American millionaire, blind him to the life he had been inhabiting, bring him to a different kind of seeing" (742). After they killed Tancredi, the men in black—reminiscent of the "men inside the auction room" in the final paragraph of *The Crying of Lot 49*, who "wore black mohair and had pale, cruel faces"—kicked his body "as forcefully as they could, shouting insults till the *fondamenta* sounded like a jailyard, while Scarsdale Vibe all but danced up and down in delighted approval," urging them on: "*Batti! Batti la faccia,* yes" (743).

It is historically counterfactual that Vibe's bodyguards in Venice would have been thugs, "newly arrived in town from strike-breaking duties in Rome and the factories of the North" (*Against* 742). John Cammett records that strikes in

Italy before World War One were few. Although striking textile worker were injured by bullets in Turin in 1906 and striking auto workers killed as well as injured in Milan in 1907, their armed assailants were the official law-enforcing *carabinieri*, not hired *teppisti* (Cammett 26, 27). Pynchon does not write historical fiction, which allows him, in this case, to intensify the passion of Tancredi's death.

The multiple interpretations of the infernal machine in *Against the Day* are likely to bewilder readers. First one thinks that the infernal machine is the accumulation of Tancredi's pointillist paintings in his studio. Then when Tancredi starts to tell Dally and Hunter that "[o]ne must begin by accepting Hell—by understanding that Hell is real and that there move through this tidy surface world a silent army of operatives who have sworn allegiance to it as to a beloved homeland," the infernal machine becomes an army of anarchists (586). Next, one gets the impression that it is an atom bomb or an information bomb. The reference to the glowing coal in the Buddhist parable suggests that it is the pent up anger in a human being. Heinz Ickstadt credits Tony Tanner for the observation that Pynchon's novels are "over-coded almost to the point of self-parody" (218).

Concluding Remarks

This essay was motivated by my hypothesis that Pynchon's *Against the Day* is in part a response to Virilio's exaggerated fears of hyper-science and hyper-technology. Because Virilio had related "the decomposition of figures in Pointillism" to the "dismantling of the space-time of the work" in *The Information Bomb* (130), I presumed that that had something to do with the role played by the pointillist artist, Tancredi, in the novel. While I was developing these hypotheses, the Wilkerson retrospective opened at the St. Louis University Museum of Art, and it occurred to me that Wilkerson might have been Pynchon's model for Tancredi. When I told Gail my idea, it brought back a memory to her of two men coming to one of Jerry's openings at the OK Harris Gallery in January 1983 and having an intense discussion with him, though she did not recall what it was about. She had a hunch that one of them could have been Pynchon, so I emailed her his well-known high-school yearbook photograph. She thought that the man that had most intrigued her resembled that student. Though I am aware that supposed Pynchon sightings, like UFOs, are legion, I like to imagine that this one was real. Many of the ideas that I present in the essays in this book were nurtured by my imagination, and I don't want to totally discredit them. Indeed, one of the claims for the essay in general that Hassan makes in the epigraph to this book is that it can "mediate our imagination and knowledge" (*Postmodern Turn* 141). In that vein I have always endeavored to bolster my imagination with knowledge and give priority to the latter.

Although I have read a number of passages and pages in *Against the Day* over and over, my reading of this 1085-page novel was in general hardly a "close" one. Instead I have put my emphasis here on intertextuality, that is, close readings of Virilio's writings *vis a vis* Pynchon's novel and subsequently *vis a vis* Wilkerson's paintings and close readings of Wilkerson's paintings *vis a vis* the novel. I was not sure that I could properly put Wilkerson's artworks in an intertextual context until I remembered that Lipan had done exactly that in her piece in the brochure for the exhibition she had curated at the St. Louis University Museum of Art, in which she wrote that "Wilkerson employed intertextuality in a complex and multilayered body of work that incorporated a range of genres, concepts and influences" (4). As to the "theoretical concept of intertexuality," she usefully wrote that it

> is often associated with postmodernism though the device itself is not new. In contemporary theory, intertexuality refers to the network of content and code interdependencies that establish meaning. The interpretation of an art work always takes [the] form of another work. (Lipan 4)

Such intertextual parallels help to establish and reinforce meaning across respective pairs of works in the same or across genres. It was not until I wrote Essay Ten that I realized that intertextuality was as important to my work as close reading. The two, in fact, have been synergistic.

From Utopian to Dystopian Modernism: Pynchon and DeLillo

For it was now like walking among matrices of a great digital computer, the zeroes and ones twinned above, hanging like balanced mobiles right and left, ahead, thick, maybe endless. Behind the hieroglyphic streets there would either be a transcendent meaning, or only the earth. (*Crying* 181)

The Banality of Vice (Pynchon)

In many ways, Pynchon's 2009 novel, *Inherent Vice*, is the antithesis of *The Crying of Lot 49*, and reading it makes for another kind of close reading of the earlier novel. I'd like to think that the later work was inspired by the earlier one, which Tony Tanner wrote was modeled after "the California detective story–an established tradition" that included "the works of writers such as Raymond Chandler, Ross MacDonald and Eric Stanley Gardner," except that

> it works in a reverse direction. With a detective story you start with a mystery and move towards a final clarification, all the apparently disparate, suggestive bits of evidence finally being bound together in one illuminating pattern; whereas in [*The Crying of Lot 49*] we move from a state of zero-degree mystery [...] to a condition of increasing mystery and dubiety. (Tanner 56)

In contrast, Pynchon's 2009 detective story works in the conventional direction.

Most importantly, *Inherent Vice* proclaims Pynchon's implicit return to modernism's "absolute moralizing judgments," which postmodernism repudiated in the 1960s in favor of a "dialectic" which went "beyond good and evil," beyond the "sense of some easy taking of sides" (Jameson 62). Pynchon characterized the absolute moralizing judgments of modernism in his descriptions of the murdered "good Duke of adjoining Faggio" and his surviving son, Niccolò, who is the "good guy of the play" (*Crying* 65, 66, 68), versus the "evil Duke of Squamuglia" (66), *i.e.*, Angelo, and the other evil guy–the acting regent of Faggio, *i.e.*, Pasquale, who is "the evil illegitimate son" of the lady Francesca and the late Duke of Faggio (65,66, 70). Francesca is the sister *and* bedded consort of Angelo, while the younger Niccolò is the legitimate son of the late Duke and his then lawful wife. Pynchon goes beyond good and evil and the easy taking of sides when he switches to the postmodern mode by focusing *The Courier's Tragedy* on "a likeable schemer named Ercole, [who] is secretly involved with dissident elements in the court of Faggio who want to keep Niccolò alive, and so [...] contrives to stuff a young goat into the cannon instead, meanwhile smuggling Niccolò out of the ducal palace disguised as an elderly procuress" to grow up in the Squamuglian "court of his father's murderer," Duke Angelo (*Crying* 66). The next we hear of

Ercole, he is persuading a childhood friend of Niccolò, named Domenico, not to inform the evil regent Pasquale that his presumed victim, Niccolò, is still alive and living in his court in Squamuglia. This is noble on Ercole's part, but the means he employs are ignoble and extreme. He entices the informer into

> putting his head into a curious black box, on the pretext of showing him a pornographic diorama. A steel vise promptly clamps onto the faithless Domenico's head and the box muffles his cries for help. Ercole binds his hands and feet with scarlet silk cords, lets him know who it is he's run afoul of, reaches into the box with a pair of pincers, tears out Domenico's tongue, stabs him a couple times, pours into the box a beaker of aqua regia, enumerates a list of other goodies, including castration, that Domenico will undergo before he's allowed to die, all amid screams, tongueless attempts to pray, agonized struggles from the victim. (*Crying* 67)

Having done the foul deed, Ercole resumes his noble deeds on behalf of the worthy Niccolò.

Whereas the modernism that postmodernism repudiated, being rooted in the Age of Enlightenment, emphasized inherent goodness—in Pynchon's own words once again, we would "do the most good, [...] cure cancer, [...], grow food for everybody, detoxify the results of industrial greed gone berserk—realize all the wistful pipe dreams of our days" (*Luddite* 41)—the hypermoderism advanced by Pynchon in the 2009 novel, emphasizes inherent evil. For Pynchon, the hyper-intensity and hyper-extensivity of moral depravity are more culturally impactive than the hyper-science and hyper-technology feared by Virilio.

Inherent Vice is set sometime after the August 1969 "Mansonoid conspiracy" that resulted in the murder of Sharon Tate and four other people, and sometime before June 1970, when "the Manson case" went on trial" (29, 280). Though these ruthless murders, as well as others described throughout the novel, were acts of pure evil, Pynchon's major focus is on the lesser but more pervasive level of evil acts called "vice," which includes sexual immorality, official corruption, and the using and selling of illegal psychedelic drugs. It's hard to imagine a reversion to the Jacobean level of immorality in *The Crying of Lot 49*, where a brother and sister are paramours and the sister is willing to accede to the brother's wishes by marrying her own son "to amalgamate the duchies of Squamuglia and Faggio" (66). There is no incest in *Inherent Vice*, but the emphasis on vice in its pages far exceeds that in *The Crying of Lot 49*. Pynchon seems to mislead when he implies that the title of the new novel is taken from what lawyers "in marine insurance liked to call inherent vice," which relates to the "stuff marine policies don't like to cover. Usually applies to cargo—like eggs break—but sometimes it's also the vessel carrying it," which is "why bilges have to be pumped out" (*Inherent* 351). When Doc's marine lawyer "Sauncho blinked, 'maybe if you wrote a marine policy on L.A., considering it, for some closely defined reason, to be a boat ... '" (351), he doesn't get a chance to complete his thought, but presumably it would have brought "inherent vice" closer to its more obvious meaning for Pynchon: that the novel is all about human vice. For Pynchon in 2009, "absolute moralizing judgments" were no longer the "impoverished luxury" they were deemed to be at the dawn of postmodernism (Jameson 62).

Pynchon's reference to Eichmann's "stand[ing] trial" in *The Crying of Lot 49* (137), together with Aunt Reet's intriguing comment in *Inherent Vice* about Mickey Wolfmann being "technically Jewish but want[ing] to be a Nazi" (7), and the very title of the new novel made me wonder if Pynchon had been influenced by Hannah Arendt's *Eichmann in Jerusalem: A Report on the Banality of Evil*. Indeed, his description of vice in Los Angeles in 1969-70 makes it sound banal, lacking in originality, freshness and novelty, compared to life in northern California in the mid-1960s in *The Crying of Lot 49*. I acquired an old copy of the 1994 Penguin edition of *Eichmann in Jerusalem* and read the first fifty pages last night, looking for clues to *Inherent Vice*. The only piece that struck me as relevant to my thesis was Eichmann's plea, as Arendt saw it, that he was

> "not guilty in the sense of the indictment." The indictment implied not only that he had acted on purpose, which he did not deny, but out of base motives and in full knowledge of the criminal nature of his deeds. As for the base motives, he was perfectly sure that he was not what he called an *innerer Schweinhund*, a dirty bastard in the depths of his heart; and as for his conscience, he remembered perfectly well that he would have had a bad conscience only if he had not done what he had been ordered to do—to ship millions of men, women, and children to their death with great zeal and the most meticulous care. (Arendt 25)

Arendt admitted that this "was hard to take," especially when "Half a dozen psychiatrists had certified him as 'normal'" (25). I am a slow reader and was not anxious, at least at this time, to spend five more nights slogging through *Eichmann in Jerusalem*. When I went to the internet for reviews, I found an excellent essay on Arendt's book by Amos Elon, who fortunately keyed his comments to the same paginated edition I had acquired. When I discovered that the final lines of his essay incorporated the word "inherent," I knew that I would want to cite Elon as well as Arendt, from whose pages 233 and 276 he based the following text, in which he asserted that Arendt believed:

> that "under conditions of terror most people will comply but *some people will not*, just as the lesson of the countries to which the Final Solution was proposed is that 'it could happen' in most places but *it did not happen everywhere*. Humanly speaking, no more is required, and no more can reasonably be asked, for this planet to remain a place fit for human habitation" (p. 233). We could take this as evidence that the only hope of preventing future catastrophes must lie in a morality that is inherent in human nature. On the other hand, Arendt considers Eichmann "terribly and terrifyingly normal" (p. 276). *Eichmann in Jerusalem* leaves us wondering not only if justice was achieved in Eichmann's case, but also

whether the lessons Arendt believes the trial has taught will make a
difference in the future. (Elon, *circa* p. viii)

It turned out that Elon's essay was actually the introduction to the 2006 edition of
Eichmann in Jerusalem published by Penguin Books in the same year that they
published Pynchon's Against the Day. It is likely that Pynchon knew of fellow
novelist Elon's introduction, read it, and reacted to his presumption of Arendt's
naive faith in the "morality that is inherent in human nature" to prevent future
catastrophes. Accordingly, that mention of "inherent" by Elon could underlies the
title of Pynchon's latest novel. If I am correct, Inherent Vice is very much about
the Nazis and the Holocaust, much more than what Louis Menand called, and I at
first agreed was, "a generally lighthearted affair." Ordinarily, I would go back
through this draft and update my earlier interpretations, but in this case I will
leave the record of my ratcheting progress, for whatever it's worth. Having been
born in 1927, I came of age during Hitler's rise to power. In a forthcoming article
in The Journal of Modern Jewish Studies, I remember hearing bits of Hitler's
blasting speeches on the radio in the 1930s. All I could understand were the
slurring references to "Juden" followed by thunderous applause, which left me
regretting that my surname was so obviously Jewish. It has taken me most of my
life to get past those feelings of shame. If Inherent Vice has to do with
antisemitism, it seems to be manifesting itself in the overly prejudicial putdowns
of hippies by Bigfoot Bjornsen, the swaggering Los Angeles police detective.
That hippies are the novel's stand-ins for Jews is affirmed by the reference to
"hippie metaphysics," which evokes the "Jewish physics" that the German
physicist and Nobel Prize laureate, Johannes Stark, intended as a slur to Albert
Einstein (Inherent 101). The substitution is again validated by Bigfoot's complaint
to Doc: "You think it's all one big monolithic funfest at the LAPD, don't you,
nothing to do all day but figure out new ways to persecute you hippie scum"
(272). That Bigfoot's contract killer was named Adrian Prussia further reinforces
the Nazi connection. Lieutenant Pat Dubonnet, another LAPD bigwig, shares
Bigfoot's "hatred of hippies" (48), but he also resents and yet envies the
detective's effectual posturing for limelight (48). The strange connection in the
novel of hippies and antisemitism is reinforced when Pat asks Doc: "Hey. You
think Bigfoot's Jewish, too" (49). "Swedish, I thought," Doc replies, but Pat,
realizing that his prejudice was revealed by that last "too," is "dimly defensive"
when he offers "Could be both, [...] there can be Swedish Jews" (49).

The massive scale of the Holocaust makes it the most evil act ever
performed by humans. Again the implicit emphasis on evil in *Inherent Vice* not
only distances Pynchon from postmodernism's repudiation of absolute moralizing
judgments, but also from modernism's preoccupation with human nobility.
Pynchon represented this change in ethos, from *The Crying of Lot 49* to *Inherent
Vice*, by a profound stylistic change; in contrast to the complex, kaleidoscopic
style of the earlier novel, the latter novel is straightforward, repetitive, almost
banal. In terms of information theory, the information potential of *Inherent Vice* is

minimal compared to that of *The Crying of Lot 49*. It's almost as though Pynchon went out of his way to manifest that change in style, even posting *Inherent Vice*, like *The Crying of Lot 49* before it, on the internet in searchable form, allowing for some heuristic experimentation under the rubric of information theory. To facilitate such endeavors, it behooves me to tackle the actual mathematics–I've been putting them off long enough, trying to get by with expert explanations–and feel my way along with simple numerical simulations of entropy levels:

The "equation" for information entropy that John Nefastis associated "with communication" in *The Crying of Lot 49* is $<\ H(X) = -\sum p(x) \log_2 p(x)\ >$ where x_1, x_2, x_3 ... x_n are the n separate informational components of a message; $p(\cdot)$ is the probability that the ith individual component is in the message; and $\sum$ sums the individual probabilities, each multiplied by the logarithm to the base 2 of that probability (*Crying* 105). The advantage of logarithms to the base 2, Thomas Cover and Joy Thomas explain, when they present the above equation, is that the "entropy will then be measured in bits" (5). A bit is a unit of computer information equivalent to the result of a choice between two alternatives, such as $<$ yes or no $>$ or even $<$ on or off $>$. When the vector X in the above formula consists of possible microstates (each x representing a different pattern of behavior of all the constituent atoms), then H(X) is a measure of thermodynamic entropy, *i.e.*, physical disorder, and is computed with natural logarithms. This is the kind of entropy that Nefastis distinguished as "having to do with heat-engines" (*Crying* 105). Because the formula for entropy is based on random sampling of the components and has nothing to do with their order, I have to presume that Maxwell's box is somewhat misleading; what makes for lower thermodynamic entropy has to do with the higher probability of well-organized miscrostates than with sorting individual atoms.

For a non-mathematician like myself, it is useful to have numerical examples demonstrating how the above formula is implemented; Arthur E. Stamps III provides a simple diagram, entitled "Basic concept of entropy as a measure of more information," on his website. In his example, there are four possible informational components, each represented by a two-dimensional caricature of a differently shaped house. Instead of houses I shall designate the four components, x, of a message by ♣, ♦, ♥, and ♠. If x is simply ♣, then $<$ $H(♣) = -1 \log_2 1 = 0$ bits $>$. Base-2 logarithm tables as well as on-site base-2 logarithm calculators may be readily accessed on the internet, though for the examples used here, all that is needed are $\log_2 1 = 0$, $\log_2 2 = 1$, $\log_2 3 = 1.58496$, and $\log_2 4 = 2$. If the message is ♣♣, then $H(♣\,♣) = -1\log_2 1 - 1\log_2 1$, which still equals zero; as it does for H(♣♣♣) and for H(♣♣♣♣). Information theory has been used as a measure of biodiversity; so it makes good sense that if only a single kind of bird, symbolized, say, by ♣, is observed, regardless of how many individuals of that species, biodiversity is zero.

If the message has two different components, or two different species are observed, say ♣ ♦, then < $H(♣ ♦) = -\frac{1}{2} (\log_2 1 - \log_2 2) - \frac{1}{2} (\log_2 1 - \log_2 2) = 1.0$ bit >. Note that I am now using the rule that < Log u/v = Log u - Log v) >. If the message is ♣ ♦ ♥, then < $H(♣ ♦ ♥) = -3 (1/3) (\log_2 1 - \log_2 3) = 1.58496$ bits >. As new components of information are added, say ♣ ♦ ♥ ♠, then < $H(♣ ♦ ♥ ♠) = -4 (1/4) (\log_2 1 - \log_2 4) = 2.0$ bits >. If the ♠ is deleted and replaced by a ♦, yielding ♣ ♦ ♥ ♦, then < $H(♣ ♦ ♥ ♦) = -2 (\frac{1}{4})(\log_2 1 - \log_2 4) - \frac{1}{2} (\log_2 1 - \log_2 2) = -\frac{1}{2} (0 - 2) - \frac{1}{2} (0 - 1) = 1.5$ bits >. If the ♥ in the previous foursome were another ♣, leaving ♣ ♦ ♣ ♦, the information entropy would be < $H(♣ ♣ ♦ ♦) = -\frac{1}{2} (\log_2 1 - \log_2 2) - \frac{1}{2} (\log_2 1 - \log_2 2) = 1.0$ bits. If the first ♦ in the last foursome were another ♣, that is, ♣ ♣ ♣ ♦, then < $H(♣ ♣ ♣ ♦) = -\frac{3}{4} (\log_2 3 - \log_2 4) - \frac{1}{4} (\log_2 1 - \log_2 4) = -\frac{3}{4} (1.58496) + 3/2 + 1/2 = 0.81128$ >. The following is a convenient sequential presentation of the above results:

$$H(♣ ♣ ♣ ♣) = 0.0 \text{ bits}$$
$$H(♣ ♣ ♣ ♦) = 0.81128 \text{ bits}$$
$$H(♣ ♣ ♦ ♦) = 1.0 \text{ bits}$$
$$H(♣ ♦ ♥ ♦) = 1.5 \text{ bits}$$
$$H(♣ ♦ ♥ ♠) = 2.0 \text{ bits}$$
$$H(♣ ♦ ♥) = 1.58496 \text{ bits}$$
$$H(♣ ♦) = 1.0 \text{ bits}$$
$$H(♣) = 0.0 \text{ bits}$$

It follows from the above series, assuming that it can be generalized, that a greater quantity of informational components increases the information of a message monotonically provided that it also includes more diversity. This is the case here when H(♣) is replaced by H(♣ ♦), H(♣ ♦) by H(♣ ♦ ♥), and H(♣ ♦ ♥) by H(♣ ♦ ♥ ♠). When the number of components increases, information decreases monotonically if the added component augments sameness. This is the case when H(♣ ♦ ♥) is replaced by H(♣ ♦ ♣ ♥), then by H(♣ ♦ ♣ ♦), then by H(♣ ♣ ♣ ♦) and finally by H(♣ ♣ ♣ ♣). I think of my numerical results as metaphorical because they are based on small numbers rather than the "very large collection of signals" on which the equations are based (Marshall Crumiller *et al.* 4). However, the simulation examples confirm Mendelson's generalization that "the more unexpected a message is, the more information it contains" (26), though Cover and Thomas help here when they alternatively define H (X) as "the number of bits on the average required to describe the random variable" (5).

Although there are fewer informational components–less than half the number of words–in *The Crying of Lot 49* as there are in *Inherent Vice*, there appears to be greater sameness across components in the latter than in the former and I heuristically surmise that the total informational entropy, H, of *Inherent Vice* is less than that of *The Crying of Lot 49*. While there are 24 repetitions of bone/s in the earlier novel, there are even more repetitions of certain nouns, all of them banal, in the later novel. There are 64 mentions of hippies in *Inherent Vice*, most of them derogatory. Often they are associated with the rolling, smoking or whatever of "joints," which appear 52 times in the novel, *not* counting the non-psychedelic homonyms, such as "massage joint," (or "pizza joint" or "seafood joints"), "joint bank account" (or "joint task force") and "joint-compound containers." In addition to "joints," the use of psychedelic drugs is evidenced by code words such as "acid," "dope," "grass," "pot," "reefer," "roach" and "weed," as well as by proper names such as "cocaine," "heroin," "LSD," "marijuana" and "Thai stick." On page 273 alone, there are references to "reefer smoke," "weed" and "do[ing] acid," and on page 353, to "pot," "reefer" and "dope." The most commonly repeated word was "fuck." Checking just the first 100-pages, I found eight mentions of this banal word referring directly to copulation (12, 14, 21, 61, 63, 64, 89, 970), nine more to "fucker" used as an expletive (3, 16, 46, 48, 69, 70, 97, 97), seven more to fucking up, in the sense of messing up (29, 29, 38, 49, 54, 68, 92), and six more to "fucking" used as an adjective (2, 8, 9, 24, 34, 34). That's a total of 30 fuck and fuck-derivatives for the first 100-pages of *Inherent Vice*. Extrapolating to all 369 pages gives an estimated total of 110 for the book. On page 122 alone, there are seven "fuck[s]", two "hippie[s]" and "pot smoke." The London *Times* reviewer picked up on these repetitions when he observed that "Almost everyone in this book is doing or dealing drugs; if not they are engaged in that other notorious Sixties vice, sex. After all, it is still gloriously pre-Aids, pre-feminism, pre-everything–the coupling is constant and primordial" (Aravind Adiga).

Another type of banality is represented by the word "ain't" which appears only once in the earlier novel (*Crying* 27). It appears 26-times in the first 184-pages (at page 184 my search engine became unreliable) of *Inherent Vice*, which extrapolates to 52-times for the entire book. These frequent repetitions heuristically imply that there is much more sameness in the information, and therefore that less total information is provided by *Inherent Vice* than by *The Crying of Lot 49*.

This conclusion seems to be reinforced by qualitative judgments. *The Crying of Lot 49* contains a myriad of variegated plots, whereas *Inherent Vice* has a handful of related plots, most of them based on Private Investigator Larry "Doc" Sportello's being asked to search for missing people:

Shasta Fey Hepworth–"She's disappeared" (34); "The one that's been missing" (64).

Mickey Wolfmann–"Wolfmann disappeared" (69); "Mickey's still missing" (143).

Bambi–"allegedly missing" (156); "She's been gone now two days and nights"(154).

Dawnette–"she seems to be missing too" (215),

Boris Spivey–"Boris has disappeared. His place is empty" (215),

Puck Beaverton–"has disappeared ... I'd like to find out what happened
    to him" (217),
Coy Harlingen–"then Coy just disappeared" (311).
Pynchon appears to have been intent on making *Inherent Vice* palpably less
complex than the information-laden *Crying of Lot 49*. Bill Millard generalizes this
observation when he notes that *Inherent Vice* creates its atmosphere more "through
American pop-culture references than through the sort of recondite material that
sent yesterday's dedicated Pynchonologists to the deepest stacks of university
libraries and sends today's arguably less fanatical ones to Google and Wikipedia"
(2). The implication of the pop-culture references for information theory–"So
many details are taken from the actual landscape of greater Los Angeles in the
given period," Millard writes, "that Wired magazine has posted an online
interactive map, open to reader submissions" (9)–is that there are relatively few
signifiers with multiple referents in *Inherent Vice*, as compared to the multiplicitous
referents per signifier in *The Crying of Lot 49*. I have no idea whether the H(X)
formula for information potential can take that important factor into account.
Whereas, "the object of a detective story is to reduce a complex and disordered
situation to simplicity and clarity," Mendelson, like Tanner, argued that "*The
Crying of Lot 49* starts with a relatively simple situation, and then lets it get out of
the heroine's control," in other words, "the simple becomes complex" (21). The
opposite is true in *Inherent Vice*, where most of the uncertainty is finally resolved.
Because information entropy is a measure of uncertainty, it must be less when
uncertainty is actually resolved.

    Fortunately, the formula for information entropy can correct for
misleading information, or, what is called in information theory, noise. Many of
the characters in *Inherent Vice* take psychedelic drugs. Doc, the protagonist, critic
Walter Kirn writes, keeps his

> workload relatively light, freeing him to stay stoned around the clock and
> live in the now, which isn't hard for him, because he's toked away his
> short-term memory. It's a wonder he can still function as a person, let
> alone make a living as a sleuth. He nods off during stakeouts, draws
> blanks while quizzing witnesses and can't seem to turn down the volume
> on the surf music playing incessantly inside his head.

Doc made a discovery that seemed significant. Watching President Richard Nixon
address the nation live on television, he realizes that the engraving of Nixon he
had seen a while back on "fake twenty-dollar bills," one of which he had in his
wallet and took out to look at again, was identical to the face on television (*Inherent*
120):

> How could this be? Unless ... sure, time travel of course ... some CIA
> engraver, in some top-security workshop far away, was busy *right now*
> copying this image off of his own screen and then would later somehow
> go slip his copy into a covert *special mailbox*, which would have to be
> located close to a power-company substation so they could bootleg the

power they needed, raising everybody else's rates, to send information *time-traveling back into the past.* (121)

In the light of wild predictions for hyper-science and hyper-technology in the writings of Virilio and Berardi, I felt that Doc's discovery might be relevant, but didn't know to what. Then I read what critics like Kirn had to say about the novel, went back to the Nixon part, and realized that Doc had fallen asleep on Penny's couch "in front of the day's sports headlights," woke up to Nixon's voice and tumultuous applause on the tube, groped around "for his stash, finding half a joint and lighting up" (*Inherent* 120). No wonder that the "two Nixons looked *just like photos* of each other!" (120). What I took to be a swirl of information coming from Doc was misinformation; he was stoned. The "*special mailbox*" in italics was idiosyncratically reminiscent of the W.A.S.T.E. mailboxes in *The Crying of Lot 49*, that it was necessary to "bootleg the power they needed, raising everybody else's rates" was ludicrous, as was sending "information time-traveling *back into the past*" (121 emphasis in the original).

Fortunately there is a companion equation for information entropy when the signals in a message include noise which can be treated like informational components, even though they are actually *misinformational* components. In their article, "Focused Review: Estimating the Amount of Information Conveyed by a Population of Neurons," Marshall Crumiller, Bruce Knight, Yunguo Yu and Ehud Kaplan "estimate the entropy due to the noise, denoted H_N, and subtract it from the total entropy [...], which we denote as H_T " (5). Note that their H_T is the $< H() = - \sum (p)Log_2(p) >$ defined and numerically simulated five paragraphs above in this essay. Their net information, I, is $< I = H_T - H_N >$, where both the informational and misinformational components are included in H_T , but only the latter in H_N. In an email to me, dated May 31, 2011, the corresponding editor, Ehud Kaplan, advised me that their article—which is easily searched for, by its unique title, on the internet—is a simple application of Shannon's original formulation and has been used by many before them. Consider the following cases in which misinformational components are represented by N, n and Greek *nu*, ν:

$$I(\clubsuit \blacklozenge \heartsuit N) = [- (Log_2 1 - Log_2 4)] - [- Log_2 1] = 2.0 \text{ bits}$$
$$I(\clubsuit \blacklozenge N) = [- (Log_2 1 - Log_2 3)] - [- (Log_2 1)] = 1.58493 \text{ bits}$$
$$I(\clubsuit \blacklozenge N n) = [- (Log_2 1 - Log_2 4)] - [- (Log_2 1 - Log_2 2)] = 1.0 \text{ bits}$$
$$I(\clubsuit N n) = [- (Log_2 1 - Log_2 3)] - [- (Log_2 1 - Log_2 2)] = 0.58493 \text{ bits}$$
$$I(\clubsuit N n \nu) = [- (Log_2 1 - Log_2 4)] - [- (Log_2 1 - Log_2 3)] = 0.41507 \text{ bits}$$
$$I(N n \nu) = [- (Log_2 1 - Log_2 3)] - [- (Log_2 1 - Log_2 3)] = 0.0 \text{ bits}$$

Note that the larger the ratio of diverse components of information to diverse components of misinformation, the greater the total amount of information, I. It is of interest that both

$$I(\clubsuit \blacklozenge \heartsuit N) = [- (Log_2 1 - Log_2 4)] - [- Log_2 1] \text{ and}$$
$$H(\clubsuit \blacklozenge \heartsuit \spadesuit) = [- (Log_2 1 - Log_2 4)]$$

equal 2.0 bits. Although this equality also holds for two diverse informational components or even one, simply because the logarithm of 1 is 0, it is a metaphor for the fact that a relatively small amount of misinformation, as in *The Crying of Lot 49*, increases information. Whether the misinformation is the consequence of mental disorders, as in the case of Oedipa's hallucinations, or drugs, in the case of Doc's, that in itself is informative. I will give an example of noise in *The Crying of Lot 49* that I take to be willful on Pynchon's part. It is all the more intriguing because the paragraph in which it is lodged is Pynchon at his most philosophical: "Tremaine the Swastika Salesman's reprieve from holocaust was either an injustice, or the absence of a wind" (181). Though I may be wrong if this sentence is an example of what Duyfhuizen calls "the fine line between randomness and pattern" in *The Crying of Lot 49* (241).

The banality of *Inherent Vice* goes beyond low information entropy. In the information-rich *Crying of Lot 49*, whose very title alludes to, among other things, the Tibetan Buddhist *bardo* that underlies Inverarity's failed plot to "survive death" (179), there is only a single explicit reference to Buddhism: "a front page story in the *Times* [...] about a Buddhist monk in Viet Nam who had set himself on fire to protest government policies" (*Crying* 114). In *Against the Day*, there are multiple allusions to Tibetan Buddhism; Cyprian had his "first encounter with release from desire" when "he found that for some undefined time now he had not even been imagining desire, its fulfillment, any occasion for it" (839). This is the profoundest goal of Buddhism, for "freedom from desire and attachment is necessary if one would be free from bondage" (Evans-Wentz *Tibetan Yoga* 69). It is symptomatic of the programmed banality of *Inherent Vice* that, for the first time in Pynchon's writing, it banalizes Tibetan Buddhism. One of the female residents of the mansion in Topango Canyon rented by the surf band, the Boards, has the unlikely name of Bodhi, a tree whose name is both the Pali and Sanskrit word for Enlightenment: "Like girls at Hawaiian airports, a couple of house groupies named Bodhi and Zinnia came forward with leis, or actually love beads, and put them around Doc's and Denis's necks" (*Inherent* 125). It doesn't detract from the irreverence of the lady's name that "everybody pronounced" Denis's name "to rhyme with 'penis'" (10). The most respect given to Buddhism in *Inherent Vice* is when the chicks "all got together and kicked in and hired an exorcist. Some Buddhist priest from the Temple downtown. He came up one day and did his thing, and now the [usually stoned] Boards and the house are all officially dezombified" (299), which is a far cry from another past novel by Pynchon, *Mason and Dixon,* in which "The Buddha sat beneath a Tree, and he was enlighten'd. A quick overview would suggest that Trees produce Enlightenment" (615). Asked about a friend who felt that the internet had "taken his soul," Sparky, ostensibly talking about the internet in *Inherent Vice,* replied in a way that could be taken as a brush-off of Tibetan Buddhism:

> The system has no use for souls. Not how it works at all. Even this thing
> about going into other people's lives? it isn't like some Eastern trip of
> absorbing into a collective consciousness. It's only finding stuff out that
> somebody else didn't think you were going to. (365)

The word *karma*, which does not even appear in *The Crying of Lot 49*–again
suggesting the "resistance of modern writers to having their archetypes 'spotted'"
(Frye 102)–emerges in *Gravity's Rainbow*, in "trapped on the Karmic wheel" (651),
where it is respectfully capitalized. In an abrupt switch, karma" appears numerous
times in *Inherent Vice*, typically in flip references such as "karmic rap sheets of surf-
sax players' (37), "Doc the kiss of death, laying bad karma on everybody he
touched" (215), "three stiffs so far that may or may not be on his karmic ticket"
(313), "the bad-karma level gets jacked up one more little two-hundred-dollar
notch" (347) and "this weird twisted cop karma" (350). Given that Virginia
Woolf's allusions to Tibetan Buddhism in *Between the Acts* unveiled an early
glimpse of postmodern fiction (Kohn *Buddhism in* 239), Pynchon's turn from it in
Inherent Vice is another marker for postmodernism's ending.

The banal world of *Inherent Vice* may have been inspired by Arendt's view
of a world in which an allegedly "normal" person would rather "ship millions of
men, women, and children to their death" than disobey "what he had been
ordered to do" by his superiors (*Eichmann in* 25). Arendt's report from Jerusalem
was controversial largely because she accepted Eichmann's dubious assertions that
he was a normal human being. Posing as a reasonable man, he revealed that

> he had received a memorandum from an S.S. man stationed in the
> Warthegau, telling him that 'Jews in the coming winter could no longer be
> fed,' and submitting for his consideration a proposal as to "whether it
> would not be the most humane solution to kill those Jews who were
> incapable of work through some quicker means. This, at any rate, would
> be more agreeable than to let them die of starvation." (*Eichmann in* 95, 96)

Arendt believed that "He 'personally' never had anything whatever against Jews"
(26), that "everybody could see this man was not a monster" (54).

It may also be that vice and evil tend to thrive in the presence of
misinformation and the absence of correct information. This seems to have been
especially true in Pynchon's portrayal in *Inherent Vice* of the late 1960s and early
70s, when postmodern rationalism was presumably flourishing. Kevin, the owner
of

> Kozmik Banana, a frozen-banana shop near the Gordita Beach pier, [...[
> instead of throwing away the banana peels, was cashing in on a hippie
> belief of the moment by converting them to a smoking product he called
> Yellow Haze. [...] Some who smoked it reported psychedelic journeys to
> other places and times. Others came down with horrible nose, throat, and
> lung symptoms that lasted for weeks. The belief in psychedelic bananas
> went on, however, gleefully promoted by underground papers which ran

learned articles comparing diagrams of banana molecules to those of LSD
and […] Kevin was raking in thousands.   (*Inherent* 140)

Adding to the vice, the local LAPD station kept a freezer full of several hundred
frozen chocolate-covered bananas:

> Bigfoot saw no reason why law enforcement shouldn't be cut in for a
> share of the proceeds. "What kind of extortion do you call that?" Doc
> wanted to know. "Ain't like it's a real drug, it doesn't get you loaded, and
> anyway it's legal, Bigfoot." "Exactly my point. If it's legal, then so is
> taking my cut. Especially, see, if it's in the form of frozen bananas instead
> of money." (140)

Inherent Vice records the culture of the late 1960s when the Beatles "Yellow
Submarine" peaked in popularity. Could there have been some connection
between "Yellow Haze" and the Beatles at that time, "implicitly recognizing the
constraints inherent in the mythologizing process […] while standing amidst a
garden of flower power and *faux* cannabis" (Kenneth Womack 183). Could the
nostalgic Jerry Wilkerson have had that early era in mind when he painted "Starry
Night with Banana," which is reproduced as Figure 2 in Essay Ten above?

Banality, uniformity, dearth of knowledge and vice take on a different
meaning in Pynchon's 2009 novel when an unusual visitor comes to see Doc:

> What made him unusual was, was he was a black guy. To be sure, black
> folks were occasionally spotted west of the Harbor Freeway, but to see
> one this far out of the usual range, practically by the ocean, was pretty
> rare. Last time anybody could remember a black motorist in Gordita
> Beach, for example, anxious calls for backup went out on all the police
> bands, a small task force of cop vehicles assembled, and roadblocks were
> set up all along Pacific Coast Highway. (*Inherent Vice* 14)

I have no idea why Pynchon juxtaposed two *was*'s in the initial sentence above,
unless it was to emphasise the text's sameness and low information. Continuing
the history of blacks west of the Harbor Freeway, the narrator goes

> back to shortly after the Second World War, when a black family had
> actually tried to move into town and the citizens, with helpful advice
> from the Ku Klux Klan, had burned the place to the ground and then, as
> if some ancient curse had come into effect, refused to allow another
> house ever to be built on the site. The lot stood empty until the town
> finally confiscated it and turned it into a park, where the youth of Gordita
> Beach, by the laws of karmic adjustment, were soon gathering at night to
> drink, dope, and fuck, depressing their parents, though not property
> values particularly. (14)

Fortunately, this is history. My son and his wife adopted three African-American
children and wouldn't think of raising them in any other state but California.

What to make of Mickey Wolfmann, the "scumbug developer" Doc's
ex-girlfriend had ran away with (40)? Aunt Reet called him:

Westside Hochdeutsch mafia, biggest of the big, construction, savings and loans, untaxed billions stashed under an Alp someplace, technically Jewish but wants to be a Nazi, becomes exercised often to the point of violence at those who forget to spell his name with two *n*'s. What's he to you?" Doc gave her a rundown on Shasta's visit and her account of the plot against the Wolfmann fortune. "In the real-estate business," Reet remarked, "God knows, few of us are strangers to moral ambiguity. But some of these developers, they make Godzilla look like a conservationist, and you might not care to get involved with this, Larry." (*Inherent* 7)

Wolfmann's giant housing development, Channel View Estates,

> stretched into the haze and the soft smell of the fog component of smog, and of desert beneath the pavement–model units nearer the road, finished homes further in, and just visible beyond them the skeletons of new construction, expanding into the unincorporated wastes. Doc drove past the gate till he got to a patch of empty contractor hardpan with street signs already in but the streets not yet paved. He parked at what would be the corner of Kaufman and Broad. (20)

The inference of those street names is that the Wolfmann character is based in part on the renowned builder Eli Broad. His name, I was quickly reminded when I visited the Broad Foundation building in Santa Monica a number of years ago, is pronounced to rhyme with road. My article "Pynchon's Transition from Ethos-Based Postmodernism to Late-Postmodern Stylistics" would never have been written if the Broad Foundation had not generously provided some of their finest examples of postmodern American art of the 1980s to Washington University for a major exhibition at the Sam Fox Arts Center in 2004-2005. My thesis in that article was that *The Crying of Lot 49* influenced American postmodern art of the 1980's, which art in turn influenced Pynchon's *Against the Day*. Only now, as I connect postmodernism to complexity do I realize that the chief attribute of the Broad artworks that I used in my article was, as Cover and Thomas might have put it, their extremely high "average uncertainty in the random variable" (5; see for example, my paragraph on David Salle's "Pound Notes" starting at the bottom of page 200 and ending near the bottom of page 201 in Kohn, *Pynchon's Transition*. This paragraph is better understood in the light of Duyfhuizen's comments on "fragments of meaning across a culture that has lost any totalizing mythology" [237]). Hassan was fifteen years ahead of his time when he wrote that "Postmodern art, viewed in a Modernist perspective, creates more anxiety than it appeases" (*POSTmodernISM* 29).

Most of what I know about Eli Broad, the man, I learned from a segment about him on the television show *60 Minutes* which aired on April 24, 2011. All that he has in common with the fictional Wolfmann is that he built major housing subdivisions in the Los Angeles area, and that like Wolfmann, who suddenly "decide[d] to change his life and give away millions" (*Inherent* 244), so are Broad and his wife fulfilling a commitment to give away 75 percent of their wealth, possibly more, to philanthropy. What astonished me most was the ending of *60 Minutes* segment, when Broad stood beside one of his best known sculptures, a large bronze casting, 29" x 67" x 69," by Tom Otterness, officially entitled "Double Foot" but evidently known as "Bigfoot" by certain Angelenos, because that's what 60-Minutes' host Morley Safer called it. That could explain why Pynchon thought of this nickname for his corrupt LAPD detective, unless it was just an amazing coincidence.

Just as smaller firms like Aunt Reet's had "major liquid-liner issues" of their own to deal with and resented Wolfmann's "latest assault on the environment–some chipboard horror known as Channel View Estates" (*Inherent* 8), competitors may have wondered whether Broad's corporate giant got breaks from police officers like Bigfoot. "People with a decent respect for preserving the environment" may even have spoken of Kaufman and Broad as "high-density tenement scum without the first idea of how to clean up after themselves," as they did of Wolfmann in the novel (347). Operating on the scale they did, Broad's contractors, like Wolfmann's, could have committed "reels' worth of Stateside environmental abuse," strangely reminiscent of "jungle clearings" (104). I don't know whether Kaufman and Broad did so, but it is relevant that Ihab Hassan, in a section on "The Imaginable" in his 1971 essay "POSTmodernISM," published a year or two after the time period in which *Inherent Vice* was set, wrote: "The litany of our disasters is all too familiar, and we recite it in the name of that unholy trinity, Population, Pollution, Power (read genocide), hoping to appease our furies, turn our fate inside out" (22). It was in the 1960s that Americans became aware of population and pollution as problems. The Eichmann trial started bringing the Nazi genocide out of the closet. It was the burgeoning of population in southern California that created the demand for the conversion of desert land to housing, for urban sprawl, and for mounting reliance on polluting automobiles, though government regulation could have mitigated the adverse effects of these pressures. To the extent that there were regulations, power and money may have subverted enforcement. That it was a world problem is registered in the epigraph to *Inherent Vice*, one of the graffiti from the May 1968 student uprising in Paris, "Under the paving-stones, the beach!", which is connected in the novel's reference to the "desert beneath the pavement" at Channel View Estates (20).

A lingering disaster in the 1960s was racial, religious, ethnic, cultural, even gender prejudice. Aunt Reet seems obsessed with Mickey Wolfmann's being Jewish. Even Doc finds it hard to take his aunt's word that Wolfmann surrounds himself with anti-Semitic bodyguards from the Aryan Brotherhood. It took Pynchon until 2009 to recognize that his repudiation of modernity's utopianism in *The Crying of Lot 49* was short-lived, superseded by the new dystopian modernism, which remained largely ignored for decades. Holocaust awareness burgeoned in 1985 with Claude Lanzmann's 500-minute film, *Shoah*, that featured clandestine interviews with former Nazi perpetrators and revelatory visits to key extermination sights. By the time that the 2006 edition of Arendt's *Eichmann in Jerusalem* appeared, gentile Germans were as conscious of, and offended by, the human disaster as anyone else. Pynchon's view of postmodernism holding sway for the latter part of the 1960s, then serving another 30-years to shield the gathering dystopia, is comparable to Berardi's European view of the "arts of the 1900s [having] favored the register of utopia in two forms: the radical utopia of Mayakovsky and the functional utopia of the Bauhaus"–followed by the "dystopian thread [which] remained hidden in the folds of the artistic and literary imagination" (*(T)error* 43). "Only today, at the beginning of the twenty-first century," added Berardi, "does dystopia take center stage and conquer the whole field of the artistic imagination"(43). Virilio, like Berardi, skipped postmodernism altogether. Having come of age in dystopian Nazi-occupied Paris, he told Armitage: "I simply cannot understand why people are talking about postmodernism. […] It doesn't make any sense to me. Hence, I do not feel linked at all with postmodernity" (Armitage 25). Even from the American experience, John Knapp may have been more literal than figurative when he spoke of treatises on postmodernism dealing with a *moment* in critical history.

I had thought in Essay Ten, based on the rising fear of dystopian developments in science and technology, that Pynchon was following in the direction of Virilio's hypermodernism. Berardi's emphasis on dystopianism, of which Pynchon appears to have been aware, overlaps Virilio's hypermodernism, when in "(T)error and Poetry," Berardi expresses concern about "the proliferation of artificial devices in the organic universe" and especially "in the body" (42). Berardi's dystopia overlaps Pynchon's when he writes of the "dystopian thread [having] remained hidden in the folds of the artistic and literary imagination," giving Fritz Lang's expressionism as an example (43). "Metropolis," Lang's 1927 film masterpiece, set in a futuristic urban dystopia, is evidence that early modernism wasn't only utopian. The dystopia in *Inherent Vice* is entirely sociological, which in fact is more consistent with Huyssen's initial philosophy than with my own interpretation of modernism, postmodernism and its sequel as being based on changing attitudes toward science and technology.

Adiga calls *Inherent Vice* "minor Pynchon, but […] the perfect entry point into his work for a new generation of readers." For Pynchon to have left this impression attests to his brilliance as a writer. The perfect entry point into Pynchon's novels is still *The Crying of Lot 49*, but a close reading of *Inherent Vice* is now a necessary complement to a close reading of the earlier novel. It's as though Pymchon intended it to be. Behind the hieroglyphic streets of San Narciso there was no "transcendent meaning"–"only the earth" and dystopia (*Crying* 181).

Dystopia Writ Large (DeLillo)

In every one of his novels except the last, *Point Omega*, published in 2010, DeLillo refers to Tibetan Buddhism. In my recent essay on this aspect of his writings

(Kohn *Tibetan*), I draw heavily on Joseph Dewey's insightful categorization of
DeLillo's first 14 novels:

> [I]nitially, he embraced the street, specifically an unabashed love for the
> reach of the alert sense; then he tested his own deep satisfaction with the
> word as our species' defining and empowering gesture [...], and most
> recently, he has turned to the implications of the soul, the difficult
> confirmation of a visible spiritual dimension. Such a schema [...]–the
> street, the word, and the soul–can provide an enticing touchtone for
> approaching DeLillo. (Dewey 8-9)

Dewey's three stages have a Tibetan Buddhist correlative in the *Tri-Kaya*, which is
Sanskrit for "the Three Divine Bodies" through which "the Buddha Essence is
present and perpetually manifested" (Evans-Wentz *Dead* 3). These are stated in
reverse order by Evans-Wentz as "the *Buddha*, the "*Dharma* (or Scriptures), [and]
the *Sangha* (or Priesthood)" (*Liberation* 14). In *Point Omega*, DeLillo abruptly
discredits his three stage/*Tri-Kaya* approach–most likely as a reaction to Dewey's
revelation of his archetypes. He demeans "street" by repeating the word no less
than 13-times in a single paragraph (*Point Omega* 67, 68). As to "words," the "true
life" says Jim Finley in the first sentence of Chapter 1 "is not reducible to words
spoken or written, not by anyone, ever" (*Point* 17). The novel's protagonist
Richard Elster, one of the "the tight minds that made the [Iraq] war" (18),
reminded me of Paul Wolfowitz–the mention in the novel that "Wolfowitz went
to the World Bank" (23), though it apparently constitutes a legal disclaimer,
suggests that DeLillo had him very much in mind–especially, given the remark
that "the hair on his [Elster's] head was a question of morale" (90) and the iconic
TV clip of Wolfowitz licking his comb before a quick coif, though in the novel,
Elster "wasn't carrying a comb" and had "to smooth down his hair with his hands
once he got in front of a mirror" (110). From Elster's mouth came this
astonishing indictment of words:

> Lying is necessary. The state has to lie. There is no lie in war or in
> preparation for war that can't be defended. We tried to create new
> realities overnight, careful sets of words that resemble advertising slogans
> in memorability and repeatability. These were words that would yield
> pictures eventually and then become three-dimensional. The reality
> stands, it walks, it squats. Even when it doesn't. (*Point* 28, 29)

In *Point Omega*, the "soul" now connotes dystopia rather than transcendence: "The
man [Elster] is a soul in distress, [...] a flawed character in a chamber drama,
justifying his war and condemning the men who made it" (99). With the
tarnishing of the street, the word and the soul, the *Tri-Kaya* and all its allusions to
Buddhism vanish from *Point Omega*. In the one exception, Dennis asks Jessie "Can
you imagine yourself living another life?" (111): we know that DeLillo has
Buddhist reincarnation in mind because he quoted Evans-Wentz's *Tibetan Book of
the Dead* in his first novel (*Americana* 324). Jessie's reply to Dennis–"That's too

easy. Ask me something else" (*Point* 111)–conveys DeLillo's intention to move past Buddhism, which had been the hallmark of his postmodernism.

As in Pynchon's *Inherent Vice*, anti-rationalization, anti-optimization, and anti-utopianism are carried to extremes in DeLillo's *Point Omega*, while the postmodern attraction to new spiritualities is displaced. Elster appeals to the visceral "I still want a war. A great power has to act. We were struck hard. We need to retake the future. The force of will, the sheer visceral need" (*Point* 30).

The most powerful image in *Point Omega* is Douglas Gordon's renowned videowork *24 Hour Pyscho*, the "old Hitchcock film projected so slowly it takes twenty-four hours to screen the whole thing" (47). With ordinary cinematic film, "the speed at which we perceive reality, at which the brain processes images," is "twenty-four frames per second" (*Point* 103). In "subliminal time, two frames per second" (*Point* 116)–more exactly, 109 frames per minute–it is the counter-image of the speed that Virilio calls the "Contamination [... of] the space-time of our planet" (*Open* 22); in its very tediousness it is disorienting. The novel incorporates the actual exhibition of Gordon's piece at the Museum of Modern Art in the late summer and early fall of 2006, and describes the visitation on September 3rd and 4th by its major fictional characters, including the young psycho, Dennis, who visits it on both days. In Dennis's case, watching the attenuated *Psycho* all day long becomes understandably addictive–"This was the fifth straight day he'd come here"(*Point* 6)–and he "kept feeling things whose meaning escaped him" (11). After the young woman walked in and spoke to him in the darkened room–she liked speaking to strangers–he imagined himself "turning and pinning her to the wall with the room emptied out except for the guard who is looking straight ahead, nowhere, motionless, the film still running, the woman pinned, also motionless, watching the film over his shoulder" (112). He follows her when she leaves and gets her telephone number. When he returns to watching the video, he "imagines the guard removing the sidearm from his holster and shooting himself in the head" (116).

In *Point Omega*, Elster carries dystopianism to its extreme: "Look at us today. We keep inventing folk tales of the end. Animal diseases spreading, transmittable cancers. [...] The climate. [...] The asteroid, the meteorite. [...] Famine, worldwide [, ...] the end of human life on earth" (51). "Father Teilhard knew this, the omega point. A leap out of our biology" (52). "Consciousness is exhausted. Back now to inorganic matter. This is what we want. We want to be stones in a field" (*Point* 53).

A few pages from the end of *The Human Phenomenon*, the latest translation of Teilhard's acclaimed *Phenomenon of Man*, he foresaw the possibility "that evil, increasing at the same time as good, will reach its paroxysm in the end, and it too, in a specifically new form. There are no summits without abysses" (Teilhard 206). Whereas, Father C.J. McNaspy emphasizes the summit–"As a Christian, he [Teilhard] identifies the omega point with the risen Christ" (387)–DeLillo's Elster foresees the paroxysmal abyss, humans wanting "to be stones in a field" (*Point* 53).

Nirvana is a Sanskrit word that means blowing out, extinguishing–
Webster's (1980) explicitly includes "wind" in the definition. What it says is
extinguished is "desire and individual consciousness." *Point Omega* ends with a
merger of *Nirvana* and paroxysm, as the young psycho separates himself from the
wall of the museum

> and waits to be assimilated, pore by pore, to dissolve into the figure of
> Norman Bates, who will come into the house and walk up the stairs in
> subliminal time, two frames per second, toward the door of Mother's
> room. Sometimes he sits by her bed and says something and then looks at
> her and waits for an answer. Sometimes he just looks at her. Sometimes a
> wind comes before the rain and sends birds sailing past the window, spirit
> birds that ride the night, stranger than dreams. (*Point* 116-17).

The "dominating tendency of mental life, and perhaps of nervous life in general,"
wrote Freud, "is the effort to reduce, to keep constant or to remove internal
tension [, …] a tendency which finds expression in the pleasure principle; and our
recognition of that fact is one of our strongest reasons for believing in the
existence of death instincts" (Freud 50).

Concluding Remarks

Teilhard foresaw evil "increasing at the same time as good" and reaching its
"paroxysm in the end," in a "specifically new form. There are no summits [of
good] without abysses [of evil]," he wrote (206). Whereas utopian modernism
over-emphasized the summits of good, which postmodernism subsequently
repudiated, postmodernism itself was engulfed by a wave of dystopian
modernism. Although Virilio blamed the dystopia on hyperscience and
hypertechnology, he sounded almost like Teilhard, when he wrote that

> the great regression of living matter has, then, begun, with the manifest
> refusal of our age to generate the succeeding ones, and the absolute
> reversal of the accepted logic of the evolution of species, with the most
> accomplished link in the chain (the human being?) re-situating itself on its
> own initiative not far from the very first cell – the point at which the first
> glimmer of terrestrial life seemingly appeared.
> (*Information Bomb* 34)

Berardi likewise recognized the great regression, the shift from the end of "the
century that believed in the future" to the "beginning of the century with no
future" (*(T)error* 39). Berardi saw that literature and culture have entered a
dystopian era, which in the present essay, I have associated with Pynchon's
Inherent Vice and DeLillo's *Point Omega*. The fact that the former is placed in the
1970th year of the common era and that Berardi specifically dates DeLillo's
"literary dystopia" back to "the second half of the twentieth century" suggests
that cultural and literary change has been happening much faster than we thought
(*(T)error* 43).

Berardi is likely to have had *Mao II* in mind as DeLillo's first dystopian novel. That John Adams' opera *The Death of Kinghoffer* and *Mao II*, both pinnacles of dystopia, were copyrighted in the same year –1991–suggests that 1990 may have marked the return to modernism that Huyssen (49) foresaw, only this time in its counter-utopian phase. Goodman's libretto of the opera is richly dystopian, bristling with accusations of murder, the desire for the deaths of enemies and vows to die for one's cause. The Chorus of Exiled Palestinians sing: "Let the supplanter look/ Upon his work. Our faith/ Will take the stones he broke/ And break his teeth" (Goodman 1). Molqi, one of the hijackers, sings: "Tell them there is a bomb/ in the engine room./ If we are betrayed / The ship will explode/ And you will be dead" (7). Mamoud, a second hijacker, sings "We are sorry/ For you. We don't worry/ As we want to die" (7) and remembers in song his mother saying "There was a raid" and "God would/ Restore threefold/ All we had called/ Ours. She was killed/ With the old men/ And children in/ Camps at Sabra/ And Chatila" (10). In his first aria, Leon Klinghoffer, the wheel-chair bound American Jew, accuses Mamoud: "You pour gasoline/ Over women/ Passengers on/ The bus to Tel Aviv/ And burn them alive./ You don't give a shit,/ Excuse me, about your grandfather's hut./ His sheep and his goat,/ And the land you wore out./ You just want to see/ People die" (18-19). Omar, a third hijacker, sings "May we be worth/ The pains of death/ And not grow old/ In the world/ Like these Jews./ My soul is/ All violence" (23). After Klinghoffer is shot offstage and Rambo, the fourth hijacker, throws his dollar bills in the air, singing "What will they buy/ That anyone wants?/ They come from the pants/ Of an old man./ They're not very clean" (26), Mamoud threateningly intones "Every fifteen/ Minutes, one/ More will be shot./ You cannot doubt/ We mean what we say" (25). The Captain pleads "They know the score. It's time for you/ To shoot another passenger -/ A guest in my house, as it were./ I speak now as a man to men:/ You should kill me. That act alone/ Would echo to your lasting fame./ [...] / Shoot me, and let that be enough" (26-27). "It's finished./ As you wished,/ It was done by talk," sings Mamoud in reply (28). When the ordeal is over and the Captain finally informs Marilyn Klinghoffer of her husband's death, she concludes her aria (and the opera) with "They should have killed me. I wanted to die" (32). Indeed, she died the year after the hijacking.

Before I conclude this essay by suggesting that Pynchon's *Inherent Vice* is as dystopian as Adams' and Goodman's *Death of Klinghoffer* and DeLillo's *Mao II* and that the latter's *Point Omega* is, perhaps, the beginning of a neo-postmodernist repudiation of dystopian modernism, I want to draw on a powerful statement that may define this neo-postmodernist ethos. At my request, Gerald Early kindly sent me a copy of his unpublished opening remarks as moderator of the May 26, 2011 panel discussion of *The Death of Klinghoffer* at the Ethical Society of St. Louis. To understand the terrorists, Early said,

> you must, for a few hours, know what it feels like to be one, to
> acknowledge the times in your own being when you actually felt that

181

someone else was not really human. To recognize evil, you must first know how seductive evil can be, how it can give false strength and corrupted pride. It is the job of the great artist not to detach you from experience, not to make you a mere tourist of human experience, but to force you to confront it by making you see yourself in repulsive human beings, to make you see both the evil in humanity and the awful humanity in evil. To believe that evil is be found only in the other, that evil is the other, is merely to delude ourselves by believing that what is horrible in human beings is alien to us. Nothing humans do is alien to any other human being. It is the belief of the great artist that we can understand what other people think and do; we can put ourselves in the place of other people. If this were not so, why do we then have art? Is it not one of the purposes of art to take us out of ourselves and to put ourselves into the place of others? (Gerald Early, May 26, 2011)

"The tragedy of *The Death of Klinghoffer*," Early concluded, "is that the characters, ultimately cannot break free. They don't know how." This is certainly true of the hijackers and of Klinghoffer himself, as revealed in some of their arias quoted above.

Doc Sportello in *Inherent Vice* could have been one of those people described by Early who can see themselves in repulsive human beings and who know how seductive evil can be. When "a crazed teenage doper of Doc's acquaintance had stolen a fire bell from his high school as part of a vandalism spree, and next morning the youth, overcome with remorse and having no idea what to do with the bell, came to Doc and offered it for sale," Doc was happy to help him out and had the bell hooked up to his office phone, which "seemed like a groovy idea at the time" (*Inherent* 154). "Forgiveness," Millard writes, "or at least a form of nonjudgementalism toward individual behavior, is in ample supply in Pynchon's work" (17). Certainly, Doc's willingness to acquire the stolen fire bell briefly exemplified the nonjudgementalism in *Inherent Vice*. However, any major forgiveness on Doc's part, the kind that met Early's standards, was hard for me to find—until the fourth to last page of the novel, when Doc learns, that Trillium Beaverton had been admitted to a Las Vegas hospital "with a concussion, cuts, and bruises" and three days later "released in the custody of her parents" (*Inherent* 366). What was strange was Doc's relief to receive this information from Sparky, one of the early surfers of the internet: "'That's her.' He looked over Sparky's shoulder at the screen. 'What do you know, that is her. Well. Thanks, man'" (366). But why is Doc happy to learn that his friend and former client, Trillium, had to be hospitalized with injuries? The answer to this question has more to do with Puck Beaverton, a neo-Nazi with a swastika tattooed on his shaved head, who married Trillium earlier in the novel (246-47). Doc learned about the state of their marriage when he was coming out of a drug coma, which he did not yet realize had been administered by Puck:

"That you again, Puck? How's the missus?"

"Who told you about that?"

"Uh-oh. What happened?"

"The paramedics gave her a good chance, better than you got right at the moment."

"What'd you do to her, Puck?"

"Nothin she didn't want. What fuckin business is it of yours?" (319) Puck has the upper hand because Doc was handcuffed after being injected. It turns out that Puck and Adrian Prussia have a contract from Bigfoot (the "silent benefactors [being] the LAPD" [324]) to kill Doc, though it appears that Bigfoot would be happiest if all three killed each other. With Doc handcuffed in a room and "the dead bolt slammed into place," it appears that the Private Investigator's life is close to over (326). "It took a lot of squirming and muscle strain and semi-headstands to get even one of the shims to fall out of his jacket, but finally Doc worked himself out of the cuffs, creaked up off the bed, and had a look around" (326). Next thing, he is out of the room, "grabbing Puck's head and continuing to beat it almost silently against the marble doorsill till everything was too slippery with blood" (327). He recovers his handgun from Puck's pocket, "keeping an ear out for Adrian" (327), whom he eventually drops with a bullet. It's too dark to see well: "'That you, Adrian?'/ 'I'm fuckin lunch meat,' sobbed Adrian. 'Oh, shit ...'/ 'Did I get you?' said Doc./ 'You got me.'/ 'Fatal, I hope?'/ 'Feels like it.'/ 'How can I know for sure?'/ 'Maybe it'll be on the news at eleven, asshole.'/ 'Stay there, try not to croak, I'll call this in.'"/ He went looking for a phone. [...] He was calling the ambulance when he heard sounds of activity from directly beneath the floor" (328). I won't divulge anymore of the ending, but before he makes it home, he knows that Adrian is dead and is pretty sure that Puck is also. Somebody on the Pynchon *Inherent Vice* Wiki website figured out that the date is Tuesday, May 5, 1970. So why is Doc so happy on Friday, May 8, 1970 to learn that Trillium was released from the hospital "last Tuesday" (366)? I would like to think that the Wiki site is wrong on the dates–Maybe the site is not peer reviewed–and that Doc was relieved to learn that Puck was still alive and well and beating up on his wife; that would have been better in his mind than him killing Puck. He didn't want to kill Adrian either and had told him, in vain; "Go on ahead Adrian, you can still get away, go in peace man, don't let me keep you or nothing" (330). The real enemy was Bigfoot, and he had told him so; "You fuckin set me up, Bigfoot, what's the matter, you don't have the balls to do this yourself?" (328).

Maybe Pynchon didn't want to imbue *Inherent Vice* with anything but inherent vice, pure dystopia-like *Mao II*, like *The Death of Klinghoffer*. In *Falling Man*, DeLillo forgave the 9/11 hijackers (See Kohn *Tibetan Buddhism*, note 4, which begins "On September 9, 2001, my wife and I ...")). In *Point Omega*, Finley forgave Elster: "Whatever Elster's sense of implication, the nature of his guilt and failure, I shared it" (88-89). "Look at him, inconsolably human" (*Point* 96). "The story was here, not in Iraq or in Washington, and we were leaving it behind and taking it with us, both" (99). Possibly Finley forgave Dennis too: "The omega point has narrowed, here and now, to the point of a knife as it enters a body" (98).

If there is a new postmodernism that repudiates inordinate self-righteousness in the censure of evil, we should find it in the writings of popular newspaper columnists as well as revered humanities scholars like Gerald Early. Consider the following excerpt from last Friday's column in the *St. Louis Post Dispatch* by Bill McClellan:

> I remember when we had a so-called voting fraud scandal. The Association of Community Organizations for Reform Now–ACORN–conducted a voter registration drive and a good number of the newly registered voters did not exist. Or they were dogs. Or they were dead. Or they were cartoon characters. I had mixed reactions to that story. My main reaction was this: I don't like voter registration drives. If you can't find the local library [where people used to go to register to vote], too bad for you. But I also have sympathy for the workers who turned in the phony names. They were paid $7 an hour but had to meet a daily quota.
>
> When I first moved to St. Louis, I was unable to get a newspaper job, so I got a job for a marketing company doing door-to-door surveys. My supervisor warned me about filling out the forms without talking to people. She said the company did random checks and cheaters were fired. I stayed honest for most of the first morning. But it was awful work. Nobody wanted to answer my questions. I couldn't blame them. One of my questions had to do with household income. People looked at me like I was working for a burglary ring. For all I knew, I was. Soon, I was sitting in a fast-food restaurant filling out the surveys myself. So, yes, I could sympathize with those ACORN workers who had falsified registration cards. (A11)

Between McClellan's inclination to look for similar flaws in his own past in order to empathize with wrong-doers, Early's willingness to see himself in repulsive human beings, Jim Finley's forgiveness of one of the tight minds that lied to make the Iraq war, and Larry "Doc" Sportello's relief that a punk he thought he'd beaten to death, to keep from being killed himself, had actually survived, we have a good insight on what the new anti-dystopian postmodernism might look like.

(It is June 24, 2011, the day after I delivered this manuscript to the printer and the morning after I finally attended the performance of *The Death of Klinghoffer* by Opera Theatre of St. Louis. According to the libretto, which I read twice, the chorus does not appear in the final scene; yet there they were quietly singing "Noah" over and over again. I perceive this to have been Opera Theatre's 2011 reaction, though I'm not sure they were the first, to the unremitting dystopia of Adams' and Goodman's original 1991 version. Whether justified or not, they felt the compunction to conclude with a neo-postmodern glimmer of hope. The horrible flood of dystopia is over, the ark has come through, and Noah reiterates his faith.)

Close Reading and F.R. Leavis

The act of a metaphor then was a thrust at truth and a lie,
depending where you were: inside, safe, or outside, lost. Oedipa
did not know where she was. (*Crying* 129)

"And something rather disturbing, Miz Maas. A new book
bidder has appeared on the scene, whom neither I nor any of the
firms in the area have heard of before. That hardly ever
happens." [...] "Then how do you know he's a stranger?" "Word
gets around [, ...] he was an outsider. So being a conservative
house, naturally, they apologized and said no." "What do you
think?" said Oedipa, already knowing pretty much. "That our
mysterious bidder may be from Tristero," Cohen said.
(*Crying* 176)

I think I understand what F.R. Leavis had in mind when he began Chapter 1 of
The Living Principle with the disclaimer: "This is not the book I have been often
reproached with having promised a quarter of a century ago, and never having
produced. "Judgment and Analysis" was the heading I put over some of the
intended contents when they were printed in *Scrutiny*" (19). Presumably, he was
widely expected to elucidate how his close reading, which he was now referring to
as "local close criticism" (Leavis 23), as "close local attention," as "close and
sensitive perception" (24), and as 'close critical study" (59), had been
"triumphantly consummated in the American New Criticism" (Eagleton 44). In
no way, however, could Leavis have believed, as Eagleton put it, that "any piece
of language, 'literary' or not, can be adequately studied or even understood in
isolation" (44). Sections i, ii, iii, and v of Chapter 2 of *The Living Principle*,
according to Paul Dean, "were originally published in [Leavis's journal] *Scrutiny*
under the running title 'Judgment and Analysis' and were already classics before
their appearance in the [1975] book" (4). In the original section i, which dates
back to 1945, written before the American New Criticism peaked as a *cause célèbre*,
Leavis closely examined a piece of poetry, not intra-textually (as in the new
criticism) but inter-textually, first contrasting a poem by William Johnson Cory
with one by Sir Walter Scott (71-72), then a poem by William Wordsworth with
one by Alfred, Lord Tennyson (72-73), next one by D.H. Lawrence with another
by Tennyson (75-76), and finally one by Lionel Pigot Johnson with one by
Andrew Marvel (82-84). To emphasize the intertextuality in each case, Leavis
pointedly identified the first excerpt as (a) and the second as (b). It was his view
that if he took "two poems, which present an obvious contrast, for a 'comparison'
that should initiate discussion" (71). Rather than renounce his reliance on

intertextuality, as devotees of the American New Criticism may have expected him to do, Leavis reproduced and featured the same four sections in his 1975 *summa*. Moreover, in the new section iv, he specifically extended the emphasis on inter-textual analysis from poetry to prose. A paragraph by (a) M.A. Chapman (1921) is contrasted with one of (b) Herbert Read (Leavis 135), and another by (a) Joseph Conrad with one by (b) William Makepeace Thackeray (139-40). No wonder that Leavis "made enemies," he had "fallen foul of the current dogma that all criticism," not just the American New Criticism, "must be underpinned by an explicitly stated theory, something he consistently refused" (Dean 3).

The "really triumphant achievement" of Leavis's *The Living Principle*, Dean argued, "comes in the new material" (4). Likewise, for me, Leavis's Chapter 1, entitled "Thought, Language and Objectivity," comes closest to my personal views, as expressed in the present book, than any other critical work I know. Ordinarily I would think myself weird to want to believe that Leavis had written Chapter 1 of his book to help explain Pynchon's work *for me*, but he himself was no less weird when he said of Joseph Conrad's 1910 story, *The Secret Sharer.* "It is brief, but obviously the work of a great writer, one notably unlike Lawrence, and *it might have been written in order to enforce my point*" (45 emphasis added). Leavis importantly contended that literature" is "the supreme creative art of language," that all "major literary creation is concerned with thought," that "the thinking" of every great writer involves "a marked distinctiveness" in the "reality that is conveyed," and that the "human quality of genius" is "inseparable" from the "intense individuality" of each writer (49). Though such thoughts apply to Pynchon and his writing, they had not crystallized in my mind, and I am grateful to Leavis for articulating them. Because I believe that Pynchon's writing is focused on and imbued with his thoughts, my underlying objective is to identify the conscious thoughts that underlie his words. I am certainly not alone in this; Geddes for one, in his blog on *Inherent Vice*, wrote that "seeing the insights of [Pynchon's] mind is just what many of his readers are looking for" (4). Because Pynchon does not ordinarily respond to criticism, I am content with Leavis's view that "there is no meaning unless individual beings can meet in it" (58). Most of the essays in this book are based on earlier interpretations of *The Crying of Lot 49* that editors and their anonymous readers have rejected. Hopefully I have strengthened my positions, in large part in response to their helpful comments, and that there will be a number of readers of the present book who will agree that Pynchon might have had the thoughts I attribute to him.

The person that I would have liked most to read this book is, not Pynchon, but Leavis. Unfortunately, he died at the age I have finally reached. The reason that I would have wanted him to read my book is that he may have had *The Crying of Lot 49* in mind when he wrote the following:

> The notion that the currently applauded American writers prove the vitality of the civilization that produced them is absurd–and significant. What, characteristically, they demonstrate, is a depressing, and often

repellent, poverty in the range of experience, satisfaction and human potentiality they seem to know of, and to think all. As for the famed and flattered American critics, who write about the 'British-English' classics, they seem, judged by what they say about them, unable to read them. (Leavis 52)

Leavis died three years after he published this book. If he had lived longer and maintained his mental vigor, I believe he would have regretted writing the above paragraph. I'm sure that there are paragraphs in the present book that, if I lived long enough, I would regret having written.

As far as the British-English classics are concerned, surely Pynchon read John Fowles's *The French Lieutenant's Woman*, which he appeared to emulate in the 1990 novel *Vineland*, with its amazing alternative ending of *The Crying Of Lot 49*. Not the least of the contributions of Fowles's famous novel is that it had three alternative endings: the first on pages 348 and 349, the second from page 350 to 473, and the third from page 474 to 480. Near the end of *Vineland*, its protagonist visits Wendell ("Mucho") Maas, now a "music-business biggie" living in a "posh Telegraph Hill town house" in San Francisco (307). "[O]riginally a disk jockey," he "had decided around 1967, after a divorce remarkable even in that more innocent time for its geniality, to go into record producing" (*Vineland* 309). How could Mucho, who was lucky to find a job in broadcasting when he couldn't endure selling used cars any longer, and who appeared to the program director at KCUF to be losing his mind, have been able two years later to start his own business producing records? This could be evidence that Pierce left his fortune in trust to Oedipa, with the intention of becoming the soul of her future child, who would eventually be the beneficiary. Perhaps the trust allowed her, at her discretion, to withdraw funds for special situations such as the congenial divorce that would take Mucho out of her life. There appeared to have been little prospect of Mucho's being able to produce a child with a woman anywhere near his own age, so a divorce was in Pierce's interest, as well as Oedipa's, and potentially Mucho's. It is not surprising that Mucho, now close to 50, had taken up with a women "forever eighteen" (*Vineland* 307), who might even have been the same Trillium, who had married the hoodlum Puck Beaverton fourteen years earlier in *Inherent Vice* (*supra* Essay Eleven). As I mentioned earlier in this book, I read *Vineland* before *The Crying of Lot 49*, so that the four or five pages in it devoted to Mucho didn't make an impression on me then. I am indebted to Duyfhuizen who concluded his essay, published for the third time by Bloom, with the information that "In *Vineland*, Pynchon briefly visits the fictional universe of *The Crying of Lot 49*" for an account of what happened to Mucho Maas between 1966 and 1984. (248). "Although hardly the continuation we may desire, at least we can infer that Oedipa got out of the auction room. Small comfort" (Duyfhuizen 248).

Pynchon was ambiguous about psychedelic drugs in the mid-1960s when he wrote *The Crying of Lot 49*. It was not clear whether Mucho had a problem with LSD–"He's losing his identity, Edna, how else can I put it? (*Crying* 140)–or whether it liberated him–his "face now smooth, amiable, at peace" (143)–or the problem was in Funch's and Oedipa's head (*supra* Essay Seven). A resident of San Francisco fourteen years later, he "figured as a responsible, even sober-sided user of psychedelics, but cocaine was another story. It hit him out of nowhere, […] furtive meetings between his nose and the illicit crystals, sudden ecstatic peaks, surprising negative cash flows" (*Vineland* 310). In *Vineland*, as Dan Geddes describes it, America has become a garrison state, "where organized political dissent is monitored and ultimately destroyed by the federal government. The Repression, as Pynchon calls it, takes many forms, including naked police power, political infiltration of the resistance, and the War on Drugs," which is symbolized on the novel's cover by a 1936 photograph by Darius Kinsey of "a burning forest, [here] suggestive of the government's attempt to stamp out marijuana use, a great nation's war on a botanical species." They called it the "Marijuana Menace," wrote Pynchon sardonically (*Vineland* 312). It's all the more absurd in 2011 when we allow private citizens to possess machine guns, but not marijuana? Perhaps, Leavis was right that "currently applauded American writers" fail to confirm "the vitality of the civilization that produced them" (52), but is it "absurd" that they should write to restore that vitality? And wouldn't Leavis have been proud that they were inspired by British writers such as Fowles and Ian McEwan to advocate change that is needed (see Kohn *Foursquare Amsterdam*). In the Introduction, on Essay Three, I recalled how my career in economics paralleled Pynchon's interest in pollution control. Our interests later crossed when I wrote a pair of articles on taxing controversial goods and services such as marijuana and prostitution, rather than *illegalizing* them (Kohn *Optimal Quantity*; Kohn *Transactions Costs*). It is a coincidence that the second of these articles was written and revised while I was a visiting professor at the University of California, Los Angeles. It did not occur to me then that laws on gun ownership would gradually be relaxed to the point where private citizens could own machine guns, and the left-hand-side headline of yesterday's *St. Louis Post-Dispatch* would read "Openly Carrying Guns is in Vogue" (Shane Anthony). If it had, I would surely have included firearms among the taxable controversial goods.

Perhaps, I relate strongly to Chapter 1 of Leavis's book because he wrote it when he was close to the age that I am now. I was particularly struck just now when I came upon a footnote in Chapter 1 that reads

> I find this, casually, in today's *Times*: "When did a Conservative minister last make a speech about patriotism: that is to say, about the objective idealism for which most human beings have some yearning as distinct from the rational self-interest which is the language of most political appeals today?" (Leavis 48)

It could be an old-age thing that makes us more apt to go off on tangents. I have purposely omitted footnotes from this book for that reason. It could also be an old-age thing that makes us want to write about past criticism we received. The introduction to this book is almost all about the earlier rejections that I have built upon. In a similar vein, Leavis wrote about "a prominent member of the Faculty" who once "proposed the elimination of [his famous] 'Practical Criticism' from among the papers set for the English Tripos" at Cambridge because it "was out of date–a now pointless inheritance from the past, so much had changed" (23). Later in the chapter he cites a critic who attacked him for "belabouring [T.S.] Eliot with what amounts to jargon" (59); given that the third chapter of *The Living Principle* is his now celebrated analysis of Eliot's *Four Quartets*, Leavis was not the least embarrassed by the critic's slur

Concluding Remarks

In the preface to their edited volume, *Close Reading: The Reader*, Frank Lentricchia and Andrew DuBois address what they "take to be the major clash in the practice of literary criticism in the past century: that between so-called formalist and so-called nonformalist (especially 'political') modes of reading." The headings of the two major sections of their book, "Formalism (Plus)" and "After Formalism?", are meant to suggest that

> formalist critics are always interested in the vast world which lies outside literature and that the nonformalists who have dominated literary criticism and theory over the last decades of the twentieth century do their most persuasive work by attending closely to the artistic character of the text before them.
>
> (Lentricchia and DuBois "Preface")

These terms, formalist and nonformalists, were new to me, and I took the above excerpt to mean that formalist critics, being interested in the vast world which lies outside literature, are not the American New Critics, whereas the nonformalists, who dominated literary criticism over the last decades of the twentieth century and did their most persuasive work by attending closely to the text before them, were the New Critics. That I was wrong was affirmed by Bressler's explanation that "the New Critics belong to a broad classification of literary criticism called formalism" which "espouse[s] what many call 'the text and text alone' approach to literary analysis" (33). Conceivably, Lentricchia and DuBois subtly conflated the two terms to "emphasize the continuity, not the clash of critical schools," in the hope that readers of their book "will emerge better equipped as close readers to deal critically with the messages, linguistically and visually encoded, that flood and threaten to drown us daily." Their thesis I believe is compatible with the way that I have implemented close reading in the present volume. I was pleased and intrigued that Eve Kosofsky Sedgwick's essay "Jane Austen and the Masturbating Girl" was included in the section "After Formalism?" of Lentricchia and DuBois's book, because ten months ago I published an article on Virginia Woolf's *Orlando* as the masturbating girl (Kohn, *Erotic Daydreams*). Whereas Sedgwick brings together the politics of disapproval with close reading, my article was able to dispense with such politics, given Woolf's liberated feminism, and concentrate on

"Formalism (Plus)," though, admittedly, I would not have dared to include "masturbation" among the keywords listed at the beginning of the article.

Just as Leavis was distressed that a particular analytical piece of his was slighted by a well known critic—it had seemed to Leavis to be "a piece of serious thinking about the fundamentals in question and one that, judged as such, deserve[d] better than to be lightly dismissed" (60)—so have I complained in my Introduction about anonymous readers who had only negative things to say about my submissions. But in the eight months that I have been working on this book— it started with my telephone call to Professor Hassan on November 6, 2010—I have realized more and more how well I have been treated by leaders in my new field. Many editors brushed me off, but a surprisingly large minority did not. It's understandable that English Studies graduates, who had taken the proper graduate courses, paid their dues as it were, and needed to publish for their livelihoods, were more deserving of journal space. At first, I was an outsider and, like Oedipa, did not know whether I was "inside, safe, or outside, lost" (*Crying* 129). My first submission, which was on *The Fan Man*, was rejected without explanation. My appeal to the editor for feedback was totally ignored. Fortunately I resubmitted the essay to Kostas Myrsiades, who if my memory is correct sent it to a half-dozen readers whose constructive responses were my first lessons in hermeneutics. Now, eleven years later, he is publishing a second essay, the one on Tibetan Buddhism in DeLillo's novels. He has rejected a number of intervening papers, but one acceptance per decade is enough to make me feel "inside." In the seven years that I have been submitting manuscripts to *Style* at Northern Illinois University, the journal has had three editors, each of which has published one of my articles; that's like "inside, safe." Most recently, since I started on this book, wonderful things have happened for me at *Soundings* and the *Journal of Modern Jewish Studies*. When I visited with Steven Moore last month, he informed me that the literary journals are being swamped with submissions. Surely, I have gotten more than my share, more than I even deserve, of what the academic humanities have to offer. I hasten to add that I have never read a published article in a current journal that struck me as less qualified than any of my papers, rejected or accepted.

It has nothing whatever to do with my being "inside, safe, or "outside, lost," but my latest close reading of the related paragraphs in *The Crying of Lot 49* makes me wonder why the new bidder at the auction of lot 49 was a threat to "the firms in the area," none of which had heard of him before (*Crying* 175). If there were some kind of collusion among the regular bidders at the philatelic auctions in little San Narciso, that would explain why Cohen "looked genuinely embarrassed" when he appeared at the auction: "Please don't call it a conflict of interests, he drawled earnestly. There were some lovely Mozambique triangles I couldn't quite resist. May I ask if you've come to bid, Miz Maas" (182). Her naive reply that she was "only being a busybody" may have reassured him that she was no threat (182). This suggests another interpretation of the last paragraph of *The*

Crying of Lot 49 in which the men in black mohair with pale, cruel faces were local bidders and Oedipa had settled back to await the crying of the auctioneer because she sensed what might be going on. If Cohen buys the Mozambique triangles without active competition, she will know. Given the intense focus on paranoia throughout *The Crying of Lot 49*, how could Oedipa have been anything but suspicious about Cohen's mailing out valuable stamps to potential buyers "willing to pay all the postage and insurance' (176) and his mention of "a conflict of interests" (182)? The implication of a man named Cohen, like mine which is Kohn, in connection with possible fraud may not have been obvious to readers, causing Pynchon, true to form, to alert them again in *Against the Day* to antisemitism in America. Kit Traverse is sounded out–"Traverse,' what sort of name ... you are not *also Hebraic*, by any chance?'" (*Against* 624)–satisfying the interrogator , who then expressed surprise that Kit is not anxious about "the millions now into your own country [...] how naïve do Americans have to be, not to see the danger?" (624). If Pynchon intentionally alluded to antisemitism by Cohen's behavior at the end of *The Crying of Lot 49*, it is important that Oedipa may also be Jewish. Charles Hollander gives a number of reasons why he thinks she is (74-75; see also Grant 2nd Ed., 13, 14). Catherine Stimpson's observation that "Pynchon's Jewish men want to sit *shivah* for the lost of the world" while "his Jewish women want to nurture and feed them" (85) further suggests that Oedipa is Jewish, for when she saw that "Genghis Cohen had a touch of summer flu, [... she] felt at once motherly" (*Crying* 94), and when, "hardly knowing what she was doing," she took the weeping old sailor "in her arms, actually held him [.] 'I can't help.' She whispered, rocking him, 'I can't help'" (126).

Pynchon's answer to antisemitism appears to be that Jews are like other people, they do good things and they do bad things. As I argue elsewhere, Kate Chopin implied the same in her 1899 masterpiece *The Awakening* (Kohn *The Jewess*; Kohn *Issues of Antisemitism*). We need go no further than the life of F.R. Leavis to show that intolerance sadly goes both ways. Quoting Denys Thompson's biography of the Leavises, G. Singh reveals that the

> total rejection by Q.D. Leavis's family of her marriage to a gentile was an act of cruelty that left a lasting wound ... The poison was never purged. Given the right kind of help and the capacity to accept it, she might have overcome the infliction; as it was, it seemed that she did not. {... Q.D. Leavis's} sense of belonging to a chosen people ... [hardened] ... into a conviction of her own infallibility {that in turn made her} intolerant, readily contemptuous of other people and their views, and arrogant. (Singh 179; braces {} denote my insertion of Singh's words in the quotation from Thompson)

Singh's reference to "psychoanalytical diagnosis" in the context of the above "infliction" suggest that religious prejudice is for the most part a mental illness (179).

New Close Readings of *The Crying of Lot 49*

******

As chance would have it, I did not discover Umberto Eco's book *Interpretation and Overinterpretation* until the last few days of my final review of the manuscript before turning it over tomorrow (June 23, 2011) to the printer for formatting. On the face of it, my interpretation of *The Crying of Lot 49* would appear to be the pinnacle in overinterpretation; it requires a greater number of pages, and these more dense, than the novel it interprets. I have assumed that Pynchon read and was influenced by particular books of E.M. Forster, Henry Adams, J.R. Pierce, Rachel Carson, Loren Eiseley, Charles Darwin, and W.Y. Evans-Wentz. I believe that he has followed breaking news and scholarly articles in the natural sciences, such as that surrounding the geological paradigm shift during the early- and mid-1960s, now called the Plate Tectonic Revolution, and in the medical sciences, such as were occasioned by the psychiatric turn from esoteric psychoanalysis to the exoteric *Diagnostic and Statistical Manual of Mental Disorders*. I have gone outside the subject novel to look at Pynchon's later novels, particularly *Vineland, Against the Day*, and *Inherent Vice*, for clues to changes in his thinking that contrasted with, and thereby elucidated *The Crying of Lot 49*. I went to writers like Andreas Huyssen, Paul Virilio, Roland Barthes, Franco Berardi, Don DeLillo, William Gaddis and even painters like Robert Longo, David Salle, Eric Fischl, Keith Haring and Jerry Wilkerson to learn more about *The Crying of Lot 49*. The list is by no means complete.

I am looking for what Pynchon "had to say" in the novel, not "what the text said independently of the intentions of its author," though Eco wrote that only through the latter can we find "what the text says by virtue of its textual coherence and of an underlying signification system." (63-64). I am led by what I have read in combination with what Eco calls my "own system of expectations"(64), though it has always been my intention to abandon any expectation that did not appear to match those of Pynchon. The same, I'm sure, apply to other writers, though certainly not to Angela Carter, who depended upon the reader's own system of expectations in the case of her poststructuralist novel, *The Infernal Desire Machines of Doctor Hoffman*. That novel will be the subject of another book I hope to write. When it comes to Pynchon and *The Crying of Lot 49*, I strongly reject Eco's view that

> the intention of the text is basically to produce a model reader able to make conjectures about it, the initiative of the model reader consists in figuring out a model author that is not the empirical one and that, in the end, coincides with the intention of the text. (Eco 64)

The only model reader that I can imagine for *The Crying of Lot 49* would be Pynchon himself. Eco rules this out when he writes:

> My ideal of textual interpretation as the discovery of a strategy intended to produce a model reader, conceived as the ideal counterpart of a model author (which appears only as a textual strategy), makes the notion of an empirical author's intention radically useless. We have to respect the text,

not the author as person so-and-so. Nevertheless, it can look rather crude to eliminate the poor author as something irrelevant for the story of an interpretation. (66)

Eco seems to think of the interpretation of a novel "as a paradigm, a theory must seem better than the other theories in the lists but need not necessarily explain all the facts with which it is concerned" (60). That would be like saying that my eleven or twelve essays are a list of competing paradigms. In the first place, my essays are mostly the rejected ones, so there are hundreds more. In the second place, those hundreds are almost all correct. Presumably, mine are low on the list because they're so late in coming. On the one hand, there are probably decreasing returns to interpretation, but, on the other hand, I had the strong shoulders of earlier critics to stand upon. And why can't we have as many theories as there are, excluding those that current consensus would reject? Why must we choose "the best" paradigm, concentrate only on it, and consign all the rest to Occam's razor?

I visualize Pynchon as a genius with an almost encyclopedic mind, who is willing to acknowledge and delight in endless interpretations of *The Crying of Lot 49*. If others share my visualization, I can understand why the man dares not interact with us—though I wish he would, even if it meant that my "fat deckful" of essays could collapse (*Crying* 11).

| | ♦\ ♠ // → ♣ // ♥ ⇓ ♠ ♣ \\\ ↓ ↓ ♠ ♦ ♣ ♥ → ⇓ /// \ ♥ ↓ \\ ♥ ♥ ♠ / ↓ ↓ ♣ =

Epilogue

It is July 18, 2011, and Martha and I have returned from a ten-day visit with our children and grandchildren in the Bay Area, where I found time to proof this book at leisure. It was also an opportunity to meet Arthur Stamps, who, via the blogosphere, had provided me with a Rosetta Stone for numerically quantifying information entropy. This meeting, in his four-story house—he romantically calls it a castle—that he had designed for a slim 750-squarefoot corner high on a steep hill overlooking San Francisco, turned out to be a sea-changing experience for me because I finally realized that the title of Stamps's paper, "Entropy, Berlyne, Kaplan: Integration of Two Aesthetic Theories," was the ultimate key to understanding a new, major connection of Information Theory and *The Crying of Lot 49*. I had been so focused on Stamps's implementation of the entropy equation that I read no further in the paper nor thought about the significance of "aesthetics" in its title. It was only when I met him in person and learned how involved he is with the application of information theory to aesthetics—since 2000, he has published almost 40 articles and books, the majority of them on information and/or aesthetics— that I realized that it was not simply Pynchon's connection of the "measure of physical disorder" that Shannon and Weaver "reinvented in 1949, as a measure of disorder in information" (Stamps 1), which was, as I originally thought, Pynchon's way of symbolizing the association of science with postmodernism's repudiation of modernism, that is most important. Instead, it is the connection of information theory and aesthetics, that according to Stamps began in 1960 with the publication of Kevin Lynch's *The Image of The City*. By explaining why the concept of "mystery" has had such a large influence in the literature on environmental aesthetics, Lynch paved the way for connecting information theory directly to what he called the aesthetic "value in mystification, labyrinth, or surprise in the environment" (Lynch 5; Stamps 3). This is stronger than Mendelson's assertion that "Information theory and aesthetics are indeed related, but only tangentially" (42), though Mendelson was remarkably prescient.

I believe that Pynchon read *The Image of the City* and signified it in *The Crying of Lot 49* by his allusions to "mystery" (89, 124, 163), to "labyrinth" (63, 162, 171), and to "surprise" (18, 74, 150, 157, 167, 170, 183). He mentions "environment" solely in regard to Oedipa's "using subliminal cues in the environment to guide her" (84), which is close to the geographic context of the built, urban environment in which Lynch used the term. Presumably, Pynchon was aware that information theory would lead to ground-breaking new understandings of literary aesthetics. Toward that end, Stamps's research investigated "how strongly impressions of mystery were caused by the promise of more information," thereby strengthening the connection between mystery and entropy (5). Stamps also reveals that Lynch's reason "for a need for clarity in the environment was that clarity of perception was fundamental to the efficiency and the very survival of animals" (Stamps 3). This focus on survival could explain why, as I suggested in the final paragraph of Essay Four above, Pynchon anticipated literary Darwinism long before it's spectacular surge at the turn of the century.

It is awkward to propose new breakthroughs in the interpretation of *The Crying of Lot 49* as late as the Epilogue. But I am excited that my book might be the prelude to a scientific theory of literary aesthetics. By contrasting the high-entropy *Crying of Lot 49* with the low-entropy *Inherent Vice*, I may, like Oedipa, "have stumbled […] onto a secret richness" (*Crying* 170) that Stamps and his peers in psychology can build upon in their applications of information theory to aesthetics. My particular approach may not lead to something operative, but that too would be useful to learn. There is enough left to be done on *The Crying of Lot 49* for another two generation of Pynchon scholars.

Works Cited

Adams, Henry, *A Letter to American Teachers of History*, Privately printed by J.H. Furst Co., Baltimore, 1910.

_____, *The Degradation of the Democratic Dogma*, New York: Macmillan, 1919.

Adiga, Aravind. *"Inherent Vice* by Thomas Pynchon." *The Times* (July 23, 2009).

Aitken, Robert. *Taking the Path of Zen*. San Francisco: North Point Press, 1982.

Anderson, Sam. "Translating the Code Into Everyday Language: Words about Words about Words: Why Criticism Matter." *New York Times Book Review*. January 2, 2011, 11

Anthony, Shane. "Openly Carrying Guns is in Vogue." *St. Louis Post-Dispatch* (June 20, 2011): A1, A4.

Arendt, Hannah. *Eichmann in Jerusalem: A Report on the Banality of Evil*. New York: Penguin, 1994.

Armitage, John. "From Modernism to Hypermodernism and Beyond: An Interview with Paul Virilio." *Theory, Culture and Society* 16.5/6 (1999): 1-23.

Arnason, H.H. *History of Modern Art: Painting, Sculpture and Architecture*. Englewood Cliffs: Prentice-Hall, 1968.

Balzac, Honoré de, *Sarrasine*. Paris: Le Livre de Poche, 1830, 2001.

Barker, Chris. *Making Sense of Cultural Studies: Central Problems and Critical Debates*. Thousand Oaks: Sage Publications, 2002.

Barthes, Roland, S/Z. New York: Hill and Wang, 1970, 1974.

_____. "The Death of the Author." *Image, Music, Text: Essays Selected and Translated by Stephen Heath*. New York: Hill and Wang, 1978, 142-148.

Batuman, Elif. "From the Critical Impulse, The Growth of Literature: Words about Words about Words: Why Criticism Matter." *New York Times Book Review*. January 2, 2011, 11.

Belsey, Catherine. *Post-Structuralism: A Very Short Introduction*. New York: Oxford UP, 2002.

Berardi, Franco. "(T)error and Poetry." Radical Philosophy 149 (May/June 2008): 39-45.

_____. *The Soul at Work: From Alienation to Autonomy*. Los Angeles: Semiotext(e), 2009.

Bird, Benjamin. "Don DeLillo's *Americana*: From Third- to First-Person Consciousness." *Critique* 47.2 (Winter 2006): 185-200.

Bressler, Charles E. *Literary Criticism: An Introduction to Theory and Practice*. Englewood Cliffs: Prentice-Hall, 1994.

Broad, William J., "The Men Who Made the Sun Rise," *New York Times* (Sunday, February 8, 1987): Sec. 7, 1.

Brooks, Peter. "The Idea of a Psychoanalytic Literary Criticism." *Discourse in Psychoanalysis and Literature, Ed., Schlomith Rimmon-Kenan*. London: Methuen, 1987, 1-18.

Browne, Janet. *Darwin's Origin of Species: A Biography*. New York: Atlantic Monthly Press, 2006.

Burn, Stephen. "Beyond the Critic as Cultural Arbiter: Words about Words about Words: Why Criticism Matter." *New York Times Book Review*. January 2, 2011, 9.

Caldwell, J. Paul. *Anxiety Disorders: Everything You Need to Know*. Buffalo: Firefly Books, 2005.

Cammett, John M. Carter *Antonio Gramsci and the Origins of Italian Communism*. Stanford: Stanford UP, 1967.

Carroll, Joseph. *Literary Darwinism: Evolution, Human Nature, and Literature*. New York: Routledge, 2004.

Carson, Rachel, *Silent Spring*, Houghton Mifflin, Boston, 1962.

Carter, Angela. *The Infernal Desire Machines of Doctor Hoffman*. New York: Penguin, 1972.

Coleman-Norton, P.R. "Venus." *The Encyclopedia Americana: International Edition, Volume 28*. Danbury: Grolier, 1993, 13.

Cover, Thomas M., and Joy A. Thomas. *Elements of Information Theory*. New York: Wiley, 1991.

Crumiller, Marshall, Bruce Knight, Yunguo Yu and Ehud Kaplan. "Focused Review: Estimating the Amount of Information Conveyed by a Population of Neurons." Draft Under Review, 2011.

Cullum, Charles. "Rebels, Conspirators, and Parrots, Oh My!: Lacanian Paranoia and Obsession in Three Postmodern Novels." *Critique*, 52.1 (2011): 1-16.

Couturier, Maurice "The Death of the Real in *The Crying of Lot 49*." *Pynchon Notes*, 20-21 (1987): 5-29.

Dean, Paul. "Introduction." In Leavis, F.R. *The Living Principle: "English" as a Discipline of Thought*. Chicago: Elephant Paperbacks, 1975.

DeLillo, Don. *Americana*. Boston: Houghton Mifflin, 1971.

———. *Great Jones Street*. Boston: Houghton Mifflin, 1973.

———. *White Noise*. New York: Penguin, 1986.

———. *Mao II*. New York: Viking, 1991.

———. *Falling Man*. New York: Scribner, 2007.

———. *Point Omega*. New York, Scribner, 2010.

Derrida, Jacques. *The Truth in Painting (1978): Translated by Geoff Bennington and Ian McLeod*. Chicago UP, 1987.

Dewey, Joseph. *Beyond Grief and Nothing: A Reading of Don DeLillo*. Columbia: South Carolina UP, 2006.

Diagnostic and Statistical Manual of Mental Disorders. Washington DC: American Psychiatric Institute, 1952 (*DSM-I*).

Diagnostic and Statistical Manual of Mental Disorders (Third Edition - Revised). Washington DC: American Psychiatric Institute, 1987 (*DSM-III-R*).

Diagnostic and Statistical Manual of Mental Disorders, Fourth Edition. Washington DC, American Psychiatric Association, 1994 (*DSM-IV*).

Dietz, Robert S. "Continent and Ocean Bay Evolution by Spreading of the Sea Floor." *Nature* 190.4779 (June 3, 1961): 854-857.

Downing, Michael. *Shoes Outside the Door: Desire, Devotion, and Excess at San Francisco Zen Center.* Washington DC: Counterpoint, 2001.

Dugdale, John. *Thomas Pynchon: Allusive Parables of Power.* New York: St. Martin's, 1990.

Duyfhuizen, Bernard. "'Hushing Sick Transmissions': Disrupting Story in *The Crying of Lot 49*." In Harold Bloom, Ed., *Bloom's Modern Critical Views: Thomas Pynchon.* Philadelphia: Chelsea House, 2003, 235-249.

Eagleton, Terry. *Literary Theory: An Introduction.* Minneapolis: Minnesota UP, 1983.

Eco, Umberto. *Interpretation and Overinterpretation: With Richard Rorty, Jonathan Culler, Christine Brooke-Rose*, Edited by Stephan Collini. Cambridge: Cambridge UP, 1996.

Eiseley, Loren, *The Immense Journey*, Random House, New York, 1957.

Eliade, Mircea. *The Sacred and the Profane: The Nature of Religion. Translated from the French by Willard R. Trask.* New York: Harcourt Brace Jovanovich, 1959.

El Naschie, M.S. "From Pointillism to E-Infinity Electromagnetism." *Chaos, Solitons & Fractals* 34.5 (December 2007): 1377-1381.

Elon, Amos. "Introduction." In Arendt, Hannah. *Eichmann in Jerusalem: A Report on the Banality of Evil - Introduction by Amos Elon.* New York: Penguin, 2006.

Evans-Wentz, W.Y. *The Tibetan Book of the Dead or The After-death Experiences on the Bardo Plane, according to Lama Kazi Dawa-Samdup's English Rendering.* New York: Oxford UP, 1927, 1960.

_____. *Tibetan Yoga and Secret Doctrines or Seven Books of Wisdom of the Great Path, according to the Late Lama Kazi Dawa-Samdup's English Rendering.* New York: Oxford UP, 1958, 1967.

_____. *The Tibetan Book of the Great Liberation.* London: Oxford University Press, 1968.

_____. *Tibet's Great Yogi Milarepa.* London: Oxford University Press, 1969.

Fields, Rick. *How the Swans Came to the Lake: A Narrative History of Buddhism in America.* Boston: Shambhala, 1992.

Forster, E.M. *Aspects of the Novel.* San Diego: Harcourt Brace, 1927.

Fowles, John. *The French Lieutenant's Woman.* Boston: Little Brown, 1969.

Foy, Jeffrey E., and Richard J. Gerrig. "How Might Literature Do Harm?" *Style* 42.2/3 (Summer/Fall 2008): 175-178.

Fremantle, Francesca, and Chögyam Trungpa. *The Tibetan Book of the Dead: The Great Liberation through Hearing in the Bardo.* Berkeley: Shambhala, 1975.

Freud, Sigmund. "Creative Writers and Day-Dreaming." *Translation in James Strachey, Ed., The Standard Edition of the Complete Psychological Works of Sigmund Freud, Vol. 9.* London: Hogarth Press, 1953, 141-154.

_____. *Beyond the Pleasure Principle: Translated and Edited by James Strachey.* London: Hogarth, 1974.

Friedman, Milton. Essays in Positive Economics. Chicago: Chicago UP, 1953.

Frye, Northrop. *Anatomy of Criticism: Four Essays.* Princeton: Princeton UP, 1957.

Gaddis, William. *Carpenter's Gothic.* New York: Viking, 1985.

Geddes, Dan. "Pynchon's Vineland: The War on Drugs and the Coming Police-State." *The Satirist: America's Most Critical Journal.*
< http://www.thesatirist.com/books/Vineland.html >

_____. "*Inherent Vice*–Pynchon for the Masses." *The Satirist: America's Most Critical Journal.* < http://www.thesatirist.com/books/Inherent-Vice.html >

Geyh, Paula E. "Assembling Postmodernism: Experience, Meaning, and the Space In-Between." *College Literature* 30.2 (Spring 2003): 1-29.

Goldford, Louis J., Janne E. Irvine, and Robert E. Kohn. "*Berio's Sinfonia: From Modernism to Hypermodernism.*" *Interdisciplinary Literary Studies* (Forthcoming 2011).

Goodman, Alice. *John Adams* The Death of Klinghoffer : *Libretto.* St. Louis: Opera Theatre of St. Louis Guild, 2011.

Grant, J. Kerry. *A Companion to* The Crying of Lot 49. Athens: Georgia UP, *1ˢᵗ Edition* 1994, *2ⁿᵈ Edition* 2008.

Grausam, Daniel. "*The Crying of Lot 49*, circa 1642; or, Pynchon and the Writing of World War Three." *Clio* 37.2 (Spring 2008): 219-38.

Gray, Richard. "Legal Bid to Stop CERN Atom Smasher from 'Destroying the World.'" *Daily Telegraph* (30 Aug. 2008).

Hägg, Samuli. *Narratologies of* Gravity's Rainbow. Joensuu: Joensuu UP, 2005.

Harland, Richard. *Superstructuralism: The Philosophy of Structuralism and Post-Structuralism.* London: Methuen, 1987.

Harris, Gardiner. "Talk Doesn't Pay, So Psychiatry Turns Instead to Drug Therapy." *New York Times*, March 6, 2011, pp. 1, 21.

Hartman, Geoffrey H. *Easy Pieces.* New York: Columbia UP, 1985.

Hassan, Ihab H. "The Problem of Influence in Literary History: Notes toward a Definition." *The Journal of Aesthetics and Art Criticism* 14.1 (September 1955): 66-76.

_____. "POSTmodernISM: A Paracritical Bibliography." *New Literary History* 3.1 (Fall 1971): 5-30.

_____. The Postmodern Turn: Essays in Postmodern Theory and Culture. Columbus: Ohio State UP, 1987.

Hawkes, John. *The Passion Artist.* New York: Harper & Row, 1979.

Herman, Luc. "Pynchon is Not a Narratologist." *Pynchon Notes* 54-55 (Spring-Fall, 2004): 261-267.

Herrigel, Eugen. *Zen in the Art of Archery: Translated by R.F.C. Hull.* New York: Vintage Books, 1971.

Hollander, Charles. "Pynchon, JFK and the CIA: Magic Eye Views of *The Crying of Lot 49.*" *Pynchon Notes* 40-41 (Spring-Fall 1997): 61-106.

Hsü, Kenneth J., "Uniformatism vs Catastrophism in the Extinction Debate," in William Glen, Ed., *The Mass-Extinction Debates: How Science Works in a Crisis,* Stanford, Stanford University Press, 1994, pp.217-229.

Hume, Kathryn. "Books of the Dead: Postmodern Politics in Novels by Mailer, Burroughs, Acker, and Pynchon." *Modern Philology* 97.3 (February 2000); 417-444.

Hutcheon, Linda. *A Poetics of Postmodernism: History, Theory, Fiction.* London: Routledge, 1988.

Huyssen, Andreas. "Mapping the Postmodern." *New German Critique* 33 (Fall 1984): 5-52.

Ickstadt, Heinz. "History, Utopia and Transcendence in the Space-Time of *Against the Day.*" *Pynchon Notes* 54-55 (Spring-Fall, 2004): 216-244.

Jackson, David P. *A Saint in Seattle: The Life of the Tibetan Mystic Dezhung Rinpoche.* Boston: Wisdom Publications, 2003.

Jameson, Fredric. *Postmodernism or, The Cultural Logic of Late Capitalism.* Durham: Duke UP, 1991, 2003.

_____. "Postmodernism and Consumer Society." In *Hal Foster, Ed., The Anti-Aesthetic: Essays on Postmodern Culture.* Port Townsend: Bay Press, 1983, 111-125.

Kapleau, Philip. *The Three Pillars of Zen: Teaching, Practice, and Enlightenment.* Boston: Beacon Press, 1970.

Kermode, Frank. *The Genesis of Secrecy: On the Interpretation of Narrative.* Cambridge: Harvard UP, 1979.

_____. "The Use of Codes in *The Crying of Lot 49.*" In *Harold Bloom, Ed., Thomas Pynchon: Modern Critical Views.* New York: Chelsea House, 1986, 11-14.

Kershner, R.B. *The Twentieth Century Novel: An Introduction.* Boston: Bedford Books, 1997.

Kilty, Kevin T. "Perpetual Motion," http://www.kilty.com/pmotion.htm#Section14

Kirn, Walter. "Drugs to Do, Cases to Solve." *New York Times* (August 23, 2009).

Kirsch, Adam. "The Will Not to Power, But to Self-understanding: Words about Words about Words: Why Criticism Matter." *New York Times Book Review.* January 2, 2011, 10-11.

Knapp, John V. "Current Conversations in the Teaching of College-Level Literature." *Style* 38.1 (Spring 2004): 50-92.

Knight, Charles. *London, Volume I,* London: Charles Knight and Co., 1841.

Kohn, Robert E. "Abatement Strategy and Air Quality Standards. *In Arthur Atkisson and Richard S. Gaines, Eds., Development of Air Quality Standards.* Columbus: Charles E. Merrill, 1970, 103-122.

_____. *A Linear Programming Model for Air Pollution Control.* Cambridge: MIT Press, 1978.

_____. "Optimal Quantity of a Controversial Good or Service." *Public Choice* 51.1 (1986): 81-86.

_____. "Transactions Costs and the Controversial Good or Service." *Public Choice* 57.1 (April 1988): 89-93.

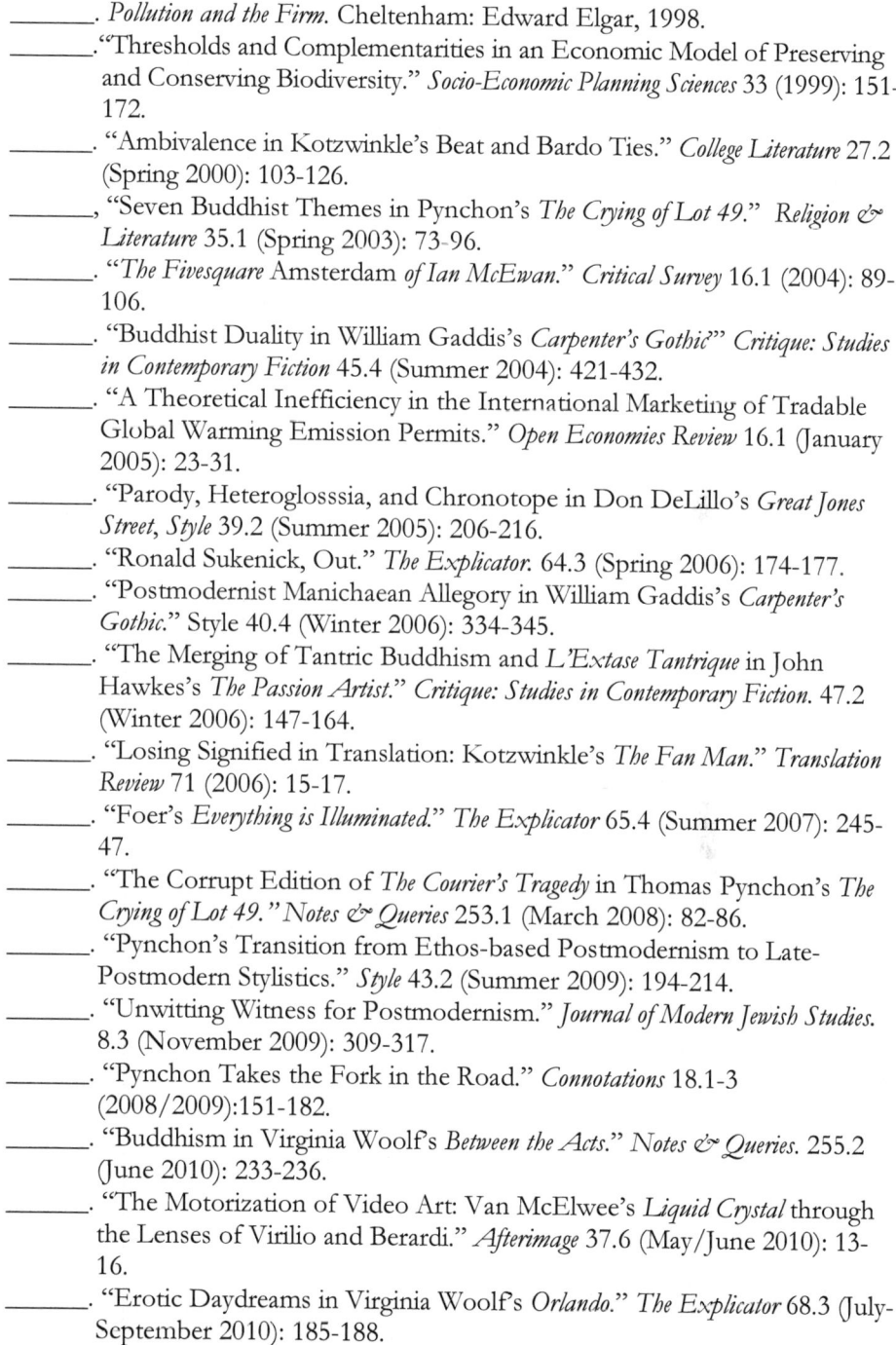

_____. *Pollution and the Firm*. Cheltenham: Edward Elgar, 1998.

_____."Thresholds and Complementarities in an Economic Model of Preserving and Conserving Biodiversity." *Socio-Economic Planning Sciences* 33 (1999): 151-172.

_____. "Ambivalence in Kotzwinkle's Beat and Bardo Ties." *College Literature* 27.2 (Spring 2000): 103-126.

_____, "Seven Buddhist Themes in Pynchon's *The Crying of Lot 49*." *Religion & Literature* 35.1 (Spring 2003): 73-96.

_____. *"The Fivesquare* Amsterdam *of Ian McEwan*." *Critical Survey* 16.1 (2004): 89-106.

_____. "Buddhist Duality in William Gaddis's *Carpenter's Gothic*" *Critique: Studies in Contemporary Fiction* 45.4 (Summer 2004): 421-432.

_____. "A Theoretical Inefficiency in the International Marketing of Tradable Global Warming Emission Permits." *Open Economies Review* 16.1 (January 2005): 23-31.

_____. "Parody, Heteroglosssia, and Chronotope in Don DeLillo's *Great Jones Street, Style* 39.2 (Summer 2005): 206-216.

_____. "Ronald Sukenick, Out." *The Explicator*. 64.3 (Spring 2006): 174-177.

_____. "Postmodernist Manichaean Allegory in William Gaddis's *Carpenter's Gothic.*" Style 40.4 (Winter 2006): 334-345.

_____. "The Merging of Tantric Buddhism and *L'Extase Tantrique* in John Hawkes's *The Passion Artist*." *Critique: Studies in Contemporary Fiction*. 47.2 (Winter 2006): 147-164.

_____. "Losing Signified in Translation: Kotzwinkle's *The Fan Man*." *Translation Review* 71 (2006): 15-17.

_____. "Foer's *Everything is Illuminated*." *The Explicator* 65.4 (Summer 2007): 245-47.

_____. "The Corrupt Edition of *The Courier's Tragedy* in Thomas Pynchon's *The Crying of Lot 49.* "*Notes & Queries* 253.1 (March 2008): 82-86.

_____. "Pynchon's Transition from Ethos-based Postmodernism to Late-Postmodern Stylistics." *Style* 43.2 (Summer 2009): 194-214.

_____. "Unwitting Witness for Postmodernism." *Journal of Modern Jewish Studies*. 8.3 (November 2009): 309-317.

_____. "Pynchon Takes the Fork in the Road." *Connotations* 18.1-3 (2008/2009):151-182.

_____. "Buddhism in Virginia Woolf's *Between the Acts*." *Notes & Queries*. 255.2 (June 2010): 233-236.

_____. "The Motorization of Video Art: Van McElwee's *Liquid Crystal* through the Lenses of Virilio and Berardi." *Afterimage* 37.6 (May/June 2010): 13-16.

_____. "Erotic Daydreams in Virginia Woolf's *Orlando*." *The Explicator* 68.3 (July-September 2010): 185-188.

_____. "The Jewess in Kate Chopin's *The Awakening.*" In Howard Schwartz and Barbara Raznick, Eds., *Winter Harvest: Jewish Writing in St. Louis, 2006-2011.* St. Louis: Brodsky Library Press, 2011, 456-458.

_____. "A Derridean Look at the Paintings of Bessie Lowenhaupt." *Soundings* (93.3-4 (Fall/Winter 2010): 385-407).

_____. "Tibetan Buddhism in Don DeLillo's Novels: The Street, The Word and The Soul." *College Literature* (Forthcoming).

_____, "Issues of Antisemitism in Kate Chopin's *The Awakening.*" *Journal of Modern Jewish Studies* (Forthcoming).

Kotzwinkle, William. *The Fan Man.* New York: Harmony, 1974.

Krauss, Lawrence M., and Glenn D. Starkman, "The Fate of Life in the Universe," *Scientific American* 281.5 (November 1999): 58-65.

_____. "Life, the Universe, and Nothing: Life and Death in an Ever-Expanding Universe." *The Astrophysical Journal* 531 (March 1, 2000): 22-30.

Kristjansson, Leo. "Iceland Spar: The Helgustadir Calcite Locality and its Influence on the Development of Science." *Journal of Geoscience Education* 50.4 (September 2002), 419-427.

Kublin, Hyman "Zen Buddhism." *The Encyclopedia Americana: International Edition.* Vol. 29. Danbury: Grolier Inc., 1993. 760-761.

Lamagna, Carlo M. "Ironies and Icons." *St. Louis University Museum of Art Brochure.* March 28, 2008, 12-15.

Leary, Timothy, Ralph Metzner and Richard Alpert. *The Psychedelic Experience: A Manual Based on the Tibetan Book of the Dead.* Secaucus: Citadel, 1964.

Leavis, F.R. *The Living Principle: "English" as a Discipline of Thought.* Chicago: Elephant Paperbacks, 1975.

LeClair, Thomas. "An Interview with Don DeLillo." *Contemporary Literature* 23.1 (Winter 1982). 19-31.

Lentricchia, Frank, and Andrew DuBois. *Close Reading: The Reader.* Durham: Duke UP, 2003.

Leopold, Aldo, *A Sand County Almanac with Other Essays on Conservation from Round River*, Oxford University Press, New York, (This is an amalgamation of the 1949 *Almanac* and the 1953 *Round River*), 1966.

Levine, George. "Risking the Moment: Anarchy and Possibility in Pynchon's Fiction." In Harold Bloom, Ed., *Bloom's Modern Critical Views: Thomas Pynchon.* Philadelphia: Chelsea House, 2003, 57-76.

Lineweaver, Charles H. "Cosmological and Biological Reproducibility: Limits on the Maximum Entropy Production Principle." *Non-Equilibrium Thermodynamics and the Production of Entropy: Life, Earth, and Beyond, Eds., A. Kleidon and R.D. Lorenz.* Heidelberg: Springer, 2005, 67-77.

Lipan, Petruta. "Jerry O. Wilkerson's Work in International Perspective." *St. Louis University Museum of Art Brochure.* March 28, 2008, 4-5.

Logan, William. "Back to the Future: *Against the Day*, by Thomas Pynchon" *Virginia Quarterly Review* 83.3 (September 2007): 226-247.

Lynch, Kevin A. *The Image of the City*. Cambridge: MIT Press, 1960.

Lyon, David. "Fear, Surveillance, and Consumption." *The Hedgehog Review*. 5.3 (Fall 2003): 81-95.

Lyotard, Jean-François. *The Postmodern Condition: A Report on Knowledge*. Minneapolis: University of Minneapolis Press, 1984.

Mangel, Anne. "Maxwell's Demon, Entropy, Information: *The Crying of Lot 49*." *Tri-Quarterly* 20 (Winter 1971): 194-208.

Maxwell, J. Clerk. *Theory of Heat*. London: Longman's, Green and Co. New Impression 1899.

McClellan, Bill. "Vote Fraud Itself is Largely a Fraud." *St. Louis Post-Dispatch* (June 3, 2011), A11.

McClure, John A. "Postmodern/Post-Secular: Contemporary Fiction and Spirituality." *Modern Fiction Studies* 41.1 (Spring 1995): 141-163.

McHale, Brian. *Postmodernist Fiction*. London: Routledge, 1989.

McLaughlin, Robert L. "Post-Postmodern Discontent: Contemporary Fiction and the Social World." *Symploke* 12.1-2 (2004): 53-68.

McPhee, John. *In Suspect Terrain*. New York: Farrar, Straus and Giroux, 1982.

Menand, Louis. "Soft-Boiled: Pynchon's Stoned Detective." *The New Yorker* (August 3, 2009)

Mendelson, Edward. "The Sacred, The Profane, and *The Crying of Lot 49*." In Harold Bloom, Ed., *Bloom's Modern Critical Views: Thomas Pynchon*. Philadelphia: Chelsea House, 2003, 11-42.

Millard, Bill. "Pynchon's Coast: Inherent Vice and the Twilight of the Spatially Specific." College Hill Review, Issue No, 4, Fall 2009. < http://www.collegehillreview.com/004/print/p0040501.html >

Miller, Sarah Bryan. "Opera is Interfaith Catalyst." *St. Louis Post-Dispatch* (May 28, 2011), A1, A10.

Mishra, Pankaj. "The Intellectual at Play in the Wider World: Words about Words about Words: Why Criticism Matter." *New York Times Book Review*. January 2, 2011, 10.

Mitchell, Elsie P. The Lion-Dog of Buddhist Asia. New York: Fugaisha, 1991.

Moore, Steven. *The Novel: An Alternative History: Beginnings to 1600*. New York: Continuum, 2010.

Naspy, C.J. "Teilhard de Chardin." *The Encyclopedia Americana: International Edition* Vol. 26 (1993): 387.

New World Encyclopedia. www.newworldencyclopedia.org/entry/Venus_(mythology)

Nicholson, Craig, Christopher C. Sorlien, Tanya Atwater, John C. Crowell and Bruce P. Luyendyk. "Microplate Capture, Rotation of the Western Transverse Ranges, and Initiation of the San Andreas Transform as a Low-Angle Fault System." *Geology* 22.6 (June 1994): 491-495.

Palmer, Alan. *Fictional Minds*. Lincoln: Nebraska UP, 2004.

Pergadia, Michele L., *et al.* "A 3p26-3p25 Genetic Linkage Finding for DSM-IV Major Depression in Heavy Smoking Families." *American Journal of Psychiatry* Published in Advance, On-Line (May 15, 2011): 1-5.

Pierce, J.R., *Symbols, Signals and Noise: The Nature and Process of Communication*, New York: Harper, 1961.

Poirier, Richard. "The Importance of Thomas Pynchon." *In Harold Bloom, Ed., Bloom's Modern Critical Views: Thomas Pynchon*. Philadelphia: Chelsea House, 2003, 43-55.

Pynchon, Thomas. *V.* New York: Bantam Windstone, 1981.

_____. *The Crying of Lot 49*. Philadelphia: Lippincott, 1966.

_____. *Gravity's Rainbow*. New York: Penguin, 1973.

_____. *Slow Learner: Early Stories*. Boston: Little, 1984.

_____. "Is it O.K. to be a Luddite?" *New York Times Book Review*, 28 October 1984, 1, 40-41.

_____. *Vineland*. Boston: Little Brown, 1990.

_____. *Mason and Dixon*. New York: Henry Holt, 1997.

_____. *Against the Day*. New York: Penguin, 2006.

_____. *Inherent Vice*. New York: Penguin, 2009.

Quinion, Michael. *World Wide Words*. http://www.worldwidewords.org/qu/qa-shr1.htm

Rabinowitz, Peter J., and Michael W. Smith. *Authorizing Readers: Resistance and Respect in the Teaching of Literature*. New York: Teachers College Press, 1998.

Raff, Arthur D. "Further Magnetic Measurements along the Murray Fault." *Journal of Geophysical Research* 67.1 (January 1962): 417-418.

Rice, Nancy Newman. "Jerry," *St. Louis University Museum of Art Brochure*. March 28, 2008, 16-17.

Rilke, Rainer Maria. *Letters to a Young Poet: Translated by Joan M. Burnham*. San Rafael: New World Library, 1992.

Roiphe, Katie. "With Clarity and Beauty, The Weight of Authority: Words about Words about Words: Why Criticism Matter." *New York Times Book Review*. January 2, 2011, 10.

Royal Society for the Protection of Birds. http://www.rspb.org.uk/ourwork/policy/species/birdsofprey/songbirds.aspx

Schaefer, Nancy A. "Y2K as an Endtime Sign: Apocalypticism in America at the *fin-de-millennium*." *Journal of Popular Culture* 38.1 (2004): 82-105.

Schaub, Thomas. "The Environmental Pynchon: *Gravity's Rainbow* and the Ecological Context." *Pynchon Notes* 42-43 (Spring-Fall 1998): 59-72.

Schnall, Marianne. "Interview with Timothy Leary" (1995). *Ecomall: A Place to Help Save the Earth*. < http://www.ecomall.com/greenshopping/tim/htm >

Scholes, Robert. *Structuralism in Literature: An Introduction*. New Haven: Yale UP, 1974.

Scott, K.M., M. Von Korff, *et al.* "Age Patterns in the Prevalence of DSM-IV Depressive/Anxiety Disorders with and without Physical Co-morbidity." *Psychological Medicine* 38.11 (November 2008): 1659-1669.

Sedgwick, Eve Kosofsky. "Jane Austen and the Masturbating Girl." In Frank Lentricchia and Andrew DuBois, Eds., *Close Reading: The Reader*. Durham: Duke UP, 2003, 301-320.

Seed, David. "Order in Thomas Pynchon's 'Entropy.'" *The Journal of Narrative Technique* 11.2 (1981): 135-153.

_____. The Fictional Labyrinths of Thomas Pynchon. Iowa City: Iowa UP, 1988.

Sherard, Tracey. "The Birth of the Female Subject in *The Crying of Lot 49.*" *Pynchon Notes* 32-33 (Spring-Fall, 1993): 60-74.

Silverman, Hugh J. *Textualities: Between Hermeneutics and Deconstruction*. New York: Routledge, 1994.

Singh, G. *F.R. Leavis (1895-1978) and Q.D. Leavis (1906-1981). Modern Age* 32.2 (Spring 1988): 179-182.

Sloan, Doris. *Geology of the San Francisco Bay Region*. Berkeley: California UP, 2006.

Smith, David Livingston. "Literature as Self-Engineering: An Evolutionary Hypothesis." *Style* 42.2/3 (Summer/Fall 2008): 272-276.

Song, Felicia Wu, "Being Left Behind: The Discourse of Fear in Technological Change," *The Hedgehog Review*, 5.3 (Fall 2003): 26-42.

Stamps, Arthur E., III. "Entropy, Berlyne, Kaplan: Integration of Two Aesthetic Theories." <

http://home.comcast.net/~InstituteOfEnvironmentalQuality/EntropyBerlyneKaplan4.pdf

Stedman, Hansell H., Benjamin W. Kozyak, Anthony Nelson, Danielle M. Thesier, Leonard T. Su, David W. Low, Charles R. Bridges, Joseph B. Shrager, Nancy Minugh-Purvis and Marilyn A. Mitchell, "Myosin Gene Mutation Correlates with Anatomical Changes in the Human Lineage," *Nature* 428, March 25, 2004, 415-418.

Stern, Laurent. "*Textualities: Between Hermeneutics and Deconstruction* by Hugh J. Silverman." *Journal of Aesthetics and Art Criticism* 55.1 (Winter 1997): 70-72.

Stimpson, Catherine R. "Pre-Apocalyptic Atavism: Thomas Pynchon's Early Fiction." *In Harold Bloom, Ed., Bloom's Modern Critical Views: Thomas Pynchon*. Philadelphia: Chelsea House, 2003, 77-92.

Sugiyama, Michelle Scalise. "Information is the Stuff of Narrative." *Style* 42.2/3 (Summer/Fall 2008): 254-260.

Sukenick, Ronald. *Out*. Chicago: Swallow Press, 1973.

Suwalsky, David J. "Discerning Palette Jerry O. Wilkerson Retrospective." *St. Louis University Museum of Art Brochure*. March 28, 2008, 2-3.

Tanner, Tony. *Thomas Pynchon*. London: Methuen, 1982.

Teilhard de Chardin, Pierre. *The Human Phenomenon: A New Edition and Translation of* Le phénomène humain *by Sarah Appleton-Weber*. Brighton: Sussex AP, 1999.

Temple, William, *Nature, Man and God: Being the Gifford Lectures Delivered in the University of Glasgow in the Academical Years 1932-1933 and 1933-1934*, Macmillan, London, 1935.

Thurman, Robert A.F. *Essential Tibetan Buddhism*. Edison: Castle Books, 1995.

Toffler, Alvin. *Future Shock*. New York: Random House, 1970.

Toker, Leona. *Eloquent Reticence: Withholding Information in Fictional Narrative*. Lexington" Kentucky UP, 1993.

Trungpa, Chögyam. "A Very Practical Joke." *Tricycle: The Buddhist Review* 64 (Summer 2007): 78-81.

Vine, F.J., and D.H. Matthews. "Magnetic Anomalies over Ocean Ridges." *Science* 199.4897 (September 7, 1963): 947-949. Reprinted in Allan Cox. Plate Tectonics and Geomagnetic Reversals. San Francisco: W.H. Freeman, 1973. 232-237.

Virilio, Paul. *The Vision Machine* (1988): *Translated by Julie Rose*. Bloomington: Indiana UP, 1994.

_____. *The Art of the Motor* (1993); *Tran., Julie Rose*. Minneapolis: Minnesota UP, 1995.

_____. *Open Sky* (1995): *Translated by Julie Rose*. London: Verso, 1997.

_____. *The Information Bomb* (1998): *Translated by Chris Turner*. London: Verso, 2000.

_____. *Ground Zero* (2002): *Translated by Chris Turner*. London: Verso, 2002.

_____. *Art and Fear* (2000): *Translated by Julie Rose*. London: Continuum, 2003.

_____. *Negative Horizon: An Essay in Dromoscopy* (1984): *Translated by Michael Degener*. London: Continuum, 2005.

Von Huene, Roland. "Geological Structure between the Murray Fracture Zone and the Transverse Ranges." *Marine Geology* 7.6 (December 1969): 475-499.

Weaver, Warren. "The Mathematics of Communication." *Scientific American* 181 (July 1949): 11-15.

Weber, Mark. "Jerry." *St. Louis University Museum of Art Brochure*. March 28, 2008, 18-19.

Wiener, Norbert. *The Human Use of Human Beings: Cybernetics and Society*. Doubleday: New York, 1954.

Wilde, Alan. *Middle Grounds: Studies in Contemporary American Fiction*. Philadelphia: Pennsylvania UP, 1987.

Womack, Kenneth. *Long and Winding Roads: The Evolving Artistry of the Beatles*. New York: Continuum, 2007.

Wu Ch'eng-en. *Monkey: Translated by Arthur Waley*. London: Penguin, 1942.

Index

Post Script (August 27, 2013)

The Crying of Lot 49 is postmodern because it defies totalization. As J. Kerry Grant famously put it in the Introduction to his Companion, there is no unitary, comprehensive account of the novel's message. Grant in turn drew on David Bennett's essay in the Winter 1985 issue of Critical Quarterly, in which Bennett added: "To say that the meaning of a text is indeterminate, however, is not to say that it signifies indeterminacy. If what a text says or means is undecidable, then it does not predetermine its interpretation, and we are free to read it in different ways" (35). This, accordingly, is what I have done in this book. Each of its chapters begins with a quotation, all but one of them from *The Crying of Lot 49*. Though their meanings may be indeterminate or at least undecidable, I was able to determine interpretations that gave me satisfaction. These have to do with Botticelli's Birth of Venus, Tibetan Bardo Rebirth, Plate Tectonics, Rachel Carson's Silent Spring, Obsessive Compulsive Disorder, and others. These particular interpretations appear and reappear, explaining other paragraphs throughout the text. They do not interrelate, but they do compensate in part for the frustration of failing to identify that grand totalization that postmodernism denies us.

What of Pynchon? Does he scorn these interpretations that I make the centerpiece of my book? I believe I know the answer. He intentionally planted hints and meant for them to be sown. Else why does he give more hints in his 2006 Against the Day? Surely, there are clues in that huge novel to other interpretations of *The Crying of Lot 49* besides Bardo Rebirth, Plate Tectonics, Silent Spring and Obsessive Compulsive Disorder, that we readers missed in the earlier novel.

This new edition of *New Close Readings of The Crying of Lot 49* corrects the worst of the typos in the first edition and prepares it for Amazon's incredible print-on-demand program. I'm grateful to my son Joel for electronically transitioning my books to that venue; his skill is not surprising given that twenty-five years ago, he was the original stand-up comedian "Computerman."

It Worked Fifteen Minutes Ago

Sea Stories Told from
Just Above Davy Jones' Locker

B. A. Ritzenthaler

A Ritzenthaler Publishing Title